THAILAND

TOP SIGHTS, AUTHENTIC EXPERIENCES

**Austin Bush,
Tim Bewer, Celeste Brash, David Eimer,
Damian Harper, Anita Isalska**

Welcome to Thailand

Thailand is blessed: exotic and mysterious yet approachable and hospitable, it has the looks and personality to entice the world to its shores.

Bangkok, the kingdom's capital, is an adrenaline rush. The pace is fast, the spaces cramped and the sights and smells dizzying. It is disorienting but addictive for urban junkies. In contrast, the tranquil southern coast will soothe modern nerves. The waters are clear, the diving is spectacular and the pace is oh-so sleepy. Thailand's famous islands and beaches specialise in fun, from beach parties to casual dining. Along the Andaman Coast dramatic limestone mountains cluster like prehistoric monuments.

Beyond the beach scene, Thailand's culture trail educates and enlightens. Intense displays of religious devotion and tangible history unfold in Bangkok, the seat of religion and monarchy. Further north, the ancient capitals of Ayuthaya and Sukhothai are peppered with gravity-ravaged ruins and serene Buddha figures. Northern Thailand is lush mountains, historic cities and border intrigue. The gateway to the region, Chiang Mai, has a well-preserved old city and university atmosphere. In higher altitudes, minority hill tribes cling to a distinct cultural identity.

In every corner of the kingdom, Thais concoct flavourful feasts from simple ingredients. Travelling from region to region becomes an edible buffet, from fiery coconut milk curries in southern Thailand to steamy bowls of noodles in Bangkok and hearty stews in Chiang Mai.

Thailand has the looks and personality to entice the world to its shores

Yi Peng Festival, part of Loi Krathong (p24), Chiang Mai

Contents

In Focus

Survival Guide

Detail in Buddhist artwork
MATT MUNRO / LONELY PLANET ©

Plan Your Trip
Thailand's Top 12

HAFIZ JOHARI / SHUTTERSTOCK ©

Bangkok

Bangkok has it all in super-sized portions

This high-energy city (p34) loves neon and noise, chaos and concrete, fashion and the future. It's an urban connoisseur's dream: a
city where the past, present and future are jammed into a steamy
pressure cooker. Zip around town in the sleek, elevated BTS; watch
the sun sink into the muddy Chao Phraya River on a commuter
ferry; or get stuck in one of the city's famous traffic jams. Then
reward your adventurousness with top-notch pampering.

THE GOATMAN / SHUTTERSTOCK ©

DAVID SALA / 500PX ©

Chiang Mai

The cultural capital of the north

Chiang Mai (p74) is a cultural darling wearing its Lanna heritage with pride. Its old walled city is crowded with temples dating to the days of the teak boom. Bookshops and ethnic-chic stores outnumber glitzy shopping centres. The dining scene celebrates the fresh and local produce of the region. Great country escapes are just an hour's journey outside the city. Nowhere else in Thailand has such a delightful mixture of big-city attractions with a provincial pace.

2

Ko Samui

Synonymous with sun, fun and, of course, comfort

Eager to please, Ko Samui (p110) is a civilised resort island that boasts a thriving health scene with yoga, massage, detoxing and other yins to the island's partying yang. Chaweng is a luxurious stretch of sand where sun-worshippers come to see and be seen, but beyond the brassy beaches are reminders of Samui's old moniker, 'Coconut Island', and a few gentle coves for families.

3

4

Chiang Rai

Ethnic diversity and dramatic mountain scenery

The days of the Golden Triangle opium trade are over, but Chiang Rai (p126) still packs intrigue in the form of fresh-air fun such as hiking and self-guided exploration. It is also a great destination for unique cultural experiences, ranging from a visit to a hill-tribe village to a stay at the Yunnanese hamlet of Doi Mae Salong. From the Mekong River to the mountains, Chiang Rai is arguably Thailand's most beautiful province. Mae Fah Luang Art & Culture Park (p136)

5

Railay

Dramatic karst towers are the main event

You'd never know that you were still on the mainland when you wade from a long-tail boat to the shore of this limestone-studded peninsula (p142). Towering karst peaks hem in all sides, creating the illusion of a rocky fortress. Rock climbers have transformed the cliffs into vertical challenges, scrambling high enough for a view of the karst-studded bay. Kayakers and snorkellers take to the sea to explore low-tide caves and peek at the marine life sheltered by hulking missile-shaped islands. Tham Phra Nang (p148)

MARTINM303 / GETTY IMAGES ©

Sukhothai

Crumbling temples and picturesque countryside

Hop on a bicycle and explore Thailand's most impressive historical park, winding past crumbling temple ruins, graceful Buddha statues and fish-filled ponds. Worthwhile museums and good-value accommodation round out the package. Despite its popularity, Sukhothai (p152) rarely feels crowded, but nearby Si Satchanalai-Chaliang Historical Park attracts only a few history adventurers willing to scale its ancient stairways. Wat Si Chum (p159)

Kanchanaburi

One of the country's easiest – and best – getaways

Given the jaw-dropping natural beauty of Kanchanaburi (p168), it seems paradoxical that the region is best known for the horrors of WWII's Death Railway. The provincial capital's war memorials are a mandatory stop before heading deeper into the parks and preserves that comprise the Western Forest Complex, one of Asia's largest protected areas. The area is home to numerous waterfalls and caves as well as an array of lush riverside resorts.

Ko Pha-Ngan
Party hard, or take it easy

Famous for its sloppy Full Moon Parties, Ko Pha-Ngan (p180) has graduated from a sleepy bohemian island to a stop on the party-people circuit. In between the lunar festivities, it excels in laid-back island life accessible to everybody. Backpackers can still find rustic, kick-back spots, and comfort seekers are attracted by Ko Pha-Ngan as an alternative to too comfortable Ko Samui. Divers will be rewarded with easy access to some of the Gulf of Thailand's best dive sites.

Ko Phi-Phi

The darling of the Andaman Coast

Arguably the prettiest island in all of Thailand, Ko Phi-Phi Don (p194; pictured left and far left) has gorgeous blonde-sand beaches, scenic lime-stone cliffs and jewel-toned waters. It's a car- and carefree island where the parties last all night and sound systems serenade the stars. If you came looking for serenity, its sister island, Ko Phi-Phi Leh (p200), is an uninhabited park with coral reefs and interior lagoons. Party boats can sail you among the scenery, tipple in hand.

CARLOS CASTILLA / SHUTTERSTOCK ©

DENIS COSTILLE / SHUTTERSTOCK ©

ANAN KAEWKHAMMUL/
SHUTTERSTOCK ©

Phuket

The ultimate beach escape

An international resort hub, Phuket (p206) is easy-peasy. You can fly in from Bangkok, cutting out the long land journey, and retreat into a five-star resort or arty boutique hotel for a trouble-free tropical vacation. There are slinky stretches of sand, hedonistic party pits and all the mod cons needed for 21st-century rest and recreation. Mix it up with day trips to mangrove forests, charming Phuket Town, water sports and gibbon-rescue centres.

10

MARTINHOSMART / GETTY IMAGES ©

Ayuthaya

Once great capital packed with temples

Ayuthaya (p234) was once Siam's vibrant, glittering capital packed with temples and hosting seafaring merchants from the east and west. Today Ayuthaya has been ravaged by war and gravity but the brick-and-stucco ruins, which form a Unesco World Heritage Site, can be visited on a cycling tour that reveals their history and artistic legacy. Ayuthaya is an easy day trip from Bangkok or an alternative landing pad for city phobics. Wat Phanan Choeng (p240)

ANNA730 / SHUTTERSTOCK ©

Nong Khai

Riverside border town with laid-back charms

Nong Khai (p248) is not a usual stop on a quick country tour but it is worth the effort for its pretty Mekong River setting. A curious sculpture garden shelters an astounding collection of avant-garde art. The riverside market displays its Indochinese links. And visitors spend the rest of their visit cycling around town, past free-range chickens, uniformed school children and tropical fruit gardens.

Plan Your Trip
Need to Know

When to Go

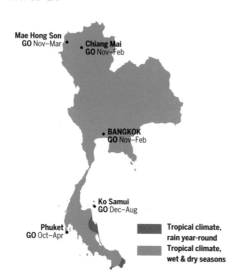

Mae Hong Son
GO Nov–Mar

Chiang Mai
GO Nov–Feb

BANGKOK
GO Nov–Feb

Ko Samui
GO Dec–Aug

Phuket
GO Oct–Apr

Tropical climate,
rain year-round

Tropical climate,
wet & dry seasons

High Season (Nov–Mar)

o A cool and dry season follows the monsoons.

o Christmas and New Year's holidays bring crowds and inflated rates.

Shoulder Season (Apr–Jun, Sep & Oct)

o April to June is very hot and dry. Coastal areas get natural sea-breeze air-con.

o September and October are ideal for the north and the gulf coast.

Low Season (Jul–Oct)

o Monsoon season ranges from afternoon showers to major flooding.

o Some islands shut down; boat service is limited during stormy weather.

o Rain is usually in short, intense bursts.

Currency
Thai baht (B)

Language
Thai

Visas
For visitors from most countries, visas are generally not required for stays of up to 30 days.

Money
ATMs are widespread and charge a 150B to 180B foreign-account fee; Visa and Master-Card accepted at most hotels and high-end restaurants but not at family-owned businesses.

Mobile Phones
Thailand is on a GSM network through inexpensive prepaid SIM cards; 4G is widespread.

Time
GMT plus seven hours

Daily Costs

Budget: Less than 1000B

- Basic guesthouse room: 600–1000B
- Market/street stall meal: 40–100B
- Small bottle of beer: 100B
- Public transport around town: 20–50B

Midrange: 1000–4000B

- Flashpacker guesthouse or midrange hotel room: 1000–4000B
- Western lunches and seafood dinner: 150–350B
- Organised tour or activity: 1000–1500B
- Motorbike hire: 150–250B

Top End: More than 4000B

- Boutique hotel room: 4000B
- Meal at fine-dining restaurant: 350–1000B
- Private tours: 2000B
- Car hire: from 800B per day

Useful Websites

Thaivisa (www.thaivisa.com) Expat site for news and discussions.
Lonely Planet (www.lonelyplanet.com/ thailand) Destination information, hotel bookings, traveller forum and more.
Richard Barrow (www.richardbarrow.com) Prolific blogger and tweeter focusing on Thai travel.
Tourism Authority of Thailand (TAT; www.tourismthailand.org) National tourism department covering info and special events.
Thai Language (www.thai-language.com) Online dictionary and Thai tutorials.

Opening Hours

All government offices and banks are closed on public holidays. Bars and clubs close during elections and certain religious holidays.

Banks 8.30am to 4.30pm; 24-hour ATMs
Bars 6pm to midnight or 1am
Clubs 8pm to 2am
Government Offices 8.30am to 4.30pm Monday to Friday; some close for lunch
Restaurants 8am to 10pm
Shops 10am to 7pm

Arriving in Thailand

Suvarnabhumi International Airport (Bangkok) Taxis cost 220B to 380B plus tolls and 50B airport surcharge. An Airport Rail Link also provides service.
Don Mueang International Airport (Bangkok) There are four bus lines from Bangkok's de facto budget airport; meter taxis run 24 hours.
Chiang Mai International Airport Taxis are a flat 120B.
Phuket International Airport Buses and minivans run to Phuket Town (100B to 150B) and beaches (180B). Metered taxis cost 550B.

Getting Around

Air Domestic routes from Bangkok are plentiful.
Bus Intercity buses are convenient; purchase tickets at bus stations to avoid unscrupulous agents.
Hired transport Bangkok has metered taxis; elsewhere túk-túk and motorcycle taxis have negotiated fares. Motorcycles and cars are easily rented.
Public transport Bangkok has an extensive public transit system. Elsewhere *sŏrng·tăa·ou* (converted pick-up trucks) on fixed routes.
Train Slow but scenic.

For more on **getting around**, see p307 →

Plan Your Trip
Hot Spots for...

MMEEE / GETTY IMAGES ©

Beaches
Bliss out on a tropical beach surrounded by jewel-coloured waters and brooding jungle-clad mountains.

Ko Pha-Ngan (p180)
Master the art of hammock-hanging, rave till dawn or dive with the fishes and whale sharks.

Hat Rin Nok Cleanest beach on the island; hosts Full Moon Parties. (p184)

Ko Samui (p110)
Quick and easy beach escape with gorgeous beaches, seaside yoga and loads of people-watching.

Mae Nam Beach Fantastic views and is gorgeous at twilight. (p115)

Railay (p142)
One of Thailand's prettiest beaches, backed by fairy-tale limestone formations (pictured) and jungle.

Hat Railay East The ultimate place for rock-climbing fans. (p146)

TAKE PHOTO / SHUTTERSTOCK ©

Historic Sites
Follow the cultural trail through the historic capitals, evolving art and architecture and regional identities.

Sukhothai (p152)
Cycle among the ruins of an early Thai kingdom for a meditative journey into the past.

Sukhothai Historical Park Expansive site, best visited on two wheels. (p156)

Ayuthaya (p234)
Tumbledown temples of a former ancient capital now surrounded by a sleepy provincial town.

Ayuthaya Historical Park The must-see ruins of Thailand's former capital. (p238)

Chiang Mai (p74)
Teak treasures stand testament to the artistic legacy of the old Lanna kingdom.

Wat Phra That Doi Suthep Gleaming stupas and mountain breezes. (p90; pictured)

Thai Food

Zesty dishes of fresh spices and ingredients with a spicy sting from chillies makes Thai food one of the globe's most beloved cuisines.

PLOIPIROON / SHUTTERSTOCK ©

Bangkok (p34)
A culinary superstar covering all the bases: humble noodles, haute cuisine and immigrant comfort food.

nahm The world's best Thai restaurant? (p67)

Chiang Mai (p74)
This northern town excels in vegetarian cuisine and Thai cooking courses.

Curry Noodles The city's famous *kôw soy,* at Kao Soi Fueng Fah. (p101)

Ko Samui (p110)
Get off the tourist track and seek out southern Thailand's infamously salty, spicy dishes.

Fish Curry *Kà·nŏm jeen gaang đai þlah* (pictured), served over thin rice noodles.

Shopping

An unofficial national pastime, shopping unfolds in exuberant street markets and high-end malls.

VASSAMON ANANSUKKASEM / SHUTTERSTOCK ©

Bangkok (p34)
From markets to malls, you can practically shop anywhere for just about anything.

Chatuchak Weekend Market Getting lost here is a Bangkok experience. (p50; pictured)

Chiang Mai (p74)
Homespun and chic handicrafts in a funfair-like atmosphere at its outdoor markets.

Walking Streets For food, fashion and entertainment. (p84)

Phuket (p206)
Phuket Town boasts both artsy boutiques and a buzzy weekend market.

Ranida Boutique with antiques and vintage-inspired fashion. (p227)

Plan Your Trip
Local Life

Activities

Thailand offers a wealth of activities to choose from. From swimming with whale sharks and other big fish to a visit to the Gulf of Thailand's premier dive spots, Sail Rock and Chumphon Pinnacle on Ko Pha-Ngan, water-based activities should be at the top of your holiday to-do list. If you prefer keeping your feet dry, Kanchanaburi Province offers historical sites, caves and national parks galore, while adrenalin junkies can scale the limestone crags or kayak the rocky monuments around Railay. If hiking is more your thing, exploring the remote hill tribes of Chiang Rai might just be the tonic for you, or indulge in a little hot-spring action.

Shopping

Your wallet will get a serious retail workout in Thailand. The capital's mega-malls are packed with designer gear, unique gifts and home decor, and Chatuchak Weekend Market and other outdoor markets will test your shopping muscles to the max. In Chiang Mai, the bustling Night Bazaar is filled with souvenirs and antiques, while boutique stores provide economic development opportunities for rural villagers and their handicrafts, such as silk textiles and basketry. And save room in your suitcase for the beautiful Lao-influenced weaving traditions of *mát·mèe* to be found in the sleepy northeastern town of Nong Khai.

Eating

Thai food is super delicious, remarkably convenient and ridiculously cheap. Each region whips up its own variation of pungent, fiery and colourful curries, and you can learn the tricks of the trade at one of Bangkok's, Phuket's or Chiang Mai's cooking schools. The northeast's triumvirate of dishes – grilled chicken, spicy green papaya

OPERATION SHOOTING / SHUTTERSTOCK ©

salad and sticky rice – have converts across the country, while along the coast you can dine on some of the finest fruits of the sea. And don't overlook the tropical fruit – sweet as candy, it can be plucked from colourful pyramid displays throughout the country.

Drinking & Nightlife

From international DJs spinning discs in the capital's clubs and cocktails flowing from the sky bars to the Full Moon Parties, whisky buckets and almighty hangovers nursed by lazy days on the beach at Ko Pha-Ngan to carousing with hip uni students and boho NGOs in the beer-garden bars of Chiang Mai, the hospitality of the Thai people is legendary.

Entertainment

There is no shortage of events to keep you entertained in Thailand. As traditional music and dance are performed in colourful street

★ Best Local Restaurants

Bang Po Seafood (p122), Ko Samui

Krua Apsorn (p64), Bangkok

Lung Eed (p138), Chiang Rai

Lung Lek (p245), Ayuthaya

Daeng Namnuang (p255), Nong Khai

parades during local festivals in Chiang Mai, Chiang Rai or Nong Khai, in Bangkok you can experience Thai boxing champions sparring at the country's premier stadium, or catch an open-mike night, jazz jam sessions and Thai folk music at cosy live-music clubs in places including Chiang Mai.

From left: Rock climbing, Railay (p148); Silk weaving

Plan Your Trip
Month by Month

SOIROOM / SHUTTERSTOCK ©

January

The weather is cool and dry, ushering in the peak tourist season.

🎎 Chinese New Year

Thais with Chinese ancestry celebrate the Chinese lunar new year (drùt jeen) with a week of house-cleaning and fireworks.

February

Still in the high season; snowbirds flock to Thailand for sun and fun.

🎎 Makha Bucha

One of three holy days marking significant moments of the Buddha's life, Makha Bucha (mah·ká boo·chah) commemorates the day when 1250 arhants (Buddhists who had achieved enlightenment) assembled to visit the Buddha and received Buddhist principles. The festival falls on the full moon of the third lunar month.

🎎 Flower Festival

Chiang Mai displays its floral beauty during a three-day period. The festival highlight is the flower-decorated floats that parade through town.

March

Hot and dry season approaches and the beaches start to empty out. This is also Thailand's semester break, and students head out on sightseeing trips.

🪁 Kite-Flying Festivals

During the windy season, colourful kites battle it out over the skies of Sanam Luang in Bangkok and elsewhere in the country.

April

Hot, dry weather sweeps across the land. Although the tourist season is winding down, make reservations well in advance as the whole country is on the move for Songkran.

MATT MUNRO / LONELY PLANET ©

✕ Golden Mango Season

Luscious mangoes are at their peak of ripeness in April, and are sliced before your eyes, packed in a container with sticky rice and accompanied with a coconut milk dressing.

✿ Songkran

Thailand's traditional new year (13 to 15 April) starts out as a respectful affair then devolves into a water war. Morning visits to the temple involve water-sprinkling ceremonies. Afterwards, Thais load up their water guns and head out to the streets for battle.

✿ Poy Sang Long

This Buddhist ordination festival is held in late March/early April in Chiang Mai and Pai. Young Shan boys are paraded in festive costumes.

May

Leading up to the rainy season, festivals encourage plentiful rains and bountiful harvests. Prices are low and tourists are few but it is still incredibly hot.

★ Best Festivals

Flower Festival, February

Songkran, April

Rocket Festival, May

Vegetarian Festival, September/October

Loi Krathong, November

✿ Royal Ploughing Ceremony

This royal ceremony employs astrology and ancient Brahman rituals to kick off the rice-planting season.

✿ Rocket Festival

In the northeast, where rain can be scarce, villagers craft bamboo rockets (*bâng fai*) that are fired into the sky to encourage precipitation. This festival is celebrated in Nong Khai.

From left: Makha Bucha, Chiang Mai; Songkran, Chiang Mai

🦋 Visakha Bucha

The holy day of Visakha Bucha (*wí·săh·kà boo·chah*) falls on the 15th day of the waxing moon in the sixth lunar month and commemorates the date of the Buddha's birth, enlightenment and *parinibbana* (passing away).

June

In some parts of the country, the rainy season is merely an afternoon shower, leaving the rest of the day for music and merriment.

July

The start of the rainy season ushers in Buddhist Lent, a period of reflection and meditation. Summer holidays bring an upsurge in tourists.

🦋 HM the King's Birthday

The current king's birthday is on 28 July, and is a public holiday.

🦋 Asanha Bucha

The full moon of the eighth lunar month commemorates the Buddha's first sermon, in which he described the religion's four noble truths. It is considered one of Buddhism's holiest days.

🦋 Khao Phansaa

The day after Asanha Bucha marks the beginning of Buddhist Lent (the first day of the waning moon in the eighth lunar month), the traditional time for men to enter the monastery.

August

Overcast skies and daily showers mark the middle of the rainy season.

🦋 Mother's Day

The Queen Mother's Birthday (12 August) is a public holiday and marks national Mother's Day.

October

Religious preparations for the end of the rainy season and the end of Buddhist Lent begin. The monsoons are reaching the finish line (in most of the country).

🦋 Vegetarian Festival

A holiday from meat is taken for nine days in adherence with Chinese beliefs of mind and body purification. In Phuket the festival gets extreme, with entranced marchers becoming human shish kebabs. Generally held late September/early October.

🦋 Ork Phansaa

The end of Buddhist lent (three lunar months after Khao Phansaa) is followed by the *gà·tǐn* ceremony, in which new robes are given to the monks by merit-makers. In Nong Khai and other river towns, long-boat races are held.

🦋 King Chulalongkorn Day

Rama V is honoured on the anniversary of his death (23 October) at Bangkok's Royal Plaza in Dusit.

November

The cool, dry season has arrived, and if you get here early enough, you'll beat the tourist crowds. The beaches are inviting and the landscape is lush.

🦋 Loi Krathong

One of Thailand's most beloved festivals, Loi Krathong is celebrated on the first full moon of the 12th lunar month. Small origami-like boats (called *krathong* or *grà·tong*) festooned with flowers and candles are sent adrift in the waterways.

December

Peak tourist season returns with fair skies, busy beach resorts and a holiday mood.

🦋 Father's Day

Honouring the former king's birthday on 5 December, this public holiday hosts parades and merit-making events.

Plan Your Trip
Get Inspired

AUSTIN BUSH / LONELY PLANET ©

Read

Very Thai: Everyday Popular Culture (Philip Cornwel-Smith; 2013) A colourful compendium.

Lai Chiwit (Many Lives; Kukrit Pramoj; translation 1996) Short stories featuring the lives of 11 different Thais.

Sightseeing (Rattawut Lapcharoensap; 2004) Fictional stories about Thai life.

Bangkok Days (Lawrence Osborne; 2010) A witty and insightful account of living in Bangkok.

King Bhumibol Adulyadej: A Life's Work (Nicholas Grossman et al; 2011) Official biography of the former king.

The Judgement (Chart Korbjitti; 1981) Award winner; about a villager wrongly accused of a crime.

Watch

How to Win at Checkers (Every Time) (Josh Kim; 2015) Based on Rattawut Lapcharoensap's short story, 11-year-old Oat deals with the military draft of his gay older brother.

36 (Nawapol Thamrongrattanarit; 2012) Indie love affair remembered through 36 static camera set-ups.

Tom-Yum-Goong (Prachya Pinkaew; 2005) Tony Jaa, the Jackie Chan of Thailand, stars in this martial arts movie, the most successful Thai film ever released in the US.

Fah Talai Jone (Tears of the Black Tiger; 2000) Wisit Sasanatieng pays tribute to Thai action flicks.

Listen

Dharmajāti (Bodyslam) Headlining alt-rock.

Best (Pumpuang Duangjan) The best from the late country diva.

Boomerang (Bird Thongchai) Beloved album from the king of Thai pop.

Romantic Comedy (Apartment Khunpa) Leading post alt-rock.

Made in Thailand (Carabao) Thailand's classic classic-rock album.

Above: Street food dining, Bangkok (p56)

Plan Your Trip
Five-Day Itineraries

Bangkok to Chiang Mai

Touch down in Bangkok, jet to Chiang Mai and escape the urban grind with an excursion to the rural village of Pai.

FROM LEFT: STEPHANE BIDOUZE / SHUTTERSTOCK ©, SERGEY EDENTOD / SHUTTERSTOCK ©

Pai (p106) ❸ Party, take a yoga course or get in touch with nature at the country's hottest inland backpacker destination.

Chiang Mai (p74) Visit the ❷ old city, stroll the fashionable Th Nimmanhaemin, or visit an elephant sanctuary. 🚌 4 hrs to Pai

Bangkok (p34) Explore the capital's temples and restaurants, shop till you ❶ drop, then kick back at a rooftop bar. ✈ 1 hr to Chiang Mai

Bangkok to Kanchanaburi

See the best of what central Thailand has to offer with this itinerary that touches on Thailand's contemporary and ancient history.

Kanchanaburi (p168) WWII comes into vivid focus at the museums and monuments of this riverside town.

3

2 **Ayuthaya** (p234) Travel back in time to Thailand's golden age with a visit to Ayuthaya Historical Park. 🚌 2 hrs to Suphanburi, then 🚌 1½ hrs to Kanchanaburi

1

Bangkok (p34) Indulge in big-city excesses before downshifting to the provincial side of central Thailand. 🚌 1 hr to Ayuthaya

FROM LEFT: VACANCYLIZM / SHUTTERSTOCK ©; THALERNGSAK MONGKOLSIN / SHUTTERSTOCK ©

②

③

Plan Your Trip

10-Day Itinerary

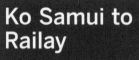

Ko Samui to Railay

Soak up the tropical scenery by surveying the beaches and islands of Thailand's famous coasts: the Gulf of Thailand and the Andaman Sea.

Ko Pha-Ngan (p180)
At full moon this relaxed island transforms into a party werewolf. 🚤 3 hrs to Surat Thani, then 🚌 2½ hrs to Krabi, then 🚤 45 mins to Railay

②

①

Ko Samui (p110)
Fly into paradise and hit the beaches, or head offshore to the limestone crags of Ang Thong Marine National Park. 🚤 20-60 mins to Ko Pha-Ngan

③ Railay (p142)
It's worth the journey here to enjoy the stunning karst mountains jutting out of jewel-coloured seas; kayak among them or strap on a harness to climb the cliffs.

Plan Your Trip
Two-Week Itinerary

Sukhothai to Chiang Rai

Explore the facets of northern Thailand, from the ancient capital of Sukhothai to the contemporary cities of Chiang Mai and Chiang Rai.

Doi Mae Salong (p134) An ethnic Chinese community perched on the spine of a mountain; an easy day trip (or overnighter).

Chiang Rai (p126) Visit Wat Rong Khun, peruse the Night Bazaar and take an NGO-led trekking tour over three or four days. 🚌 1½ hrs to Doi Mae Salong

Chiang Mai (p74) Leave three or more days for wandering around old city temples, handicraft shops and fashionable Th Nimmanhaemin. 🚌 3-4 hrs to Chiang Rai

Sukhothai (p152) Spend a few days visiting the historical parks. 🚌 6 hrs to Chiang Mai

Plan Your Trip
Family Travel

ANEKOHO / SHUTTERSTOCK ©

Thais are so family focused that even grumpy taxi drivers want to pinch your baby's cheeks and play a game of peek-aboo (called *já ǎir*). On crowded buses, adults will stand so that children can sit, and hotel and restaurant staff willingly set aside chores to become a child's playmate.

Sights & Activities

Children will especially enjoy the beaches, as most are in gentle bays appropriate for beginner swimmers. For the more experienced, some of the Gulf and Andaman islands have near-shore reefs for snorkelling. Some beaches have strong currents and riptides, especially during the monsoon season.

Crocodile farms, monkey shows and tiger zoos abound in Thailand, but conditions are inhumane. Eco-tour projects in Chiang Mai provide a better alternative. The elephant sanctuaries are excellent places to see the revered pachyderm in a dignified setting. Older children will enjoy jungle tours and other outdoor activities. Many

of the beach resorts, such as Phuket, also have waterfall spotting and water sports.

In urban areas, kids might feel cooped up, in which case a hotel swimming pool will provide necessary play space. Playgrounds are neither widespread nor well maintained, though every city has an exercise park where runners and families go in the early evening. Though Bangkok is lean on green, it is still fun for little ones in awe of construction sites and for older ones obsessed with shopping malls. If you're worried about long-distance journeys with a fussy passenger, opt for the train. Kids can walk around the carriage and visit the friendly locals; they are assigned the lower sleeping berths which have views of the stations and dust-kicking motorcycles.

Kid-Friendly Eats

In general, Thai children don't start eating spicy food until primary school; before then they seemingly survive on rice and junk food. Child-friendly meals include chicken

FOTOS593 / SHUTTERSTOCK ©

in all of its nonspicy permutations – *gài yâhng* (grilled chicken), *gài tôrt* (fried chicken) and *gài pàt mét má·môo·ang* (chicken stir-fried with cashews).

Some kids will even branch out to *kôw pàt* (fried rice), though the strong odour of *nám plah* (fish sauce) might be a deal breaker. Helpful restaurant staff will recommend *kài jee·o* (Thai-style omelette), which can be made in a jiffy. If all else fails, tropical fruits and juices are ubiquitous and will keep the kids hydrated. Of course, most tourist centres also have Western restaurants catering to homesick eaters of any age.

Need to Know

Changing facilities Non-existent.

Cots By special request at midrange and top-end hotels.

Highchairs Sometimes available in resort areas.

Nappies (diapers) Minimarkets and 7-Elevens carry small sizes; try Tesco Lotus or Tops Market for size 3 or larger.

★ Best Destinations for Kids
Ko Samui (p110)
Ko Pha-Ngan (p180)
Bangkok (p34)

Strollers Bring a compact umbrella stroller.

Transport Car seats and seat belts are not widely available on public or hired transport.

Health & Safety

For the most part, parents needn't worry too much about health concerns. Drink lots of water. Enforce regular hand washing. Thai children are bathed at least twice a day and powdered afterwards to reduce skin irritation from the humid climate; foreigners should aim for at least daily showers.

From left: Kayaking in the Gulf of Thailand; Elephant Nature Park (p87), Chiang Mai

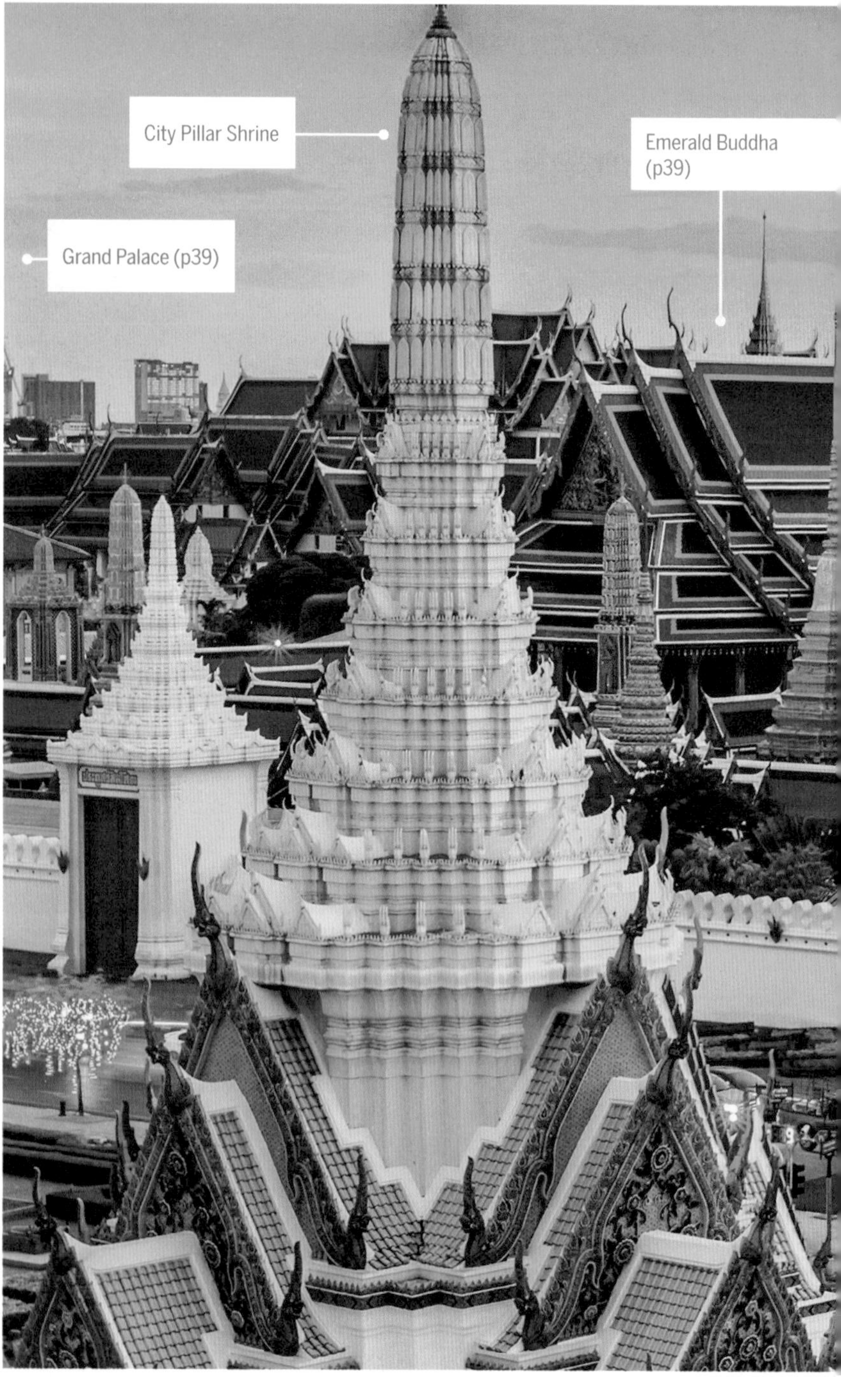

City Pillar Shrine

Emerald Buddha (p39)

Grand Palace (p39)

BANGKOK

Three Spires (p41)

Wat Phra Kaew (p38)

Murals of the Ramakian (p38)

Ko Ratanakosin & Banglamphu

Buddhist temples, royal palaces, leafy lanes, antique shophouses, buzzing wet markets and golden temples.

CHATUCHAK WEEKEND MARKET

Chinatown

The streets are crammed with bird's-nest restaurants, gaudy gold and jade shops, and flashing neon signs in Chinese characters.

CHAO PHRAYA RIVER

JIM THOMPSON HOUSE

Sukhumvit

Japanese enclaves, burger restaurants, Middle Eastern nightlife zones, tacky 'sexpat' haunts: it's all here along Th Sukhumvit.

Khlong Samsen

Hualamphong Train Station

Siam Square

Multistorey malls, outdoor shopping precincts and neverending markets – this is modern Bangkok's commercial district.

Suvarnabhumi International (20km)

WAT PHO

Silom & Riverside

Palpable history in the riverside area's crumbling architecture, while Silom, Bangkok's de facto financial district, is frenetic and modern.

WAT PHRA KAEW & GRAND PALACE

Ko Ratanakosin, Banglamphu & Chinatown (p62)
Siam Square, Silom & Riverside (p66)
Sukhumvit (p70)

Bang Sue

Don Mueang International (13km)

Bangkok at a Glance...

Formerly the epitome of the steamy Asian metropolis, Bangkok has undergone decades worth of renovations and emerged an international starlet. The Bangkok of today is tidier and easier to navigate than ever before and will impress with awesome urban exploration, and sophisticated dining and nightlife.

Supplement your fun with scholarly pursuits such as historic sightseeing and courses ranging in topic from cooking to meditation. And don't worry, the city's famous temples, palaces and markets still deliver just as they always have done.

Bangkok in Two Days

Hit the temples of **Ko Ratanakosin** (p60), followed by lunch in **Banglamphu** (p64). On the second day visit **Jim Thompson House** (p49) and indulge in a Thai **massage** (p63), followed by an upscale Thai dinner at **nahm** (p67).

Bangkok in Four Days

Spend a day at **Chatuchak Weekend Market** (p50). Hit **Chinatown** (p65) for a street-food dinner. Hang out with Bangkok's hipsters at **Sukhumvit's** (p52) bars and clubs.

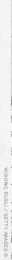

Suvarnabhumi International Airport (p68)

Arriving in Bangkok

Suvarnabhumi International Airport
The Airport Rail Link (30 minutes) operates from 6am to midnight. Meter taxis make the run to town at all times.

Don Mueang International Airport
Meter taxis run into town 24 hours.

Sleeping

Bangkok is home to a diverse spread of modern hostels, guesthouses and hotels. To make matters better, much of Bangkok's accommodation offers excellent value, and competition is so intense that fat discounts are almost always available.

For more information on the best neighbourhood to stay in, see p73.

TRAVEL MANIA / SHUTTERSTOCK ©

Wat Phra Kaew & Grand Palace

Bangkok's biggest tourist attraction is this fantastical complex, the spiritual core of Thai Buddhism and the monarchy, symbolically united in what is the country's most holy image, the Emerald Buddha.

Great For...

☑ **Don't Miss**

The Ramakian Murals depicting the *Ramakian* (the Thai version of the Indian *Ramayana* epic) in its entirety.

The Complex

This ground was consecrated in 1782, the first year of Bangkok rule, and is today a pilgrimage destination for devout Buddhists and nationalists. The 94.5-hectare grounds encompass more than 100 buildings that represent 200 years of royal history and architectural experimentation.

Ramakian Murals

Outside the main *bòht* (ordination hall) of Wat Phra Kaew is a stone statue of the Chinese goddess of mercy, Kuan Im; nearby are two cow figures, representing the birth year of Rama I (King Phraphutthayotfa Chulalok; r 1782–1809). In the 2km-long cloister that defines the perimeter of the complex are 178 murals depicting the *Ramakian* in its entirety, beginning at the

Detail of the Ramakian murals

Th Na Phra Lan

Wat Phra Kaew & Grand Palace

NICEPIX / SHUTTERSTOCK ©

❶ Need to Know

วัดพระแก้ว, พระบรมมหาราชวัง; Map p62; Th Na Phra Lan; 500B; ⏱8.30am-3.30pm; 🚢Chang Pier, Maharaj Pier, Phra Chan Tai Pier

✖ Take a Break

Pa Aew (Map p62; Th Maha Rat; mains 20-60B; ⏱10am-5pm Tue-Sat; 🚢Tien Pier) is a basic, open-air curry stall, but it's one of our favourite places to eat in this part of town.

★ Top Tip

At Wat Phra Kaew and in the Grand Palace grounds, dress rules are strictly enforced. If you're wearing shorts or a sleeveless shirt you will not be allowed into the temple grounds.

north gate and moving clockwise around the compound.

If the temple grounds seem overrun by tourists, the mural area is usually mercifully quiet and shady.

Emerald Buddha

Upon entering Wat Phra Kaew you'll meet the *yaksha,* brawny guardian giants from the *Ramakian.* Beyond them is a courtyard where the central *bòht* houses the Emerald Buddha. The spectacular ornamentation inside and out does an excellent job of distracting first-time visitors from paying their respects to the image. Here's why: the Emerald Buddha is only 66cm tall and sits so high above worshippers in the main temple building that the gilded shrine is more striking than the small figure it cradles. No

one knows exactly where it comes from or who sculpted it, but it first appeared on record in 15th-century Chiang Rai (in northern Thailand).

Photography inside the *bòht* is not permitted.

Grand Palace

Adjoining Wat Phra Kaew is the Grand Palace (Phra Borom Maharatchawang), a former royal residence that is today only used on ceremonial occasions. Visitors can survey a portion of the Grand Palace grounds, but are allowed to enter only one of the remaining palace buildings.

Wat Phra Kaew & Grand Palace

EXPLORE BANGKOK'S PREMIER MONUMENTS TO RELIGION & REGENCY

The first area tourists enter is the Buddhist temple compound generally referred to as Wat Phra Kaew. A covered walkway surrounds the area, the inner walls of which are decorated with the ❶ ❷ murals of the Ramakian. Originally painted during the reign of Rama I (r 1782–1809), the murals, which depict the Hindu epic the *Ramayana*, span 178 panels that describe the struggles of Rama to rescue his kidnapped wife, Sita.

After taking in the story, pass through one of the gateways guarded by ❸ **yaksha** to the inner compound. The most important structure here is the ❹ **bòht (ordination hall)**, which houses the ❺ **Emerald Buddha**.

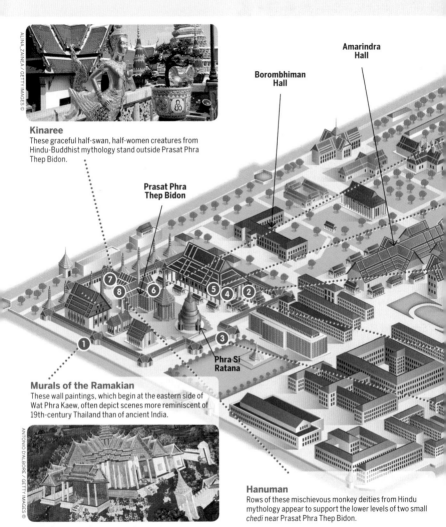

Kinaree
These graceful half-swan, half-women creatures from Hindu-Buddhist mythology stand outside Prasat Phra Thep Bidon.

Prasat Phra Thep Bidon

Borombhiman Hall

Amarindra Hall

Phra Si Ratana

Murals of the Ramakian
These wall paintings, which begin at the eastern side of Wat Phra Kaew, often depict scenes more reminiscent of 19th-century Thailand than of ancient India.

Hanuman
Rows of these mischievous monkey deities from Hindu mythology appear to support the lower levels of two small *chedi* near Prasat Phra Thep Bidon.

Head east to the so-called Upper Terrace, an elevated area home to the **6 spires of the three primary chedi**. The middle structure, Phra Mondop, is used to house Buddhist manuscripts. This area is also home to several of Wat Phra Kaew's noteworthy mythical beings, including beckoning **7 kinaree** and several grimacing **8 Hanuman**.

Proceed through the western gate to the compound known as the Grand Palace. Few of the buildings here are open to the public. The most noteworthy structure is **9 Chakri Mahaprasat**. Built in 1882, the exterior of the hall is a unique blend of Western and traditional Thai architecture.

The Three Spires
The elaborate seven-tiered roof of Phra Mondop, the Khmer-style peak of Prasat Phra Thep Bidon, and the gilded Phra Si Ratana *chedi* are the tallest structures in the compound.

LEPNEVA IRINA / SHUTTERSTOCK ©

Emerald Buddha
Despite the name, this diminutive statue (it's only 66cm tall) is actually carved from nephrite, a type of jade.

ALEXEY STIOP / GETTY IMAGES ©

The Death of Thotsakan
The panels progress clockwise, culminating at the western edge of the compound with the death of Thotsakan, Sita's kidnapper, and his elaborate funeral procession.

Chakri Mahaprasat
This structure is sometimes referred to as *fa·ràng sài chá·dah* (Westerner in a Thai crown) because each wing is topped by a *mon·dòp*: a spire representing a Thai adaptation of a Hindu shrine.

DESIGN PICS / BLAKE KENT / GETTY IMAGES ©

Dusit Hall

Yaksha
Each entrance to the Wat Phra Kaew compound is watched over by a pair of vigilant and enormous *yaksha*, ogres or giants from Hindu mythology.

ZZVET / GETTY IMAGES ©

Bòht (Ordination Hall)
This structure is an early example of the Ratanakosin school of architecture, which combines traditional stylistic holdovers from Ayuthaya along with more modern touches from China and the West.

Reclining Buddha

Wat Pho

Of all Bangkok's temples, Wat Pho is arguably the one most worth visiting, for both its remarkable Reclining Buddha image and its sprawling, stupa-studded grounds.

Great For...

☑ **Don't Miss**

The Reclining Buddha, the granite statues and the massage pavilions.

Reclining Buddha

In the northwest corner of the site you'll find Wat Pho's main attraction, the enormous Reclining Buddha. The figure was originally commissioned by Rama III (King Phranangklao; r 1824–51), and illustrates the passing of the Buddha into nirvana. It is made of plaster around a brick core and finished in gold leaf, which gives it a serene luminescence that keeps you looking, and looking again, from different angles.

Phra Ubosot

Phra Ubosot, the compound's main *bòht* (ordination hall), is constructed in Ayuthaya style and is strikingly more subdued than Wat Phra Kaew's. A temple has stood on this site since the 16th century, but in 1781 Rama I ordered the original Wat Photharam

Phra Buddha Deva Patimakorn

ℹ Need to Know

วัดโพธิ์/วัดพระเชตุพน, Wat Phra Chetuphon; Map p62; Th Sanam Chai; 100B; ☺8.30am-6.30pm; 🚢Tien Pier

✗ Take a Break

Sip a cocktail at **Amorosa** (Map p62; www.arunresidence.com; rooftop, Arun Residence, 36-38 Soi Pratu Nokyung; ☺5pm-midnight Mon-Thu, to 1am Fri-Sun; 🚢Tien Pier), while enjoying views of the river and Wat Arun opposite.

★ Top Tip

Enter via Th Chetuphon or Th Sanam Chai to avoid the touts and tour groups of the main entrance on Th Thai Wang.

to be completely rebuilt as part of his new capital. Rama I's remains are interred in the base of the presiding Buddha figure in Phra Ubosot. The images on display in the four *wí·hǎhn* (sanctuaries) surrounding Phra Ubosot are worth investigation, as is a low marble wall with 152 bas-reliefs depicting scenes from the *Ramakian*.

Royal Chedi

On the western side of the grounds is a collection of four towering tiled *chedi* (stupa) commemorating the first four Chakri kings. The surrounding wall was built on the orders of Rama IV (King Mongkut; r 1851–68). Among the compound's additional 91 smaller *chedi* are clusters containing the ashes of lesser royal descendants.

Massage Pavilions

A small pavilion west of Phra Ubosot has Unesco-awarded inscriptions detailing the tenets of traditional Thai massage. These and other similar inscriptions led Wat Pho to be regarded as Thailand's first university. Today it maintains that tradition as the national headquarters for the teaching and preservation of traditional Thai medicine, including Thai massage. The famous school has two **massage pavilions** (Thai massage per hour 420B; ☺9am-4pm) located within the temple area and additional rooms within the **training facility** (Map p62; ☎02 622 3551; www.watpomassage.com; 392/32-33 Soi Phen Phat; lessons from 2500B; Thai massage per hour 420B; ☺lessons 9am-4pm, massage 9am-8pm) outside the temple.

Wat Pho

A WALK THROUGH THE BIG BUDDHAS OF WAT PHO

The logical starting place is the main *wí·hǎhn* (sanctuary), home to Wat Pho's centrepiece, the immense ❶ **Reclining Buddha**. In addition to its enormous size, note the ❷ **mother-of-pearl inlay** on the soles of the statue's feet. The interior walls of the *wí·hǎhn* are covered with murals that depict previous lives of the Buddha, and along the south side of the structure there are 108 bronze monk bowls; for 20B you can buy 108 coins, each of which is dropped in a bowl for good luck.

Exit the *wí·hǎhn* and head east via the two ❸ **stone giants** who guard the gateway to the rest of the compound. Directly south of these are the four towering ❹ **royal chedi**.

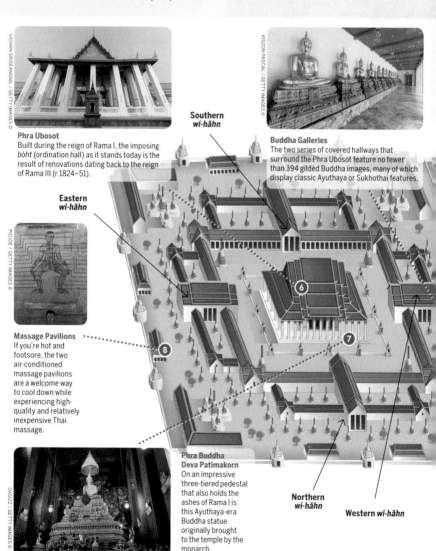

Phra Ubosot
Built during the reign of Rama I, the imposing *bòht* (ordination hall) as it stands today is the result of renovations dating back to the reign of Rama III (r 1824–51).

Buddha Galleries
The two series of covered hallways that surround the Phra Ubosot feature no fewer than 394 gilded Buddha images, many of which display classic Ayuthaya or Sukhothai features.

Southern *wí·hǎhn*

Eastern *wí·hǎhn*

Massage Pavilions
If you're hot and footsore, the two air-conditioned massage pavilions are a welcome way to cool down while experiencing high-quality and relatively inexpensive Thai massage.

Phra Buddha Deva Patimakorn
On an impressive three-tiered pedestal that also holds the ashes of Rama I is this Ayuthaya-era Buddha statue originally brought to the temple by the monarch.

Northern *wí·hǎhn*

Western *wí·hǎhn*

VICHAN SRISEANGNIL / GETTY IMAGES ©

KISZON PASCAL / GETTY IMAGES ©

PIDJOE / GETTY IMAGES ©

OASISZZ / GETTY IMAGES ©

Continue east, passing through two consecutive **⑤ galleries of Buddha statues** linking four *wí·hǎhn*, two of which contain notable Sukhothai-era Buddha statues; these comprise the exterior of **⑥ Phra Ubosot**, the immense ordination hall that is Wat Pho's second-most noteworthy structure. The base of the building is surrounded by bas-relief inscriptions, and inside is the notable Buddha statue, **⑦ Phra Buddha Deva Patimakorn**.

Wat Pho is often referred to as Thailand's first university, a tradition that continues today in an associated traditional Thai medicine school and, at the compound's eastern extent, two **⑧ massage pavilions**.

Interspersed throughout the eastern half of the compound are several additional minor *chedi* and rock gardens.

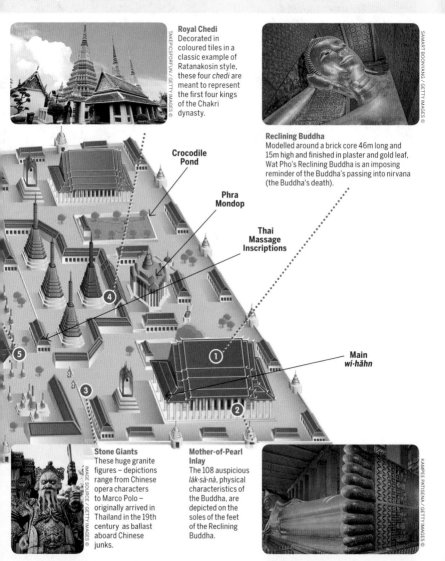

Royal Chedi
Decorated in coloured tiles in a classic example of Ratanakosin style, these four *chedi* are meant to represent the first four kings of the Chakri dynasty.

TAKEPICSFORFUN / GETTY IMAGES ©

Reclining Buddha
Modelled around a brick core 46m long and 15m high and finished in plaster and gold leaf, Wat Pho's Reclining Buddha is an imposing reminder of the Buddha's passing into nirvana (the Buddha's death).

SAMART BOONYANG / GETTY IMAGES ©

Crocodile Pond

Phra Mondop

Thai Massage Inscriptions

Main *wí·hǎhn*

Stone Giants
These huge granite figures – depictions range from Chinese opera characters to Marco Polo – originally arrived in Thailand in the 19th century as ballast aboard Chinese junks.

IMAGE SOURCE / GETTY IMAGES ©

Mother-of-Pearl Inlay
The 108 auspicious *lák·sà·nà*, physical characteristics of the Buddha, are depicted on the soles of the feet of the Reclining Buddha.

KAMPEE PATISENA / GETTY IMAGES ©

Taling Chan Floating Market

SANIT FUANGNAKHON / SHUTTERSTOCK ©

Chao Phraya River

The River of Kings (Mae Nam Chao Phraya) is the symbolic lifeblood of the Thai nation. Revered riverside temples stand sentry as boats and barges industriously move cargo and passengers, and cool breezes provide evening refreshment.

Great For...

☑ **Don't Miss**

Catch the Chao Phraya Express Boat as the sun sets across this throbbing metropolis.

Wat Arun

Claiming a powerful riverside position, **Wat Arun** (วัดอรุณฯ; Map p62; www.watarun.net; off Th Arun Amarin; 50B; ⊙8am-6pm; ⛴cross-river ferry from Tien Pier) marks the rebirth of the Thai nation after the fall of Ayuthaya to the invading Burmese army in the 1700s. The temple's facade is decorated with delicate porcelain mosaics, a common temple adornment from the days when Chinese porcelain was used for ship ballasts.

Thonburi's Canals

Bangkok's past as the Venice of the East lives, bathes and plays along Thonburi's network of canals, including Khlong Bangkok Noi and Khlong Mon. Traditional homes are built on stilts with front doors leading to the water.

Wat Arun

SAIKOOP / SHUTTERSTOCK ©

❶ Need to Know

Tour the river and riverside attractions aboard chartered long-tail boats (1½ to two hours, 1300B to 1500B) or the Chao Phraya Express commuter boats.

✕ Take a Break

Make a dinner date with the river at **Khinlom Chom Sa-Phan** (Map p62; ☑02 628 8382; www.khinlomchomsaphan.com; 11/6 Soi 3, Th Samsen; mains 100-2500B; ☺11.30am-midnight; 🚢Thewet Pier).

★ Top Tip

People shouldn't sit in the last seats on the commuter boats; these are reserved for monks.

Royal Barges National Museum

Travel by boat used to be a majestic affair. Historic vessels dating back to the Ayu-thaya period are on display at the **Royal Barges National Museum** (พิพิธภัณฑสถาน แห่งชาติ เรือพระราชพิธี/เรือพระที่นั่ง; Map p62; Khlong Bangkok Noi or 80/1 Th Arun Amarin; admission 100B, camera 100B; ☺9am-5pm; 🚢Phra Pin Klao Bridge Pier). *Suphannahong* (the king's personal barge) is bestowed with a huge swan head carved into the bow. Lesser barges feature bows that are carved into other Hindu-Buddhist mythological shapes such as the *naga* (mythical sea serpent) and *garuda* (Vishnu's bird mount).

Floating Market

The nearly extinct floating markets (*dà·làht nám*) have been rescued by nostalgic Thais and tourists. **Taling Chan Floating Market** (ตลาดน้ำตลิ่งชัน; off Map p62; Khlong Bangkok Noi, Thonburi; ☺7am-4pm Sat & Sun; 🚇Wongwian Yai exit 3 & taxi), located along Khlong Bangkok Noi, is a hybrid market with fruit vendors on the road and floating docks serving as informal dining rooms. Meals are prepared aboard tethered canoes.

Ko Kret

An easy rural getaway, Ko Kret is a car-free island and home to the Mon people, known for their hand-thrown terracotta pots. Locals flock to Ko Kret on weekends to snack and shop. Ko Kret is in Nonthaburi, about 15km north of central Bangkok. Take bus 166 from the Victory Monument or a taxi to Pak Kret, before boarding the cross-river ferry (from 5am to 9pm) that leaves from Wat Sanam Neua.

COWARDLION / SHUTTERSTOCK ©

Jim Thompson House

The former home of an American silk entrepreneur is a beautiful repository for Thai art and architecture. On display are museum-quality examples of Thai craftsmanship, Buddhist sculpture and textiles.

Great For...

☑ **Don't Miss**

Wandering the lushly landscaped grounds.

A socialite and former spy, Jim Thompson's life is as intriguing as his belongings. He served briefly in the Office of Strategic Services (the forerunner to the CIA) in Thailand during WWII. Settling in Bangkok after the war, he established a successful Thai silk export business, introducing the textile to international fashion houses. He mysteriously disappeared in 1967 while out for a walk in Malaysia's Cameroon Highlands. His disappearance was never explained and some suspect foul play.

Art

A collector with eclectic tastes, Thompson bought art and antiques from travelling merchants and neighbouring countries. He collected objects that were not well known at the time, including from the Dvaravati period.

COWARDLION / SHUTTERSTOCK ©

❶ Need to Know

เรือนไทยจิมทอมป์สัน; Map p66; www.jim
thompsonhouse.com; 6 Soi Kasem San 2;
adult/student 150/100B; ⊙9am-6pm,
compulsory tours every 20min; 🚤klorng boat
to Sapan Hua Chang Pier, Ⓢ National Stadium
exit 1

✗ Take a Break

MBK Food Island (Map p66; 6th fl, MBK
Center, cnr Rama I & Th Phayathai; mains
35-150B; ⊙10am-9pm; ❄🖊; Ⓢ National
Stadium exit 4) is a quintessential mall
food court selling regional Thai and
international dishes.

★ Top Tip

Read *The Ideal Man* by Joshua Kur-
lantzick for a profile of Jim Thompson.

Architecture

Thompson collected six teak houses
from different regions in the country as a
showcase for his art collection. Some of the
houses were brought from Ayuthaya, while
others were transported across the canal
from Baan Khrua. The homes were given a
landscaped jungle garden to further highlight Thailand's natural beauty. The home,
however, is organised like a Western residence with an entrance hall and all rooms
arranged on the same level overlooking the
terrace and the canal.

Baan Khrua

Just across the canal is the silk-weaving
community of **Baan Khrua** (บ้านครัว; Map
p66). This neighbourhood was settled
by Cham Muslims from Cambodia and

Vietnam, who relocated to Bangkok after
fighting on the side of the Thai king during
the wars of the end of the 18th century.
Their silk-weaving skills attracted the attention of Jim Thompson in the 1950s and
'60s when he hired the weavers for his bur-
geoning silk export business. Since then
commercial silk production and many of
the original families have moved elsewhere
but two family-run outfits, **Phamai Baan
Krua** (ผ้าไหมบ้านครัว; www.phamaibaankrua.
com; Soi 9, Soi Phaya Nak; ⊙8.30am-5pm) and
Aood Bankrua Thai Silk (ลุงอู๊ดบ้านครัว
ไหมไทย; ☏02 215 9864; Soi 9, Soi Phaya Nak;
⊙9am-8pm), continue the tradition. Baan
Khrua can be reached by the bridge over
the canal at the end of Soi Kasem San 3.

ARTAPARTAMENT / SHUTTERSTOCK ©

Chatuchak Weekend Market

An outdoor market on steroids, Chatuchak Weekend Market sells everything under the sun. Vendors are packed into claustrophobic warrens creating a shopping obstacle course. It is crowded and chaotic but one of a kind.

Great For...

☑ Don't Miss

If you aren't in town on the weekend, visit nearby **Or Tor Kor Market** (องค์กร ตลาดเพื่อเกษตรกร; Map p66; Th Kamphaeng-phet 1; ⊙8am-6pm; Ⓜ Kamphaeng Phet exit 3), a fruit and vegetable market.

A little pre-planning goes a long way. Nancy Chandler's *Map of Bangkok* has a handy schematic map and the clock tower provides an essential landmark.

Antiques, Handicrafts & Souvenirs

Section 1 is the place to go for Buddha statues, old LPs and other random antiques. More secular arts and crafts, such as musical instruments and hill-tribe items, can be found in Sections 25 and 26.

Clothing & Accessories

Clothing dominates most of Chatuchak, starting in Section 8 and continuing through the even-numbered sections to 24. Sections 5 and 6 deal in used clothing for every youth subculture, from punks to

Th Kamphaengphet
Chatuchak Mo Chit
Park
**Chatuchak
Weekend
Market**
Th Phahonyothin
Chatuchak
Park
Kamphaeng
Phet
Th Kamphaengphet 2
Th Kamphaengphet 1

ⓘ Need to Know

ตลาดนัดจตุจักร, Talat Nat Jatujak; Map p66; www.chatuchakmarket.org; 587/10 Th Phahonyothin; ⊙7am-6pm Wed & Thu plants only, 6pm-midnight Fri wholesale only, 9am-6pm Sat & Sun; ⓂChatuchak Park exit 1, Kamphaeng Phet exits 1 & 2, ⓈMo Chit exit 1

✕ Take a Break

Sections 6 and 8 have food and drink vendors, a necessary antidote to Chatuchak fatigue.

★ Top Tip

Come early to beat the crowds and the heat.

cowboys, while Soi 7, where it transects Sections 12 and 14, is heavy on hip-hop and skate fashions. More sophisticated independent labels can be found in Sections 2 and 3, while tourist-sized clothes and textiles are in Sections 8 and 10.

Housewares & Decor

The western edge of the market, particularly Sections 8 to 26, specialises in housewares, from cheap plastic buckets to expensive brass woks. This area is a particularly good place to stock up on inexpensive Thai ceramics, ranging from celadon to the traditional rooster-themed bowls from Lampang. For less utilitarian goods, Section 7 is a virtual open-air gallery with stalls selling Bangkok-themed murals and other unique artwork. Burmese lacquerware can be found in Section 10, while Section 26 has dusty collections of real and reproduction antiques from Thailand and Myanmar.

Eating & Drinking

Lots of Thai-style eating and snacking will stave off Chatuchak rage, and numerous food stalls set up shop between Sections 6 and 8. Established standouts include Foontalop, a popular Isan restaurant; Café Ice, a Western-Thai fusion joint that does good, if overpriced, *pàt tai* (fried noodles) and tasty fruit shakes; Toh-Plue, which does all the Thai standards; and Saman Islam, a Thai-Muslim restaurant that serves a tasty chicken *biryani*. Viva 8 features a DJ and, when we stopped by, a chef making huge platters of paella. As evening draws near, down a beer at Viva's, a cafe-bar that features live music.

The Commons

CARLO BOLLO / ALAMY STOCK PHOTO ©

Hipster Bangkok

In recent years, Bangkok has become host to dozens of new and sophisticated bars, clubs, art galleries and markets. The hippest of all seem to be the places that intertwine all of these elements.

Great For ...

☑ Don't Miss

WTF (Map p70; www.wtfbangkok.com; 7 Soi 51, Th Sukhumvit; ⊗6pm-1am Tue-Sun; ☎; ⑤Thong Lo exit 3), Bangkok's best bar, combines excellent cocktails, an art gallery and friendly clientele.

Bars & Clubs

Animal-themed domestic beers and cocktails with names like 'blue kamikaze' no longer cut it with Bangkok's hip crowd; these days, craft beers and complicated cocktails have become the norm.

○ **Ku Bar** (Map p62; www.facebook.com/ku.bangkok; 3rd fl, 469 Th Phra Sumen; 7pm-midnight Thu-Sun) Fruit- and food-heavy cocktails.

○ **Ba Hao** (Map p62; www.ba-hao.com; 8 Soi Nana; ⊗6pm-midnight Tue-Sun; ⛴Ratchawong Pier, ⒨Hua Lamphong exit 1) Craft beer, inventive cocktails and excellent Chinese-style bar snacks.

○ **Q&A Bar** (Map p70; www.qnabar.com; 235/13 Soi 21/Asoke, Th Sukhumvit; ⊗7pm-2am Mon-Sat) Like drinking in a mid-century modern airport lounge.

Roast

PHILIP GAME / ALAMY STOCK PHOTO ©

o Studio Lam (Map p70; www.facebook.com/
studiolambangkok; 3/1 Soi 51, Th Sukhumvit;
⊙6pm-1am Tue-Sun; ⑤Thong Lo exit 3)
Retro-Thai DJ sets and the occasional
live show.

o Beam (Map p70; www.beamclub.com; 72
Courtyard, 72 Soi 55/Thong Lor, Th Sukhumvit;
⊙9pm-late Wed-Sat; ⑤Thong Lo exit 3 & taxi)
Bangkok's club of the moment.

o Teens of Thailand (Map p62; 76 Soi
Nana; ⊙7pm-midnight Tue-Sun; ⓂHua
Lamphong exit 1) Speakeasy vibe and an
emphasis on gin.

o Roast (Map p70; ☑02 185 2865; www.roast
bkk.com; The Commons, 335 Soi Thong
Lor 17; ⊙10am-11pm Mon-Thu, from 9am Fri
& Sat, to 10pm Sun; ⑤Thong Lo) Bangkok's
coolest coffee specialist.

ⓘ Need to Know

Bars and clubs close at midnight, 1am
or 2am, depending on their designation
and if the rules are enforced.

✕ Take a Break

A good time for Thais always involves
food, and most bars have tasty snacks;
markets and malls also have lots of food
options.

★ Top Tip

Nearly all of Bangkok's hotel-based
rooftop bars have strictly enforced
dress codes barring access to those
wearing shorts and/or sandals.

Restaurants

Thais who have spent time abroad are
bringing home the flavours of their travels
– as well as taking a new look at their own
cuisine.

o Tonkin-Annam (Map p62; ☑093 469 2969;
www.facebook.com/tonkinannam; 69 Soi Tha
Tien; mains 140-300B; ⊙10am-10pm Wed-Mon;
❄; ⛴Tien Pier) Exquisite Vietnamese in a
riverside shophouse.

o The Commons (Map p70; www.the
commonsbkk.com; 335 Soi 17, Soi 55/Thong
Lor, Th Sukhumvit; mains 500-2000B;
⊙8am-midnight; ❄; ⑤Thong Lo exit 3 & taxi)
The Bangkok foodcourt – taken upscale.

o Baan Nual (Map p62; ☑081 889 7403; 372
Soi 2, Th Samsen, no roman-script sign; mains
70-390B; ⊙noon-9pm Tue-Fri, 4-9pm Sat & Sun;
⛴Phra Athit/Banglamphu Pier) Tiny, retro-
themed Thai restaurant.

o Guss Damn Good (Map p66; ☑081 901
1787; www.facebook.com/gussdamngood; Soi
Sala Deang 1; ice cream 85-100B; ⊙11am-11pm;
❄; ⓂSi Lom exit 2, ⑤Sala Daeng exit 4) Edgy
ice creams.

o Daniel Thaiger (Map p70; ☑084 549 0995;
www.facebook.com/danielthaiger; Soi 11, Th
Sukhumvit; mains from 140B; ⊙11am-late;
⑤Nana exit 3) Bangkok's best burgers.

○ **80/20** (Map p62; ☎02 639 1135; www.
facebook.com/8020bkk; 1052-1054 Th Charoen
Krung; mains from 240B; ☯6pm-midnight Wed-
Mon; ❄; ⛴Ratchawong Pier, Ⓜ Hua Lamphong
exit 1) Fusion that works.

Shopping & Markets

In Bangkok, commerce is the glue that
binds people together. Yet in recent years,
the city's famous malls have become
edgier, and alternatives, often taking the
form of renovated structures, are popping
up across town.

○ **Warehouse 30** (Map p62; 52-60 Soi 30,
Th Charoen Krung; ☯11am-8pm Mon-Fri,
10am-9pm Sat & Sun) Shops in a string of
WWII–era godowns.

○ **Siam Discovery** (Map p66; www.siam
discovery.co.th; cnr Rama I & Th Phayathai;
☯10am-10pm; Ⓢ Siam exit 1) Recently renovated, now the most design-conscious mall
in town.

○ **Siam Center** (Map p66; www.siamcenter.
co.th; Rama I; ☯10am-9pm; Ⓢ Siam exit 1)
The 3rd floor of this mall is local designer
central.

○ **ZudRangMa Records** (Map p70; www.
zudrangmarecords.com; 7/1 Soi 51, Th Sukhumvit;
☯2-9pm Tue-Sun; Ⓢ Thong Lo exit 1) Where
record-browsing and drinking meet.

○ **Talat Rot Fai** (ตลาดรถไฟ; www.facebook.
com/taradrodfi; Soi 51, Th Srinakharin;
☯5pm-1am Thu-Sun; Ⓢ Udom Suk exit 2 & taxi)
Retro-themed outdoor market.

Art Galleries

Bangkok's art scene has graduated from
dusty, state-funded museums to small,

Stall, Talat Rot Fai

independently run, increasingly edgy, multimedia art spaces.

○ Bangkok CityCity Gallery (Map p66; ☎083 087 2725; www.bangkokcitycity.com; 13/3 Soi 1, Th Sathon Tai/South; ◷1-7pm Wed-Sun; ⓜLumphini exit 2) **FREE** Small, modern-feeling art space.

○ Bangkok Art & Culture Centre (BACC; หอศิลปวัฒนธรรมแห่งกรุงเทพมหานคร; Map p66; www.bacc.or.th; cnr Th Phayathai & Rama I; ◷10am-9pm Tue-Sat; ⓢNational Stadium exit 3) **FREE** One of the more significant players in the city's contemporary arts scene.

> ★ **Top Tip**
> Check in with BK (www.bk.asia-city.com) to see what's on or new when you're in town.

CHUMPHON_TH / SHUTTERSTOCK ©

○ Gallery VER (☎02 103 4067; www.vergallery.com; 10 Soi 22, Th Narathiwat Ratchanakharin/Chong Nonsi; ◷noon-6pm Tue-Sun; ⓢChong Nonsi exit 2 & taxi) **FREE** Vast art space hosting work by established and emerging domestic artists.

○ Subhashok The Arts Centre (SAC; Map p70; www.sac.gallery; 160/3 Soi 33, Th Sukhumvit; ◷10am-5.30pm Sat, noon-6pm Sun; ⓢPhrom Phong exit 6 & taxi) New gallery that's one of the city's most ambitious art spaces.

Hipster Hubs

In recent years, Bangkok has seen an explosion in venues that link art, commerce, drinking and food.

○ Chang Chui (ช่างชุ่ย; off Map p62; www.en.changchuibangkok.com; 460/8 Th Sirindhorn; 20-40B; ◷11am-11pm Tue-Sun) Eclectic marketplace that's one of the most exciting openings Bangkok has seen in years.

○ Jam Factory (Map p62; ☎02 861 0950; www.facebook.com/thejamfactorybangkok; 41/1-5 Th Charoen Nakon; ◷11am-8pm; 🚢river-crossing ferry from River City Pier) Renovated warehouses transformed into eateries, shops and galleries.

○ Whiteline (Map p66; ☎087 061 1117; www.facebook.com/whitelinebangkok; Soi 8, Th Silom; ◷7pm-midnight Thu-Sun; ⓜSi Lom exit 2, ⓢSala Daeng exit 1) Shophouse hosting film screenings, concerts, gallery nights and parties.

○ Soy Sauce Factory (Map p62; www.facebook.com/soysaucefactory; Soi 24, Th Charoen Krung; ◷10am-7pm Tue-Sun; ⓜHua Lamphong exit 1) A former factory turned gallery/event space/bar/photo studio.

○ YELO House (Map p66; www.yelohouse.com; 20/2 Soi Kasem San 1; ◷11am-8pm Tue-Sun) Dig through vintage clothes and ceramics, check out the latest exhibition, or enjoy an espresso in the cafe.

> ★ **Did You Know?**
> Smoking is banned indoors at bars and restaurants.

Noodle dish being prepared

STOCKPHOTO MANIA / SHUTTERSTOCK ©

Culinary Bangkok

Nowhere else is the Thai reverence for food more evident than in Bangkok. Life in the city can appear to be a never-ending meal with a little bit of work and commuting thrown into the mix.

Great For ...

☑ **Don't Miss**

You don't need a restaurant and linens to have a fine meal in this city. Bangkok foodies adore several famous street vendors.

Dining Scene

All of Thailand's culinary traditions converge in Bangkok. Simple market meals fuel the working class and transform the sidewalk into a communal dining room. High-end makeovers of Thai classics and royal recipes define the fine-dining scene. Mom-and-pop restaurants anchor a neighbourhood, be it an immigrant community from Arabia or from southern Thailand.

Bangkok's Must-Have Meals

○ **Pàt tai** Thailand's famous noodle dish at **Thip Samai** (Map p62; 313 Th Mahachai; mains 50-250B; ⊙5pm-2am; 🚤klorng boat to Phanfa Leelard Pier).

○ **Gŏo•ay dĕe•o reua** Pork/beef 'boat noodle' soups at **Bharani** (Sansab Boat

Pàt tai

CATHERINE SUTHERLAND / LONELY PLANET ©

❶ Need to Know

Restaurants are generally open from 10am to 8pm. Street vendors are prohibited from operating on Monday.

✕ Take a Break

Mall food courts offer a great introduction to Thai street food.

★ Top Tip

Thais use their spoon like a fork and their fork like a knife. They only use chopsticks for noodle dishes.

Noodle; Map p70; 96/14 Soi 23, Th Sukhumvit; mains 60-250B; ⏲11am-10pm; ❄; Ⓜ Sukhumvit exit 2, Ⓢ Asok exit 3).

○ **Mèe gròrp** A palace recipe for crispy noodles at **Chote Chitr** (Map p62; 146 Th Phraeng Phuthon; mains 60-200B; ⏲11am-10pm; ⛴klorng boat to Phanfa Leelard Pier).

○ **Hǒy tôrt** Oyster crêpe, a Bangkok Chinatown staple, at **Nai Mong Hoi Thod** (Map p62; 539 Th Phlap Phla Chai; mains 50-70B; ⏲5-10pm Tue-Sun; ⛴Ratchawong Pier, Ⓜ Hua Lamphong exit 1).

○ **Má·đà·bà** Meat-filled flatbread, a Southeast Asian Muslim favourite, at **Karim Roti-Mataba** (Map p62; 136 Th Phra Athit; mains 40-130B; ⏲9am-10pm Tue-Sun; ❄✎; ⛴Phra Athit/Banglamphu Pier).

Cooking Courses

Better than a souvenir, Thai cooking courses teach students how to recreate standard dishes back home. Courses are half-day and include a recipe book and lunch.

○ **Amita Thai Cooking Class** (✆02 466 8966; www.amitathaicooking.com; 162/17 Soi 14, Th Wutthakat, Thonburi; classes 3000B; ⏲9.30am-1pm Thu-Tue; ⛴klorng boat from Maharaj Pier)

○ **Cooking with Poo & Friends** (✆080 434 8686; www.cookingwithpoo; classes 1500B; ⏲8.30am-1pm; ♿)

○ **Bangkok Bold Cooking Studio** (Map p62; ✆098 829 4310; www.facebook.com/bangkok boldcookingstudio; 503 Th Phra Sumen; classes 2500-4500B; ⏲11am-2pm; ⛴klorng boat to Phanfa Leelard Pier)

Bangkok Walking Tour

Stroll around the former royal district of Ko Ratanakosin. Start early to beat the heat, dress modestly for the temples, and ignore shopping advice from well-dressed touts.

Start Wat Phra Kaew & Grand Palace
Distance 5km
Duration Three hours

5 Wander along Trok Mahathat, the alley leading to the **Amulet Market** (p60).

Thammasat University

Th Phra Chan

Th Maha Rat

Take a Break

Savoey (www.savoey.co.th; 1st fl, Maharaj Pier, Th Maha Rat; mains 125-1800B; ⊙10am-10pm) **provides an air-conditioned rest stop.**

Silpakorn University

Th Na Phra Lan

Th Maha Rat

4 Explore the classic architecture in the narrow alleyway of **Trok Tha Wang**.

Mae Nam Chao Phraya

3 Catch the cross-river ferry from Tien Pier to the military-looking **Wat Arun** (p46).

N

0   1 km
0   0.5 miles

6 Continue east until you reach **Sanam Luang (Royal Field)**, the location of elaborate, albeit infrequent, royal cremations, and seasonal festivals.

Classic Photo
Gold *garuda* decoration at Wat Phra Kaew.

Th Na Phra That

Sanam Luang

6
FINISH

Th Ratchadamnoen Nai

KO RATANAKOSIN

Th Sanam Chai

Th Kanlaya Namit

1 Start with the architecturally flamboyant and domestically revered **Wat Phra Kaew & Grand Palace** (p38).

1
START

Saranrom Royal Garden

Th Thai Wang

Th Charoen Krung

Th Chetuphon

2

Th Maha Rat

2 Head to **Wat Pho** (p42) temple where you can enjoy a traditional healing massage.

◎ SIGHTS

◎ Ko Ratanakosin & Banglamphu

National Museum
Museum

(พิพิธภัณฑสถานแห่งชาติ; Map p62; 4 Th Na Phra That; 200B; ⏰9am-4pm Wed-Sun; 🚢Chang Pier, Maharaj Pier, Phra Chan Tai Pier) Often touted as Southeast Asia's biggest museum, Thailand's National Museum is home to an impressive, albeit occasionally dusty, collection of items, best appreciated on one of the museum's free twice-weekly guided **tours** (free with museum admission; ⏰9.30am Wed & Thu). Most of the museum's structures were built in 1782 as the palace of Rama I's viceroy, Prince Wang Na. Rama V turned it into a museum in 1874, and today there are three permanent exhibitions spread out over several buildings. When we stopped by, several of the exhibition halls were being renovated.

Museum of Siam
Museum

(สถาบันพิพิธภัณฑ์การเรียนรู้แห่งชาติ; Map p62; www.museumsiam.org; Th Maha Rat; 300B; ⏰10am-6pm Tue-Sun; 👶; 🚢Tien Pier) Although temporarily closed for renovation when we stopped by, this fun museum's collection employs a variety of media to explore the origins of the Thai people and their culture.

ⓘ Dress for the Occasion

Many of Bangkok's biggest tourist attractions are sacred places, and visitors should dress and behave appropriately. In particular, you won't be allowed to enter Wat Phra Kaew and Grand Palace and Wat Arun unless you're well covered. Shorts, sleeveless shirts, spaghetti-strap tops, short skirts, cropped pants – basically anything that doesn't cover to your elbows or ankles – are not allowed. Expect to be shown into a dressing room and loaned a sarong before entry if you don't comply.

Housed in a European-style 19th-century building that was once the Ministry of Commerce, the exhibits are presented in a contemporary, engaging and interactive fashion not typically found in Thailand's museums. They are also refreshingly balanced and entertaining, with galleries dealing with a range of questions about the origins of the nation and its people.

Golden Mount & Wat Saket
Buddhist Temple

(ภูเขาทอง & วัดสระเกศ; Map p62; Th Boriphat; admission to summit of Golden Mount 10B; ⏰7.30am-5.30pm; 🚢klorng boat to Phanfa Leelard Pier) Even if you're wát-ed out, you should tackle the brisk ascent to the Golden Mount (Phu Khao Thong). Serpentine steps wind through an artificial hill shaded by gnarled trees, and past graves and pictures of wealthy benefactors. At the peak, you'll find a breezy 360-degree view of Bangkok's most photogenic side.

Next door, seemingly peaceful Wat Saket contains murals that are among both the most beautiful and the goriest in the country; proceed to the pillar behind the Buddha statue for explicit depictions of Buddhist hell.

Amulet Market
Market

(ตลาดพระเครื่องวัดมหาธาตุ; Map p62; Th Maha Rat; ⏰7am-5pm; 🚢Chang Pier, Maharaj Pier, Phra Chan Tai Pier) This arcane and fascinating market claims both the footpaths along Th Maha Rat and Th Phra Chan, as well as a dense network of covered market stalls that runs south from Phra Chan Pier; the easiest entry point is clearly marked 'Trok Maha That'. The trade is based around small talismans carefully prized by collectors, monks, taxi drivers and people in dangerous professions.

◎ Chinatown

Wat Traimit (Golden Buddha)
Buddhist Temple

(วัดไตรมิตร, Temple of the Golden Buddha; Map p62; Th Mittaphap Thai-China; 100B; ⏰8am-5pm; 🚢Ratchawong Pier, Ⓜ Hua Lamphong exit 1) The attraction at Wat Traimit is undoubt-

Lumphini Park

edly the impressive 3m-tall, 5.5-tonne, solid-gold Buddha image, which gleams like, well, gold. Sculpted in the graceful Sukhothai style, the image was 'discovered' some 60 years ago beneath a stucco/plaster exterior, when it fell from a crane while being moved to a new building within the temple compound.

Talat Mai
Market

(ตลาดใหม่; Map p62; Soi Yaowarat 6/Charoen Krung 16; ☉6am-6pm; ☷Ratchawong Pier, ᴹHua Lamphong exit 1 & taxi) With nearly two centuries of commerce under its belt, New Market is no longer an entirely accurate name for this strip of commerce. Regardless, this is Bangkok's, if not Thailand's, most Chinese market, and the dried goods, seasonings, spices and sauces will be familiar to anyone who's ever spent time in China. Even if you're not interested in food, the hectic atmosphere (be on guard for motorcycles squeezing between shoppers) and exotic sights and smells create something of a surreal sensory experience.

◉ Riverside, Silom & Lumphini

Lumphini Park
Park

(สวนลุมพินี; Map p66; bounded by Th Sarasin, Rama IV, Th Witthayu/Wireless Rd & Th Ratchadamri; ☉4.30am-9pm; ᴨ; ᴹLumphini exit 3, Si Lom exit 1, ˢSala Daeng exit 3, Ratchadamri exit 2) Named after the Buddha's place of birth in Nepal, Lumphini Park is the best way to escape Bangkok without actually leaving town. Shady paths, a large artificial lake and swept lawns temporarily blot out the roaring traffic and hulking concrete towers.

There are paddleboats for lovers, playgrounds for the kids and enormous monitor lizards for the whole family. One of the best times to visit the park is before 7am, when the air is fresh (well, relatively so for Bangkok) and legions of Thai-Chinese are practising t'ai chi. The park reawakens with the evening's cooler temperatures – aerobics classes collectively sweat to a techno soundtrack. Late at night the borders of the park are frequented by streetwalking sex workers, both male and female.

Ko Ratanakosin, Banglamphu & Chinatown

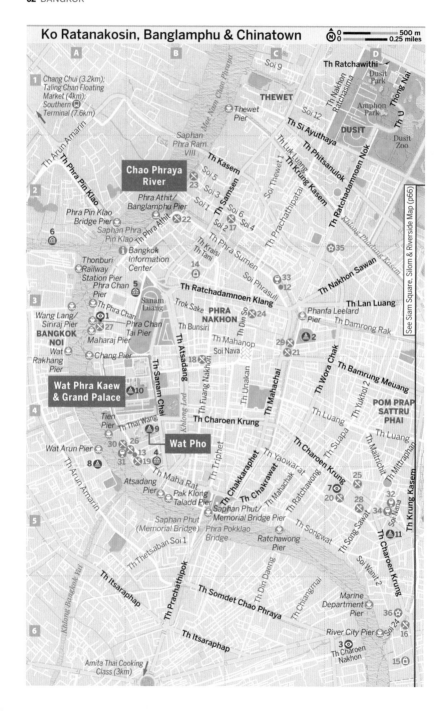

Ⓝ 0 — 500 m
0 — 0.25 miles

A · B · C · D

1

Chang Chui (3.2km);
Taling Chan Floating
Market (4km);
Southern Ⓢ
Terminal (7.6km)

Soi 9

Th Ratchawithi

Dusit
Park

Th Nakhon Ratchasima

Thong Nai

Th U

THEWET

Thewet
Pier

Soi 12

Amphon
Park

DUSIT

Dusit
Zoo

Th Arun Amarin

Mae Nam Chao Phraya

Saphan
Phra Ram
VIII

Th Si Ayuthaya

Th Phitsanulok

**Chao Phraya
River**

Th Kasem

Soi 5

Soi 3

Soi 1

23

Th Samsen

Th Luk Luang

Th Krung Kasem

Th Ratchadamnoen Nok

Th Phra Pin Klao

Phra Athit/
Banglamphu Pier

Soi 6 Soi 4

Soi 2 17

22

Th Phra Athit

Soi Thewet 1

Th Prachathipatai

2

Phra Pin Klao
Bridge Pier

Saphan Phra
Pin Klao

Th Phra Sumen

Th Phra Sumen

35

6

Th Kraisi
Th Tani

Soi Phrasuli

33

12

Khlong Phadung Krung Kasem

Thonburi
Railway
Station Pier

Ⓘ Bangkok
Information
Center

14

Th Nakhon Sawan

See Siam Square, Silom & Riverside Map (p66)

Phra Chan
Pier

5

Th Ratchadamnoen Klang

Th Lan Luang

3

Wang Lang/
Siriraj Pier

Th Phra Chan

Sanam
Luang

Trok Sake

**PHRA
NAKHON**

24

Phanfa Leelard
Pier

Th Damrong Rak

29

2

**BANGKOK
NOI**

1

27

Phra Chan
Tai Pier

Th Din So

Th Bunsiri

Maharaj Pier

Th Mahanop

Soi Nava

21

Th Wora Chak

Th Bamrung Meuang

Wat Ⓢ
Rakhang
Pier

Chang Pier

18

Th Mahachai

**POM PRAP
SATTRU
PHAI**

Th Yukhol 2

**Wat Phra Kaew
& Grand Palace**

10

Th Sanam Chai

Th Atsadang

Th Fuang Nakhon

Th Unakan

Th Luang

Th Maitrichit

Th Mittraphan

4

Tien
Pier

9

Th Thai Wang

Khlong Lod

Th Charoen Krung

Th Luang

Th Suapa

Th Krung Kasem

Wat Arun Pier

30 26

13 4

Wat Pho

Th Charoen Krung

25

Th Arun Amarin

8

31 19

Th Maha Rat

Th Triphet

Th Chakkaraphet

Th Yaowarat

Th Chakrawat

Th Charoen Krung

7

32

Atsadang
Pier

Pak Klong
Taladd Pier

Th Mahachak

Th Ratchawong

20

28

34

5

Saphan Phut
(Memorial Bridge)

Saphan Phut/
Memorial Bridge Pier

Phra Pokklao
Bridge

Phra Pokklao
Bridge

Ratchawong
Pier

Th Songwat

11

Soi Nana

Th Thetsaban Soi 1

Th Song Sawat

Soi Charoen Krung

Th Itsaraphap

Th Prachathipok

Th Somdet Chao Phraya

Th Din Daeng

Th Chiangmai

Soi Wanit 2

6

Khlong Bangkok Yai

Th Itsaraphap

Marine
Department
Pier

36

River City Pier

Soi 24

16

3

Th Charoen
Nakhon

15

Amita Thai Cooking
Class (3km)

Ko Ratanakosin, Banglamphu & Chinatown

Bangkokian Museum   Museum
(พิพิธภัณฑ์ชาวบางกอก; Map p66; 273 Soi 43, Th Charoen Krung; admission by donation; ⏲10am-4pm Wed-Sun; ⛴Si Phraya/River City Pier) A collection of three antique structures built during the early 20th century, the Bangkokian Museum illustrates an often-overlooked period of the city's history, and functions as a peek into a Bangkok that, these days, is disappearing at a rapid pace.

❸ ACTIVITIES
Health Land   Massage
(Map p70; ☎02 261 1110; www.healthlandspa.com; 55/5 Soi 21/Asoke, Th Sukhumvit; Thai massage 2hr 550B; ⏲9am-11pm; Ⓜ Sukhumvit exit 1, ⓢAsok exit 5) A winning formula of affordable prices, expert treatments and pleasant facilities has created a small empire of Health Land centres across Bangkok.

Eight Limbs   Martial Arts
(Map p70; ☎090 987 9590; www.facebook.com/8limbsluaythaigym; Soi 24, Th Sukhumvit; lessons from 580B; ⏲10am-8.30pm Tue-Sun; ⓢPhrom Phong exit 2) This small gym in downtown Bangkok offers 1½-hour walk-in lessons in *moo·ay tai* (Thai boxing; also spelt *muay Thai*) for all skill levels. See the Facebook page for times.

⌂ SHOPPING
MBK Center   Shopping Centre
(Map p66; www.mbk-center.com; cnr Rama I & Th Phayathai; ⏲10am-10pm; ⓢNational Stadium exit 4) This eight-storey market in a mall has emerged as one of Bangkok's top attractions. On any given weekend half of Bangkok's residents (and most of its tourists) can be found here combing through a seemingly inexhaustible range of small stalls, shops and merchandise.

Asiatique   Market
(Soi 72-76, Th Charoen Krung; ⏲4-11pm; ⛴shuttle boat from Sathon/Central Pier) One of Bangkok's more popular night markets, Asiatique takes the form of warehouses

From left: Th Khao San; Asiatique (p63); Siam Discovery mall (p54)

of commerce next to Chao Phraya River. Expect clothing, handicrafts, souvenirs and quite a few dining and drinking venues.

Frequent, free shuttle boats depart from Sathon/Central Pier from 4pm to 11.30pm.

Siam Square
Shopping Centre

(Map p66; Rama I; ⊙11am-9pm; 🐾; ⑤Siam exits 2, 4 & 6) This open-air shopping zone is ground zero for teenage culture in Bangkok. Pop music blares out of tinny speakers, and gangs of hipsters in various costumes ricochet between fast-food restaurants and closet-sized boutiques. It's a great place to pick up labels and designs you're guaranteed not to find anywhere else, though most outfits require a barely there waistline.

Thanon Khao
San Market
Gifts & Souvenirs

(Map p62; Th Khao San; ⊙10am-midnight; ⛴Phra Athit/Banglamphu Pier) The main guesthouse strip in Banglamphu is a day-and-night shopping bazaar peddling all the backpacker 'essentials': profane T-shirts, bootleg MP3s, hemp clothing, fake student ID cards, knock-off designer wear, selfie

sticks, orange juice and, of course, those croaking wooden frogs.

House of Chao
Antiques

(Map p66; 9/1 Th Decho; ⊙9.30am-7pm; ⑤Chong Nonsi exit 3) This three-storey antique shop, appropriately located in an antique shophouse, has everything necessary to deck out your fantasy colonial-era mansion. Particularly interesting are the various weather-worn doors, doorways, gateways and trellises that can be found in the covered area behind the showroom.

EATING

Ko Ratanakosin
& Banglamphu

Krua Apsorn
Thai $$

(Map p62; www.kruaapsorn.com; Th Din So; mains 100-450B; ⊙10.30am-8pm Mon-Sat; 🐾; ⛴klorng boat to Phanfa Leelard Pier) This cafeteria-like dining room is a favourite of members of the Thai royal family and restaurant critics alike. Just about all of the central and southern Thai dishes are tasty, but regulars never miss the chance to order

ARTAPARTMENT / SHUTTERSTOCK ©

the decadent stir-fried crab with yellow pepper chilli or the *tortilla Española*–like fluffy crab omelette.

Jay Fai
Thai $$$

(Map p62; 327 Th Mahachai; mains 180-1000B; ⏱3pm-2am Mon-Sat; 🛥klorng boat to Phanfa Leelard Pier) With its bare-bones dining room, it's hard to believe Jay Fai is renowned for serving Bangkok's most expensive *pàt kêe mow* ('drunkard's noodles': wide rice noodles fried with seafood and Thai herbs). The price, however, is justified by the copious fresh seafood, plus a distinct frying style resulting in an almost oil-free finished dish.

It's in a virtually unmarked shophouse, opposite a 7-Eleven.

Err
Thai $$

(Map p62; www.errbkk.com; off Th Maha Rat; mains 65-360B; ⏱11am-late Tue-Sun; ❄; 🛥Tien Pier) Think of all those different smoky, spicy, crispy, meaty bites you've encountered on the street. Now imagine them assembled in one funky, retro-themed locale, and coupled with tasty Thai-themed cocktails and domestic microbrews. If Err

(a Thai colloquialism for agreement) seems too good to be true, we empathise, but insist that it's true.

Chinatown

Thanon Phadungdao Seafood Stalls
Street Food $$

(Map p62; cnr Th Phadungdao & Th Yaowarat; mains 100-600B; ⏱4pm-midnight Tue-Sun; 🛥Ratchawong Pier, Ⓜ Hua Lamphong exit 1 & taxi) After sunset, these two opposing open-air restaurants – each of which claims to be the original – become a culinary train

---

🍽◯ **Get Cooking**

A popular cooking course, Cooking with Poo & Friends (p57) was started by a native of Khlong Toey's slums and is held in her neighbourhood. Courses, which must be booked in advance, span three dishes and include a visit to Khlong Toey Market and transport to and from Emporium Shopping Centre.

Siam Square, Silom & Riverside

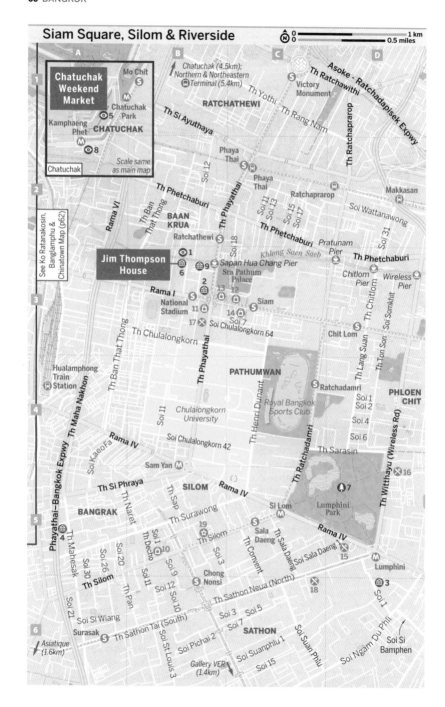

Siam Square, Silom & Riverside

wreck of outdoor barbecues, screaming staff, iced seafood trays and messy pavement seating. True, the vast majority of diners are foreign tourists, but this has little impact on the cheerful setting, the fun experience and the cheap bill.

Hoon Kuang   Chinese $$

(Map p62; 381 Th Yaowarat; mains 90-240B; ⏱11am-7.45pm Mon-Sat; ❄; 🚢Ratchawong Pier, 🚇Hua Lamphong exit 1 & taxi) Serving the food of Chinatown's streets in air-con comfort is this low-key, long-standing staple. The must-eat dishes are pictured on the door, but it'd be a pity to miss the 'prawn curry flat rice noodle', a unique mash-up of two Chinese-Thai dishes – crab in curry powder and flash-fried noodles – that will make you wonder why they were ever served apart.

🍴 Silom & Riverside

nahm   Thai $$$

(Map p66; 📞02 625 3388; www.comohotels. com; ground fl, Metropolitan Hotel, 27 Th Sathon Tai/South; set lunch 600-1600B, set dinner 2500B, mains 310-800B; ⏱noon-2pm Mon-Fri, 7-10.30pm daily; ❄; 🚇Lumphini exit 2) Australian chef-author David Thompson is the man behind one of Bangkok's – and if you believe the critics, the world's – best Thai restaurants. Using ancient cookbooks as his inspiration, Thompson has given new life to previously extinct dishes with exotic descriptions such as 'smoked fish curry

with prawns, chicken livers, cockles, chillies and black pepper'.

Kai Thort Jay Kee   Thai $$

(Polo Fried Chicken; Map p66; 137/1-3 Soi Sanam Khli/Polo; mains 50-350B; ⏱11am-9pm; ❄; 🚇Lumphini exit 3) Although the *sôm·đam* (spicy green papaya salad), sticky rice and *lâhp* (a spicy salad of minced meat) of this former street stall give the impression of a northeastern-Thai-style eatery, the restaurant's namesake deep-fried bird is more southern in origin. Regardless, smothered in a thick layer of crispy deep-fried garlic, it is none other than a truly Bangkok experience.

🍴 Sukhumvit

Soul Food Mahanakorn   Thai $$

(Map p70; 📞02 714 7708; www.soulfood mahanakorn.com; 56/10 Soi 55/Thong Lor, Th Sukhumvit; mains 140-290B; ⏱5.30pm-midnight; ❄📶; 🚇Thong Lo exit 3) This contemporary staple gets its interminable buzz from its dual nature as both an inviting restaurant – the menu spans tasty interpretations of rustic Thai dishes – and a bar serving deliciously boozy, Thai-influenced cocktails. Reservations recommended.

Bo.lan   Thai $$$

(Map p70; 📞02 260 2962; www.bolan.co.th; 24 Soi 53, Th Sukhumvit; set meals 1200-3500B; ⏱6-10.30pm Tue-Sun, noon-2.30pm Sat & Sun; ❄📶; 🚇Thong Lo exit 1) Upscale Thai is often more garnish than flavour, but Bo.lan has proved to be the exception. Bo and Dylan (Bo.lan is a play on words that means Ancient) take a scholarly approach to Thai cuisine, and generous set meals featuring full-flavoured Thai dishes are the results of this tuition (à la carte is not available; meat-free meals are). Reservations recommended.

🍸 DRINKING & NIGHTLIFE

See Hipster Bangkok Top Experience (p52) for bar and club recommendations.

✪ ENTERTAINMENT

Rajadamnern Stadium
Spectator Sport

(สนามมวยราชดำเนิน; Map p62; www.raja damnern.com; off Th Ratchadamnoen Nok; tickets 3rd class/2nd class/ringside 1000/1500/2500B; Thewet Pier, S Phaya Thai exit 3 & taxi) Rajadamnern Stadium, Bangkok's oldest and most venerable venue for *moo·ay tai*,

hosts matches on Monday, Wednesday and Thursday from 6.30pm to around 11pm, and Sunday at 3pm and 6.30pm. Be sure to buy tickets from the official ticket counter or online, not from the touts and scalpers who hang around outside the entrance.

ℹ INFORMATION

Bangkok Information Center (Map p62; ☑02 225 7612-4; www.bangkoktourist.com; 17/1 Th Phra Athit; ⏰8am-7pm Mon-Fri, 9am-5pm Sat & Sun; Phra Athit/Banglamphu Pier) City-specific tourism office providing maps, brochures and directions. Seldom-staffed kiosks and booths are found around town; look for the green-on-white symbol of a mahout on an elephant.

ℹ GETTING THERE & AWAY

AIR

Suvarnabhumi International Airport (☑02 132 1888; www.suvarnabhumiairport.com) Located 30km east of central Bangkok, Suvarnabhumi

From left: Street food; statue, Wat Saket (p60); sculpture exhibition, National Museum (p60)

International Airport began commercial international and domestic service in 2006. The airport's name is pronounced *sù·wan·ná·poom,* and it inherited the airport code (BKK) previously held by the old airport at Don Mueang. The airport website has real-time details of arrivals and departures.

Don Mueang International Airport (☎02 535 2111; www.donmueangairportthai.com) Bangkok's other airport, Don Mueang International Airport, 25km north of central Bangkok, was retired from service in 2006 only to reopen later as Bangkok's de facto budget airline hub. Terminal 1 handles international flights while Terminal 2 handles domestic destinations.

BUS

Eastern Bus Terminal (off Map p70; ☎02 391 2504; Soi 40, Th Sukhumvit; ⑤Ekkamai exit 2) The departure point for buses to Pattaya, Rayong, Chanthaburi and other points east, except for Aranya Prathet (for the border with Cambodia). Most people call it *sà·tǎh·nee èk·gà·mai* (Ekamai station). It's near the Ekkamai BTS station.

Southern Bus Terminal (Sai Tai Mai; off Map p62; ☎02 422 4444, call centre 1490; Th Boro-

Public Transport at a Glance

BTS The elevated Skytrain runs from 6am to midnight. Tickets 16B to 44B.

MRT The Metro runs from 6am to midnight. Tickets 16B to 42B.

Taxi Outside of rush hours, Bangkok taxis are a great bargain. Flag fall 35B.

Chao Phraya Express Boat Runs 6am to 8pm, charging 10B to 40B.

Klorng boat Bangkok's canal boats run from 5.30am to 8pm most days. Tickets 9B to 19B.

Bus Cheap but a slow and confusing way to get around Bangkok. Tickets 5B to 30B.

maratchachonanee) Bangkok's southern bus terminal lies a long way west of the city centre. Commonly called *sǎi đâi mài,* it's among the more pleasant and orderly in the country, serving as the departure point for all buses south of Bangkok. Transport to Kanchanaburi and western Thailand also departs from here.

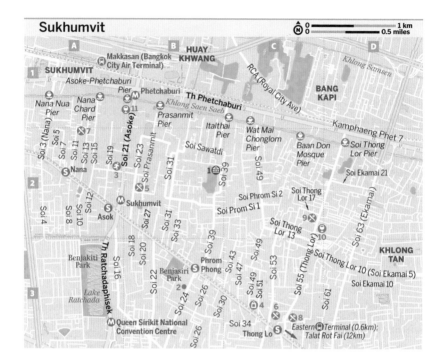

Sukhumvit

Northern & Northeastern Bus Terminal (Mo Chit; off Map p66; ☑northeastern routes 02 936 2852, ext 602/605, northern routes 02 936 2841, ext 325/614; Th Kamphaengphet; MKamphaeng Phet exit 1 & taxi, SMo Chit exit 3 & taxi) Located just north of Chatuchak Park, this hectic bus station is also commonly called kŏn sòng mŏr chít (Mo Chit station) – not to be confused with Mo Chit BTS station. Buses depart from here for all northern and northeastern destinations, as well as international destinations including Pakse (Laos), Phnom Penh (Cambodia), Siem Reap (Cambodia) and Vientiane (Laos).

TRAIN

Hualamphong Train Station (Map p66; ☑02 220 4334, call centre 1690; www.railway.co.th; off Rama IV; MHua Lamphong exit 2) Hualamphong is the terminus for the main rail services to the south, north, northeast and east.

The station has the following services: shower room, mailing centre, luggage storage, cafes

and food courts. To get to the station from Sukhumvit take the MRT to the Hua Lamphong stop. From western points (Banglamphu, Thewet), take bus 53.

🛈 GETTING AROUND

Bangkok may seem impenetrable at first, but its transport system is gradually improving. Taxis are the most expedient choice – although it's important to note that Bangkok traffic is nothing if not unpredictable. During rush hour, opt for public transport.

Keep the following in mind to survive the traffic and avoid joining the list of tourists sucked in by Bangkok's numerous scam artists:

• Ignore 'helpful', often well-dressed, English-speaking locals who tell you that tourist attractions and public transport are closed for a holiday or cleaning; it's the beginning of a con, most likely a gem scam.

Sukhumvit

○ Skip the 50B túk-túk ride unless you have the time and willpower to resist a heavy sales pitch in a tailor or gem store.

○ Good jewellery, gems and tailor shops aren't found through a túk-túk driver.

○ Don't expect any pedestrian rights; put a Bang-kokian between you and any oncoming traffic, and yield to anything with more metal than you.

○ Walk away from the tourist strip to hail a taxi that will actually use the meter. Tell the driver 'meter'. If the driver refuses to put the meter on, get out.

BTS & MRT

BTS (📞02 617 6000, tourist information 02 617 7341; www.bts.co.th) Also known as the Skytrain (*rót fai fáa*), the elevated BTS whisks you through 'new' Bangkok (Silom, Sukhumvit and Siam Sq). The interchange between the two lines is at Siam station. Most ticket machines only accept coins, but change is available at the information booths.

MRT (📞02 354 2000; www.bangkokmetro.co.th), Bangkok's Metro is most helpful for people staying in the Sukhumvit or Silom area to reach the train station at Hualamphong.

BUS

Bangkok's public buses are run by the **Bangkok Mass Transit Authority** (📞02 246 0973, call centre 1348; www.bmta.co.th).

As the routes are not always clear, and with Bangkok taxis being such a good deal, you'd really have to be pinching pennies to rely on buses as a way to get around Bangkok. However, if you're

determined, air-con bus fares range from 10B to 23B, and fares for fan buses start at 6.50B. Most of the bus lines run between 5am and 10pm or 11pm, except for the 'all-night' buses, which run from 3am or 4am to mid-morning.

You'll most likely require the help of thinknet's *Bangkok Bus Guide* or download Transit Bangkok's transport guide at www.transitbangkok.com.

TAXI

All taxis are required to use their meters, which start at 35B, and fares to most places within central Bangkok cost 60B to 90B. Freeway tolls – 25B to 70B – must be paid by the passenger.

Never agree to take a taxi that won't use the meter. If a driver refuses to take you some-where, it's probably because he needs to return his hired cab before a certain time. Very few Bangkok taxi drivers speak much English, so an address written in Thai is helpful.

Older cabs may be less comfortable but typically have more experienced drivers because they are driver-owned, as opposed to the new cabs, which are usually hired.

Taxi Radio (📞1681; www.taxiradio.co.th) and other 24-hour 'phone-a-cab' services are avail-able for 20B above the metered fare.

If you leave something in a taxi your best chance of getting it back (still pretty slim) is to call 📞1644

TÚK-TÚK

Bangkok's iconic túk-túk (pronounced *đúk đúk*; a type of motorised rickshaw) are used by Thais for short hops not worth paying the taxi flag

The Sex Industry

Prostitution has been widespread in Thailand since long before the country became famous for it. Throughout Thai history the practice was tolerated though not respected.

Due to pressure from the UN, prostitution was declared illegal in 1960, though entertainment places (go-go bars, beer bars, massage parlours, karaoke bars and bathhouses) are governed by a separate law passed in 1966. These establishments are licensed and can legally provide nonsexual services (such as dancing, massage, a drinking buddy); sexual services occur through these venues but they are not technically the businesses' purpose.

With the arrival of the US military in Southeast Asia in the 1960s and '70s, enterprising forces adapted prostitution to suit foreigners, in turn creating an industry that persists today. Indeed, this foreigner-oriented sex industry is still a prominent part of Thailand's tourist economy. In 1998 the International Labour Organization, a UN agency, advised Southeast Asian countries, including Thailand, to recognise prostitution as an economic sector and income generator. It is estimated that one-third of the entertainment establishments are registered with the government and the majority pay an informal tax in the form of police bribes.

In 1996, Thailand passed a reform law to address the issue of child prostitution. Help stop child-sex tourism by reporting suspicious behaviour on a dedicated hotline (🖉1300) or by reporting perpetrators directly to the embassy of their home country.

fall. For foreigners, however, they are part of the Bangkok experience, despite their inflated prices. The vast majority of túk-túk drivers ask too much from tourists. A short hop should cost 60B.

BOAT

KLORNG

Canal boats run along Khlong Saen Saep (Banglamphu to Ramkhamhaeng) and are an easy way to get between Banglamphu and Jim Thompson House and the Siam Sq shopping centres. Disembark at Saphan Hua Chang Pier after changing boats at Pratunam Pier.

These boats are mostly used by daily commuters and pull into the piers for just a few seconds – jump straight on or you'll be left behind.

Fares range from 9B to 19B and boats run from 5.30am to 7.15pm from Monday to Friday, from 6am to 6.30pm on Saturday and from 6am to 6pm on Sunday.

RIVER

The **Chao Phraya Express Boat** (🖉02 623 6001; www.chaophrayaexpressboat.com) operates the main ferry service along Chao Phraya River. The central pier is known as Tha Sathon, Saphan Taksin or sometimes Sathon/Central Pier, and connects to the BTS at Saphan Taksin station.

● Boats run from 6am to 8pm. You can buy tickets (10B to 40B) at the pier or on board; hold on to your ticket as proof of purchase (an occasional formality).

● The most common boats are the orange-flagged express boats. These run between Wat Rajsingkorn, south of Bangkok, to Nonthaburi, north, stopping at most major piers (15B, frequent from 6am to 7pm).

● A blue-flagged tourist boat (40B, every 30 minutes from 9.30am to 5pm) runs from Sathon/Central Pier to Phra Athit/Banglamphu Pier, with stops at eight major sightseeing piers and barely comprehensible English-language commentary. Vendors at Sathon/Central Pier tout a 150B all-day pass, but unless you plan on doing a lot of boat travel, it's not great value.

● There are also dozens of cross-river ferries, which charge 3B and run every few minutes until late at night.

● Private long-tail boats can be hired for sightseeing trips at Phra Athit/Banglamphu Pier, Chang Pier, Tien Pier and Oriental Pier.

Where to Stay

Because Bangkok is a sprawling metropolis, it is best to pick your neighbourhood and then shop within your budget range. Otherwise pick a spot on the BTS for easy neighbourhood-hopping.

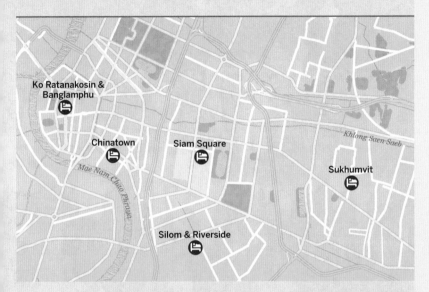

Neighbourhood	Atmosphere
Ko Ratanakosin & Banglamphu	Close to sights, old-school Bangkok feel; lots of touts and tourists
Chinatown	Interesting budget and midrange options, easy access to sights and train station; noisy and hectic
Siam Square	Convenient access to shopping and BTS; overly commercial; lack of dining and entertainment
Silom & Riverside	Upscale accommodation, convenient to transport, lots of dining and nightlife; noisy and hectic
Sukhumvit	Sophisticated hotels, easy access to BTS and MRT; international dining and bars; touristy, sexpat hang-outs

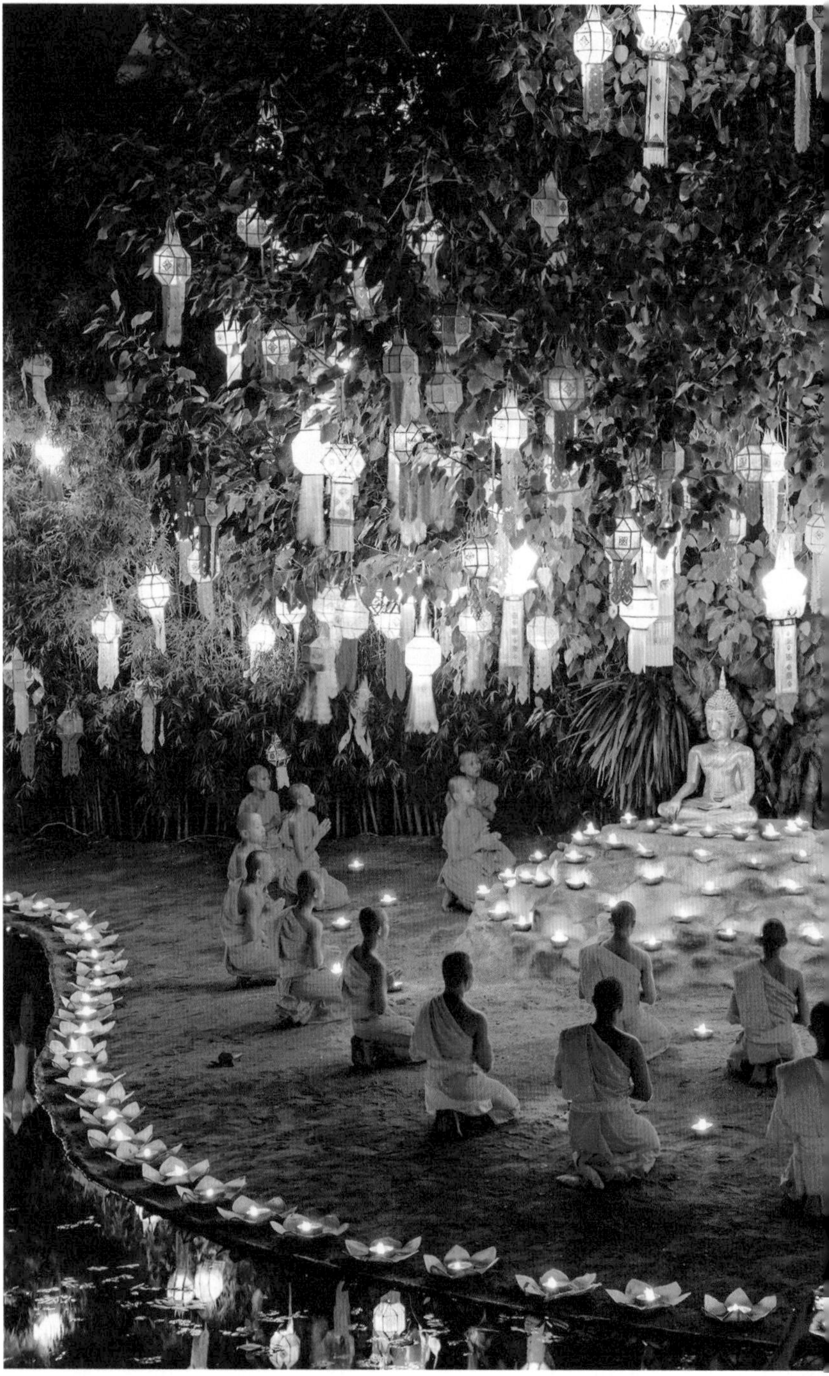

TAKE PHOTO / SHUTTERSTOCK ©

CHIANG MAI

Chiang Mai at a Glance...

The cultural capital of the north, Chiang Mai is beloved by temple-spotters, culture vultures and adventure-loving families. The narrow streets steeped in history provide an atmosphere more like a country town than a modern city. Beyond the old city, modern Chiang Mai offers fantastic dining thanks to imports from Myanmar and Japan, as well as local specialities. Great escapes from the city lie just an hour away and tours shuttle visitors to jungle treks, elephant sanctuaries and minority villages.

Chiang Mai in Two Days

Visit the **temples** (p78) and **museums** (p82) of the old city. Have either lunch or dinner at **Kao Soi Fueng Fah** (p101). Spend your second day doing a Thai **cooking course** (p95) then visit the **Saturday Walking Street** (p84) or **Sunday Walking Street** (p84).

Chiang Mai in Four Days

On your third day join a full-day **outdoor activity** (p86), such as trekking, zip-lining or mountain biking. The next day, tour the shops and restaurants of **Th Nimmanhaemin** (p88) – try Tong Tem Toh for northern Thai cuisine – and stay for the nightlife.

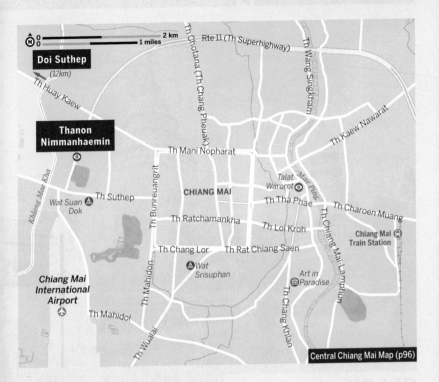

Central Chiang Mai Map (p96)

Arriving in Chiang Mai

Chiang Mai International Airport
Airport taxis charge a flat fare. Some hotels also provide hotel transfer.

Arcade Bus Terminal Take a chartered *rót daang* ('red car') or túk-túk to the city centre.

Chiang Mai Train Station Hop on a chartered *rót daang* or túk-túk.

Sleeping

Accommodation prices in the city are slowly creeping up, but you can still find a respectable air-con room from 650B. Make reservations far in advance if visiting during Chinese New Year, Songkran and other holiday periods.

For more information on the best neighbourhood to stay in, see p105.

Wat Phra Singh

Old City Temples

Chiang Mai's temples show-case traditional Lanna art and architecture, using teak harvested in the once-dense frontiers and demonstrating traditions inherited from Myanmar and China.

Great For...

☑ Don't Miss

Learn about Buddhism and being a monk at Wat Chedi Luang's Monk Chat.

The temples featured here are all located in the old city, but other beautiful temples lie outside of the city walls.

Wat Phra Singh

Chiang Mai's most revered temple, **Wat Phra Singh** (วัดพระสิงห์; Th Singharat; 20B; ⏰5am-8.30pm) sits regally at the end of Th Ratchadamnoen. Behind its whitewashed walls are lavish monastic buildings and immaculately trimmed grounds, dotted with coffee stands and massage pavilions. Pilgrims flock here to venerate the famous Buddha image known as Phra Singh (Lion Buddha), housed in Wihan Lai Kham, a small chapel immediately south of the *chedi* (stupa) to the rear of the temple grounds.

This elegant idol is said to have come to Thailand from Sri Lanka and was enshrined

Wat Chedi Luang

GABOR KOVACS PHOTOGRAPHY / SHUTTERSTOCK ©

Wat Phra Singh

Th Singharat

Th Phra Pokklao

Wat Chiang Man

Wat Inthakhin
Saduemuang

Wat Chedi Luang

Wat Phan Tao

Th Ratchamankha

❶ Need to Know

Temples are open during daylight hours and donations are appreciated.

✗ Take a Break

Akha Ama Cafe (p102), near Wat Phra Singh, is a cute cafe with an economic development mission for Akha hill tribes.

★ Top Tip

Visitors must remove their shoes before entering a temple building.

in 1367. The chapel is similarly striking, with gilded *naga* (mythical serpent) gables and sumptuous *lai·krahm* (gold-pattern stencilling) inside.

Despite Phra Singh's exalted status, very little is actually known about the image, which has more in common with images from northern Thailand than with Buddha statues from Sri Lanka. Adding to the mystery, there are two nearly identical images elsewhere in Thailand, one in the Bangkok National Museum and one in Nakhon Si Thammarat. Regardless of its provenance, the statue has become a focal point for religious celebrations during the Songkran festival, when it is ceremoniously paraded for worshippers to bathe.

As you wander the monastery grounds, note the raised temple library, housed in a dainty teak and stucco pavilion known as Ho

Trai, decorated with bas-relief angels. The temple's main *chedi*, rising over a classic Lanna-style octagonal base, was constructed by King Pa Yo in 1345; it's often wrapped in bolts of orange cloth by devotees.

Wat Chedi Luang

Wat Chedi Luang (วัดเจดีย์หลวง; Th Phra Pokklao; adult/child 40/20B; ⊘7am-10pm) is not quite as grand as Wat Phra Singh, but its towering, ruined Lanna-style *chedi* (built in 1441) is much taller and the sprawling compound is powerfully atmospheric. The famed Phra Kaew (Emerald Buddha), now held in Bangkok's Wat Phra Kaew, resided in the eastern niche of the *chedi* until 1475; today you can view a jade replica, given as a gift from the Thai king in 1995 to celebrate the 600th anniversary of the *chedi*.

In the main *wí·hǎhn* (sanctuary) is a revered standing Buddha statue, known as Phra Chao Attarot, flanked by two disciples. There are more chapels and states in teak pavilions at the rear of the compound, including a huge reclining Buddha and a handsome Chinese-influenced seated Buddha barely contained by his robes. The daily Monk Chat under a tree in the grounds always draws a crowd of interested travellers.

Next to the main entrance on Th Phra Pokklao, you'll pass Wat Chedi Luang's other claim to fame: the Làk Meuang (city pillar), allegedly raised by King Mengrai himself when Chiang Mai was founded in 1296. Buddhist rules dictate that only men can enter the pavilion to view the pillar. The gateway to the shrine on Th Phra Pakklao is flanked by *yaksha* (guardian demons) and Lanna warriors are depicted in bas-relief on the gates.

Wat Phan Tao

Without doubt the most atmospheric wát in the old city is **Wat Phan Tao** (วัดพันเถา; Th Phra Pokklao; donations appreciated; ☉daylight hours). This teak marvel sits in the shadow of Wat Chedi Luang. Set in a compound full of fluttering orange flags, the monastery is a monument to the teak trade, with an enormous prayer hall supported by 28 gargantuan teak pillars and lined with dark teak panels, enshrining a particularly graceful gold Buddha image. The juxtaposition of the orange monks' robes against this dark backdrop during evening prayers is particularly sublime.

Above the facade is a striking image of a peacock over a dog, representing the astrological year of the former royal resident's birth. The monastery is one of the focal points for celebrations during the Visakha

Wat Chiang Man

Bucha festival in May or June, when monks light hundreds of butter lamps around the pond in the grounds.

Wat Chiang Man

Chiang Mai's oldest temple, **Wat Chiang Man** (วัดเชียงมั่น; Th Ratchaphakhinai; donations appreciated; ☉daylight hours), was established by the city's founder, Phaya Mengrai, sometime around 1296. In front of the *ubosot* (ordination hall), a stone slab, engraved in 1581, bears the earliest known

> **★Did You Know?**
> Phra Singh is said to have come from Sri Lanka but it has more in common with images from northern Thailand than with Buddha statues from Sri Lanka.

reference to the city's founding. The main *wí·hǎhn* also contains the oldest known Buddha image created by the Lanna kingdom, cast in 1465.

A smaller second *wí·hǎhn* enshrines the city's guardian images; the bas-relief marble Phra Sila Buddha, believed to have been carved in Sri Lanka more than 1000 years ago; and the tiny crystal Phra Sae Tang Khamani Buddha, reportedly crafted for the king of Lopburi in around 200 AD.

The sacred images are housed inside a handsome, *mon·dòp*–like altar known as a *khong phra chao*, a distinctive feature of ancient Lanna temples. The monastery has a glorious *chedi,* with an elephant-flanked stucco base and a gilded upper level.

Wat Inthakhin Saduemuang

Tucked to the side of the Chiang Mai City Arts & Cultural Centre, **Wat Inthakhin Saduemuang** (วัดอินทขิลสะดือเมือง; donations appreciated; ☉6am-6pm) was the original location of the Làk Meuang (city pillar); part of its name refers to the 'city navel', or geographic centre, which was chosen some 700 years ago. The city pillar was moved to Wat Chedi Luang in 1800 after this temple fell into disrepair. It has since been given an intense makeover, making it one of the old city's most glittering temples. Marooned in the middle of Th Inthwarorot, its gilded teak *wí·hǎhn* is one of the most perfectly proportioned monuments in the city.

SAIKO3P / SHUTTERSTOCK ©

Old City Museums

Modern and providing an excellent introduction to the former Lanna kingdom's culture and history, these historical showcases are conveniently clustered in renovated colonial-style government buildings.

Great For...

☑ Don't Miss

A string of shops on Th Inthawarorot, near the museums, sells Thai sweets and other local dishes. It's packed with workers at lunchtime.

Just when you think you've got this country figured out, you land in a place like Chiang Mai and discover a whole new regional identity. Thankfully these museums explain the unique aspects of the Lanna kingdom, a closer cousin to southern China and Myanmar than Bangkok.

Chiang Mai City Arts & Cultural Centre

The **Chiang Mai City Arts & Cultural Centre** (หอศิลปวัฒนธรรมเชียงใหม่; www.cmo city.com; Th Phra Pokklao; adult/child 90/40B; ⊙8.30am-5pm Tue-Sun) provides an excellent primer on Chiang Mai history. Dioramas, photos, artefacts and audiovisual displays walk visitors through the key battles and victories in the Chiang Mai story, from the first settlements to wars with Myanmar and to the arrival of the railroad. Upstairs is a

ⓘ Need to Know

The museums are closed on Monday. They have a central location within walking distance to most old city accommodation.

✖ Take a Break

Get a massage and help inmates learn work skills at the Vocational Training Center of the Chiang Mai Women's Correctional Institution (p95).

★ Top Tip

Combination tickets (180B) gain entry to all three museums.

charming re-creation of a wooden Lanna village.

The museum gift shop is exceptionally well stocked with lacquerware, jewellery and even decorative fingernails for the Thai traditional dance. The building previously housed the provincial hall and is a handsomely restored Thai-colonial-style building dating from 1927. Restoration of the building was recognised by the Royal Society of Siamese Architects in 1999.

Lanna Folklife Museum

A real gem, the **Lanna Folklife Museum** (พิพิธภัณฑ์พื้นถิ่นล้านนา; Th Phra Pokklao; adult/child 90/40B; ⊘8.30am-5pm Tue-Sun) is set inside the former 1935 provincial court and re-creates Lanna village life in a series of life-sized dioramas that explain everything from *lai·krahm* stencilling and *fon lep* (tra-ditional Lanna dance) to the intricate symbolism of different elements of Lanna-style temples. Each room is designed like an art installation with engaging lessons on cultural titbits. You'll leave knowing a little more Lanna than before.

Chiang Mai Historical Centre

Housed in an airy building, this **museum** (หอประวัติศาสตร์เมืองเชียงใหม่; Th Ratwithi; adult/child 90/40B; ⊘8.30am-5pm Tue-Sun) covers the history of Chiang Mai Province, with displays on the founding of the capital, the Burmese occupation and the modern era of trade and unification with Bangkok. Downstairs is an archaeological dig of an ancient temple wall. There is a bit of overlap between the Chiang Mai City Arts & Culture Centre but sometimes an air-conditioned building is all one really needs.

Soap flowers

Evening Shopping

The evening market is a popular fixture across Thailand but Chiang Mai invented the 'walking street', which transforms streets into a pedestrian zone for itinerant vendors, a tradition that dates back to the Silk Road days.

Great For...

☑ Don't Miss

Local vendors selling refreshing ice cream, advertised as 'ancient' ice cream, at the walking streets.

Saturday Walking Street

The **Saturday Walking Street** (ถนนเดินวัน เสาร์; Th Wualai; ⊙4pm-midnight Sat) takes over Th Wualai, running southwest from Pratu Chiang Mai at the southern entrance to the old city. There is barely space to move as locals and tourists haggle for carved soaps, novelty dog collars, woodcarvings, Buddha paintings, hill-tribe trinkets and more.

The market unfolds along the city's historic silversmithing neighbourhood. Come early enough and you can see the craftspeople tapping out a rhythm as they impress decorative patterns into bowls, jewellery boxes and decorative plaques made from silver or, more often, aluminium.

Sunday Walking Street

Th Ratchadamnoen is taken over by the boisterous **Sunday Walking Street** (ถนน

① Need to Know

The walking streets and the night market get under way in the late afternoon and continue to midnight.

✕ Take a Break

Grab dinner at **Talat Pratu Chiang Mai** (Th Bamrungburi; mains from 40B; ⊘4am-noon & 6pm-midnight) before hitting the Saturday Walking Street.

★ Top Tip

Remember to stand respectfully when the national anthem is played at 6pm.

เดินวันอาทิตย์; Th Ratchadamnoen; ⊘4pm-midnight Sun), which feels even more animated than the Saturday Walking Street because of the energetic food markets that open up temple courtyards along the route. There's not a lot of breathing room as crowds slowly pass stalls selling woodcarvings, Buddha paintings, hill-tribe trinkets, Thai musical instruments, T-shirts, paper lanterns and umbrellas, silver jewellery and herbal remedies.

The market is a major source of income for local families and many traders spend the whole week hand-making merchandise to sell on Saturday and Sunday.

Chiang Mai Night Bazaar

You don't have to wait for a weekend to scratch your shopping itch. The **Chiang Mai Night Bazaar** (Th Chang Khlan; ⊘7pm-midnight) is one of the city's main night-time attractions and is the modern legacy of the original Yunnanese trading caravans that stopped here along the ancient trade route between China and Myanmar's Gulf of Martaban coast.

The night bazaar sells the usual tourist souvenirs. In true market fashion, vendors form a gauntlet along the footpath of Th Chang Khlan from Th Tha Phae to Th Loi Kroh. In between are dedicated shopping buildings: the Chiang Mai Night Bazaar Building is filled mainly with antique and handicraft stores. Across the street is the Kalare Night Bazaar selling upmarket clothes and home decor.

PHOTO: QUEROL / SHUTTERSTOCK ©

Outdoor Activities

Outdoor escapes are easy in Chiang Mai thanks to nearby looming mountains, rushing rivers, hill-tribe villages and elephant sanctuaries and camps. Dozens of operators offer adventure tours on foot, bike, raft and zipline.

Great For...

☑ Don't Miss

Chiang Mai's climate quickly transitions from the tropical plains to fern-filled mountain forests.

Trekking & Outdoor Adventuring

Thousands of visitors trek into the hills of northern Thailand hoping for adventure. Recommended companies include **Green Trails** (☏053 141356; www.green-trails.com; treks for 2 people from 2900B), which has a strong environmental ethos, and **Peak Adventure Tour** (☏053 800567; www.thepeakadventure.com; 302/4 Th Chiang Mai-Lamphun; tours 1600-2800B), for soft-adventure. Everyone loves Flight of the Gibbon (p98), a nearly 2km zipline course through the forest.

Elephant Parks

Elephant camps can look a lot like a prison but Chiang Mai has many humane alternatives.

Elephant Nature Park

ℹ Need to Know

Most tours travel about an hour outside of the city for full- and half-day tours. Trips usually include hotel transfer and lunch.

✖ Take a Break

After a sweaty adventure, reward yourself with a massage at **Lila Thai Massage** (☏053 327243; www.chiangmaimassage.com; Th Ratchadamnoen; standard/herbal massage from 200/350B; ☺10am-10pm).

★ Top Tip

Book your tickets directly with the tour operator to cut out agent commission charges.

The **Elephant Nature Park** (☏053 818754, 053 272850; www.elephantnaturepark.org; 1 Th Ratchamankha; 1-/2-day tours 2500/5800B) 🌿 provides a semi-wild state where visitors observe the natural interactions of elephants, while **Thai Elephant Care Center** (☏053 206247; www.thaielephantcarecenter.com; Mae Sa; half-/full day 2000/3000B) was set up to provide care for elderly elephants retired from logging camps and elephant shows; there are no rides and visitors feed the old-timers and help out at bath time.

Bicycling

The city's closest green space, Doi Suthep, has mountain-biking trails traversed by **Chiang Mai Mountain Biking & Kayaking** (☏053 814207; www.mountainbikingchiangmai.com; 1 Th Samlan; tours 1250-2700B; ☺8am-8pm). **Click and Travel** (☏053 281553; www.chiangmaicycling.com; half-/full/multi-day tours from 950/1500/5350B; 🚲) cycles through cultural sights outside the city centre.

Water Sports

White-water rafting takes on the wild and frothy part of Mae Taeng (best from July to March). **Siam River Adventures** (☏089 515 1917; www.siamrivers.com; 17 Th Ratwithi; rafting per day from 1800B; ☺8am-8pm) has well-regarded safety standards for the 10km stretch. Chiang Mai Mountain Biking & Kayaking paddles down a remote part of Mae Ping.

BLUR LIFE 1975 / SHUTTERSTOCK ©

Thanon Nimmanhaemin

The epicentre of 'new' Chiang Mai, Th Nimmanhaemin is the place to wine, dine and stay up all night (or at least until closing time). The main road and its tributary soi are frequented by hip uni students and NGO expats.

Great For...

☑ Don't Miss

The food stalls near Soi 10 sell fried chicken, cut fruit and noodle dishes. Simple is amazing in Thailand.

Dining

There is a bewildering array of food to be found on Nimmanhaemin.

Tong Tem Toh (Soi 13, Th Nimmamnhaemin; mains 50-170B; ⏰11am-9pm) is set in an old teak house and serves northern Thai cuisine, such as *nám prík ong* (a chilli dip with vegetables for dipping) and *gaang hang lay* (Burmese-style pork curry with peanut and tamarind).

Need a break from Thai? **Tengoku** (☑053 215801; Soi 5, Th Nimmanhaemin; mains 200-1650B; ⏰11am-2pm & 5.30-10pm; 🛜) serves superior sushi, yakitori, spectacular sukiyaki and wonderful wagyu steaks, plus cheaper bento boxes.

The farm-to-table dishes at **Rustic & Blue** (☑053 216420; www.rusticandblue. com; Soi 7, Th Nimmanhaemin; mains 180-360B; ⏰8.30am-9.30pm; ❄🛜) are in perfect

harmony with the decor. And **Italics** (☏05 321 6219; www.theakyra.com; 22/2 Nimmana Haeminda Soi 9; pizzas 260-550B; ⏱7am-11pm) does some of the best pizzas in town.

Ice cream with star power, **I-Berry** (off Soi 17, Th Nimmanhaemin; single scoop 69B; ⏱10am-10pm; 📶) is owned by Thai comedian Udom Taepanich (nicknamed 'Nose' for his signature feature). This kitschy shop in a leafy garden is mobbed day and night.

Drinking & Nightlife

Nimman draws in an eclectic crowd of night owls, from rowdy uni students to Thai yuppies and in-the-know foreigners.

Check out the urban tribe at **Sangdee Gallery** (www.sangdeeart.com; 5 Soi 5, Th Sirimungklajarn; ⏱3pm-midnight Tue-Sat), part gallery, music club, bar and cafe.

The trendy spots change but the formula stays the same: beer garden venues with brews, food and friends. The more people who can pack in, the merrier. The most impressive (and long-standing) of the lot, **Beer Republic** (www.beerrepublicchiangmai. com; Soi 11, Th Nimmanhaemin; ⏱4pm-midnight) offers 15 draught beers.

Warmup Cafe (www.facebook.com/ warmupcafe1999; 40 Th Nimmanhaemin; ⏱6pm-2am) is a Nimman club survivor, rocking out since 1999. Each room does a different music genre: hip-hop, electronica and rock.

Doi Suthep

Switchback roads leave behind the lowland plains and you ascend into a cool cloud belt filled with mosses and ferns. The mountain shelters a national park, holy temple, royal palace and hill-tribe villages.

Great For...

☑ Don't Miss

The spectacular views of Chiang Mai from Wat Phra That Doi Suthep.

Wat Phra That Doi Suthep

Overlooking the city from its mountain throne, **Wat Phra That Doi Suthep** (วัดพระ ธาตุดอยสุเทพ; Th Huay Kaew; 30B; ⊙6am-6pm) is one of northern Thailand's most sacred temples, and its founding legend is learned by every school kid in Chiang Mai. The wát itself is a beautiful example of northern Thai architecture, reached via a strenuous, 306-step staircase flanked by mosaic *naga* (serpents); the climb is intended to help devotees accrue Buddhist merit, but less energetic pilgrims can take a funicular lift (20B).

The monastery was established in 1383 by King Keu Naone to enshrine a piece of bone, said to be from the shoulder of the historical Buddha. The bone shard was brought to Lanna by a wandering monk

Pavilion, Bhubing Palace

CHRISTOPHER PB / SHUTTERSTOCK ©

ⓘ Need to Know

Public *rót daang* ('red car') leave from the zoo for Wat Phra That Doi Suthep (40B per passenger). A charter ride will cost 300/500B one-way/return.

✕ Take a Break

Ban Khun Chang Kian has a small coffee shop overlooking its coffee plants.

★ Top Tip

Bring a long-sleeved shirt because it can be cool on the mountain.

its union with Thailand. Pilgrims queue to leave lotus blossoms and other offerings at the shrines surrounding the *chedi*.

Bhubing Palace

Above Wat Phra That Doi Suthep, the grounds of the royal family's **winter palace** (พระตำหนักภูพิงค์, Phra Tamnak Bhu Bing; www. bhubingpalace.org; Th Huay Kaew; 50B; ⊙8.30-11.30am & 1-3.30pm) are open to the public. Thanks to the mountain's cool climate, the royal gardeners are able to raise 'exotic' species such as roses. More interesting is the reservoir, brought to life by fountains that dance to the king's own musical compositions.

Ban Kun Chang Kian

Ban Kun Chang Kian is a Hmong coffee-producing village about 500m down a dirt track just past the Doi Pui campground. You'll need private transport to reach the village.

from Sukhothai and it broke into two pieces at the base of the mountain, with one piece being enshrined at Wat Suan Dok (p94). The second fragment was mounted onto a sacred white elephant who wandered the jungle until it died, in the process selecting the spot where the monastery was later founded.

The terrace at the top of the steps is dotted with small shrines, rock gardens and a statue of the white elephant that carried the Buddha relic. Before entering the inner courtyard, children pay their respects to a lizard-like guardian statue known as 'Mom'.

Steps lead up to the inner terrace, where a walkway circumnavigates the gleaming golden *chedi* enshrining the relic. The crowning five-tiered umbrella marks the city's independence from Myanmar and

Chiang Mai Walking Tour

Chiang Mai's famous temples reside in the historic old city. Start in the morning hours, dress modestly (covering shoulders and knees) and remove your shoes before entering and sit in the 'mermaid' position inside the sanctuary halls.

Start Wat Phra Singh
Distance 1km
Duration Four hours

7 Get a massage at the **Vocational Training Centre of the Chiang Mai Women's Correctional Institution** (p95).

Th Ratwithi

7

FINISH

Th Singharat

Th Inthawararot

START

1

Th Ratchadamnoen

Th Jhaban

1 Start at **Wat Phra Singh** (p78), a textbook example of Lanna architecture.

2 Before condo towers, the now ruined **Wat Chedi Luang** (p79) was Chiang Mai's tallest structure.

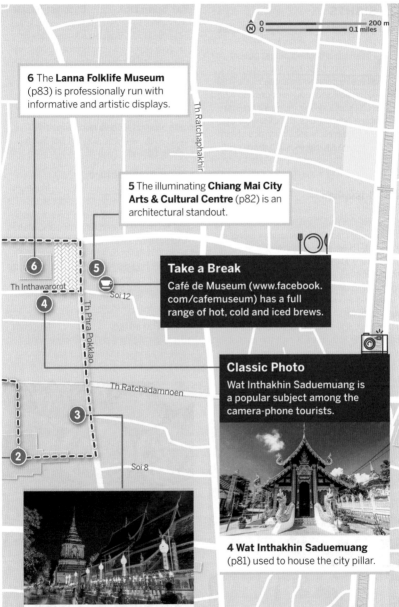

6 The **Lanna Folklife Museum** (p83) is professionally run with informative and artistic displays.

Th Ratchaphakhi

5 The illuminating **Chiang Mai City Arts & Cultural Centre** (p82) is an architectural standout.

⑥
Th Inthawarorot
⑤
④
Soi 12
Th Phra Pokklao

Take a Break

Café de Museum (www.facebook.com/cafemuseum) has a full range of hot, cold and iced brews.

Th Ratchadamnoen

③

Soi 8

Classic Photo

Wat Inthakhin Saduemuang is a popular subject among the camera-phone tourists.

4 Wat Inthakhin Saduemuang (p81) used to house the city pillar.

3 Next door is **Wat Phan Tao** (p80), a teak temple that is more photogenic than venerated.

◉ SIGHTS

Talat Warorot   Market
(ตลาดวโรรส; cnr Th Chang Moi & Th Praisani; ⊙6am-5pm) Chiang Mai's oldest public market, Warorot (also spelt Waroros) is a great place to connect with the city's Thai soul. Alongside souvenir vendors you'll find numerous stalls selling items for ordinary Thai households: woks, toys, fishing nets, pickled tea leaves, wigs, sticky-rice steamers, Thai-style sausages, *kâab mŏo* (pork rinds), live catfish and tiny statues for spirit houses.

Wat Srisuphan   Buddhist Temple
(วัดศรีสุพรรณ; Soi 2, Th Wualai; donations appreciated; ⊙6am-6pm) It should come as no surprise that the silversmiths along Th Wualai have decorated their patron monastery with the same fine artisanship shown in their shops. The 'silver' *ubosot* (ordination hall) is covered with silver, nickel and aluminium panels, embossed with elaborate repoussé-work designs. The effect is like a giant jewellery box, particularly after dark, when the monastery is illuminated by coloured lights.

Wat Suan Dok   Buddhist Temple
(วัดสวนดอก; Th Suthep; donations appreciated; ⊙daylight hours) Built on a former flower garden in 1373, this important monastery enshrines one half of a sacred Buddha relic; the other half was transported by white elephant to Wat Phra That Doi Suthep (p90). The main *chedi* is a gilded, bell-shaped structure that rises above a sea of white memorial *chedi* honouring the Thai royal family, with the ridge of Doi Suthep soaring behind.

Lanna Architecture
Center   Museum
(ศูนย์สถาปัตยกรรมล้านนา; www.lanna-arch.net; 117 Th Ratchadamnoen; ⊙8.30am-4.30pm Mon-Fri) **FREE** Formerly owned by prince Jao Maha In, this handsome mansion, built in a hybrid Lanna and European style between 1889 and 1893, houses a small education centre with some interesting models showing the changing face of Lanna architecture through the centuries.

Art in Paradise   Museum
(พิพิธภัณฑ์ อาร์ต อิน พาราไดซ์ เชียงใหม่; www.chiangmai-artinparadise.com; 199/9 Th Chang

From left: Wat Suan Dok; food stall, Talat Warorot; Wat Srisuphan

Khlan; 400B; ⊙9am-7pm) Just a whole lot of fun, this museum has a range of 3D optical illusion art displays from cliff faces and mummy tombs to tiny chairs and giant toilet paper rolls where you can get in the scene, snap photos and just be silly. Kids in particular will enjoy it but adults often love it too.

✪ ACTIVITIES

Vocational Training Centre of the Chiang Mai Women's Correctional Institution
Massage

 053 122340; 100 Th Ratwithi; massage from 200B; ⊙8am-4.30pm Mon-Fri, 9am-4.30pm Sat & Sun) Offers fantastic massages performed by female inmates participating in the prison's job-training rehabilitation program. The cafe next door is a nice spot for a post-massage brew.

Zira Spa
Spa

(☑053 222288; www.ziraspa.com; 8/1 Th Rajvithi; treatments 700-6000B; ⊙10am-10pm) Located on one of the main streets in the

 Cooking Courses in Chiang Mai

Small House Chiang Mai Thai Cooking School (☑095 674 4550; www.chiang maithaicooking.com; 19/14 Th Thipanet; 1-day/evening-only classes 1500/1300B)
Thai Farm Cooking School (☑081 288 5989; www.thaifarmcooking.com; 38 Soi 9, Th Moon Muang; courses 1500B)
Asia Scenic Thai Cooking (☑053 418657; www.asiascenic.com; 31 Soi 5, Th Ratchadamnoen; half-day courses 800-1000B, full-day courses 1000-1200B; ⊙half-day courses 9am-1pm & 5-9pm, full-day courses 9am-3pm)

centre of Chiang Mai, Zira Spa offers some of the best spa treatments and massages in the region, all for a decent price. You need to book in advance for the larger spa packages, but same-day service is available for one or two of the 30-, 60- or 90-minute treatments.

Central Chiang Mai

Lanna Muay Thai Boxing Camp (1km);
Studio Naenna (4km);
Wat Phra That Doi Suthep (13km);
Bhubing Palace (18km)

Mae Sa Valley (26km)

Th Morakot
41

Soi 4

Th Chotana (Th Chang Pheuak)

Soi 1
34
62
53
Th Huay Kaew
Soi 5
49
Soi 7
Soi 9
42
7
54
56
Soi 13
Soi 11
67
63

Thanon Nimmanhaemin

40

Th Ratchaphuek

Th Hutsadisawee

Chiang Mai
Ram Hospital

Th Si Phum
66

Soi 4
Th Wiang Kaew

Th Sirimungklajarn

Th Saijai

Th Arak

Th Singharat

Th Jhaban

Th Ratwithi
25
3
2
44
10
20

Th Suthep
15
27

Th Suthep

Th Inthawarorot
13
55
17
28
Th Ratchadamnoen

47

51

8

60
Th Ratchamankha

Th Bunreuangrit

31

Th Samlan

Soi 7

Suan
Buak Hat

Th Chang Lor
Th Bamrungburi

Kanchanaphisek
Park

23

Th Thiphanet

14
Th Wualai

Chiang Mai
International
Airport

Th Mahidon

Th Hai Ya

32

Thai Rent
a Car (320m)
Th Mahidol

Th Wualai

Chiang Mai on
Three Wheels (12km)

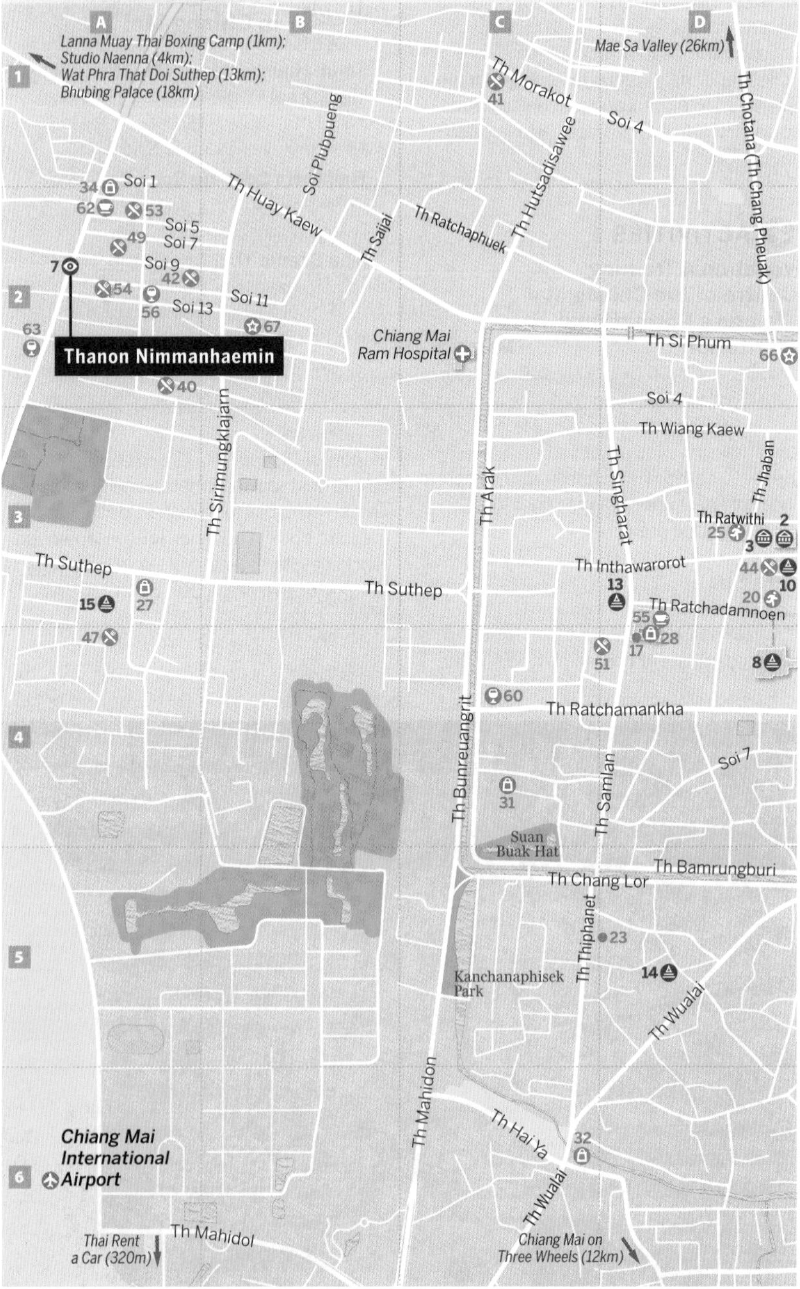

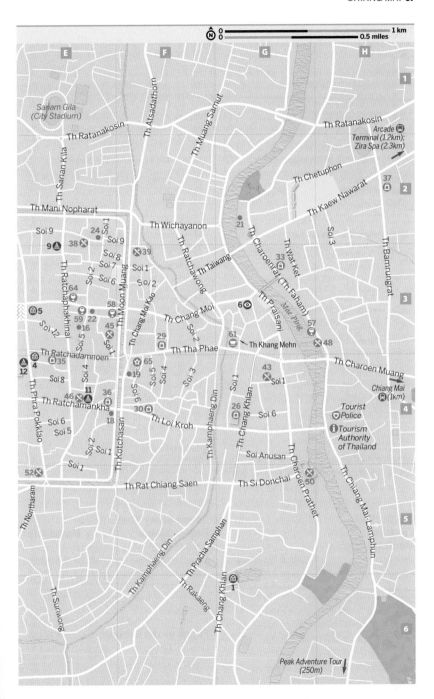

Sanam Gila
(City Stadium)

Th Ratanakosin

Th Ratanakosin

Arcade
Terminal (1.2km);
Zira Spa (2.3km)

Th Sanan Kila

Th Atsadathorn

Th Muang Samut

Th Chetuphon

Th Kaew Nawarat

37

Th Bamrungrat

Th Mani Nopharat

Th Wichayanon

21

Th Charoenrat (Th Faham)

Soi 9

24

Soi 9

38

Soi 8

9

Th Ratchaphakhinai

Soi 2

Soi 7

39

Th Ratchawong

Th Taiwang

Th Wat Ket

Soi 3

Soi 6

Soi 1

Mae Ping

64

Soi 2

Soi 2

Th Moon Muang

Th Chang Moi

Th Chang Mai Kao

58

6

Th Prai Sani

5

59 22

45

Soi 2

Soi 1

16

29

61 → Th Khang Mehn

57

48

Soi 12

Soi 6

Th Tha Phae

12

Th Ratchadamnoen

4

35

65

Soi 5

Soi 4

Soi 3

43

Soi 1

Th Charoen Muang

19

Soi 4

Chiang Mai
(1km)

Soi 8

Th Phra Pokklao

46 11

36

Th Ratchamankha

Soi 6

18

30

Th Loi Kroh

26

Soi 6

Tourist
Police

Th Kotchasan

Soi 5

Soi 2 Soi 1

Th Kamphaeng Din

Th Chang Khlan

Soi 1

Tourism
Authority
of Thailand

52

Soi 1

Th Rat Chiang Saen

Soi Anusan

Th Si Donchai

50

Th Charoen Prathet

Th Chiang Mai-Lamphun

Th Nontharam

Th Kamphaeng Din

Th Pracha Samphan

Th Rakaeng

Th Chang Khlan

1

Th Suriwong

Peak Adventure Tour
(250m)

Central Chiang Mai

Doi Suthep Vipassana Meditation Center
Health & Wellbeing

(☑053 295012; www.fivethousandyears.org; Wat Phra That Doi Suthep, Th Huay Kaew; by donation) Set within the grounds of Wat Phra That Doi Suthep (p90), this centre offers meditation training retreats for all levels, lasting from four to 21 days.

Lanna Muay Thai Boxing Camp
Martial Arts

(☑053 892102; 161 Soi Chang Khian, Th Huay Kaew; day/week/month 400/2200/8000B) Offers instruction to foreigners and Thais. The gym is famous for having trained the title-winning, transgender boxer Parinya Kiatbusaba.

Flight of the Gibbon
Ziplining

(☑053 010660; www.treetopasia.com; 29/4-5 Th Kotchasan; day tours 4000B; ⊙9.30am-6.30pm)

Much copied but never equalled, this adventure outfit started the zipline craze, with nearly 5km of wire strung up like spiderwebs in the gibbon-populated (you may see some) forest canopy near Ban Mae Kampong, an hour's drive east from Chiang Mai. The day-tour includes an optional but highly recommended village visit, waterfall walk and delicious lunch cooked by the community. As well as day trips, it offers multiday, multiactivity tours that include a night at a village homestay.

TOURS

Chiang Mai on
Three Wheels   Tours
(www.chiangmaionthreewheels.com; Don Kaeo, Saraphi; 4hr tours for 2 people 1700B) ✈ There are few better ways to tour Chiang Mai than by slow, quiet, culturally immersive săhm·lór (three-wheel pedicabs; also spelt săamláw). This organisation helps promote this dying industry by connecting tourists with the often non-English-speaking drivers and pairs you with an English-speaking guide. Profits go entirely to the drivers and to support their industry.

Scorpion Tailed
River Cruise   Boating
(☏081 960 9398; www.scorpiontailedrivercruise. com; Th Charoenrat; cruises 500B) This river cruise focuses on the history of Mae Ping using traditional-style craft, known as scorpion-tailed boats. Informative cruises (five daily) last one to 1½ hours. They depart from Wat Srikhong pier near Rim Ping Condo and stop for a snack at the affiliated Scorpion Tailed Boat Village.

SHOPPING

Old City

Mengrai Kilns   Ceramics
(www.mengraikilns.com; 79/2 Th Arak; ◷8am-5pm) In the southwestern corner of the old city, Mengrai Kilns keeps the tradition of Thai celadon pottery alive, with cookware,

dining sets, ornaments and Western-style nativity scenes.

HQ Paper Maker   Arts & Crafts
(www.hqpapermaker.com; 3/31 Th Samlan; ◷9am-6pm) This intriguing shop sells reams of handmade mulberry paper (sǎh), in a remarkable range of colours and patterns, including gorgeous marbled sheets that resemble the end leaves of bound 19th-century books. Ask about its low-key, three-hour paper-making course for 800B per person.

East of the Old City

John Gallery   Art
(Th Tha Phae; ◷daily but variable) Opened in 1980, this place is a warren of paintings on cotton, cards and rocks, often inscribed with feel-good or creative quotes. Between John's art are dusty hill tribe embroidery, ancient opium farming tools and even a 'witch doctor' recipe book or two. Be sure to head upstairs for views of the crumbling *chedi* out back.

KukWan Gallery   Clothing
(37 Th Loi Kroh; ◷10am-7pm) Set slightly back from the road, this charming little shop sells scarves, runners, bedspreads and natural cotton and silk by the metre.

Sop Moei Arts   Clothing, Handicrafts
(www.sopmoeiarts.com; 150/10 Th Charoenrat/ Th Faham; ◷9am-6pm) High-end hill-tribe crafts, from off-the-loom textiles to baskets, are sold at this economic-development shop, which provides assistance for Karen villagers in Mae Hong Son Province.

Thai Tribal
Crafts Fair Trade   Arts & Crafts
(www.ttcrafts.co.th; 25/9 Th Moon Muang; ◷9.30am-6pm Mon-Sat) A branch of the missionary-backed **fair-trade store** (208 Th Bamrungrat; ◷9am-5pm Mon-Sat), selling fine hill-tribe needlework and baskets.

From left: Ceremic elephants; fabric stall; Kiat Ocha

West of the Old City

Studio Naenna Clothing, Homewares
(www.studio-naenna.com; 138/8 Soi Chang Khian;
9am-5pm Mon-Fri, plus Sat Oct-Mar only) The
colours of the mountains have been woven
into the naturally dyed silks and cottons
here, part of a project to preserve traditional weaving and embroidery. You can see the
whole production process at this workshop.

Srisanpanmai Fashion & Accessories
(6 Soi 1, Th Nimmanhaemin; 10am-6.30pm)
The display cases here are like a library
of Lanna textiles, with reams of silk and
cotton shawls, scarves and hill-tribe costumes. You're guaranteed to find something to surprise the folks at home.

Hill-Tribe Products Promotion
Centre Clothing, Handicrafts
(21/17 Th Suthep; 9am-5pm) Hill-tribe
textiles, bags, boxes, lacquerware and other
crafts are sold at this large store near Wat
Suan Dok; profits go to hill-tribe welfare
programs.

EATING

Old City

SP Chicken Thai $
(9/1 Soi 1, Th Samlan; mains 50-170B; 11am-
9pm) Chiang Mai's best chicken emerges
daily from the broilers at this tiny cafe near
Wat Phra Singh. The menu runs to salads
and soups, but most people just pick a half
(90B) or whole (170B) chicken, and dip the
moist meat into the spicy, tangy dipping
sauces provided.

Mit Mai Chinese $$
(Th Ratchamankha; mains 60-900B; 10am-
10pm) If you didn't make it to northern
Thailand's mountaintop Chinese outposts,
this decades-old restaurant is the place
to go for Yunnanese specialities. Just
about anything flash-fried is tasty, and
you can't go wrong with the air-dried
Yunnanese ham. There's no roman-script
sign, but it's adjacent to **Wat Pha Khao** (วัด
ผ้าขาว; Th Ratchmankha; donations appreciated;
daylight hours).

EAKKAPHAN SMTABHINDHU / SHUTTERSTOCK ©

Kiat Ocha Chinese, Thai $
(Th Inthawarorot; mains 50-90B; ☺6am-3pm)
This humble Chinese-style canteen is
mobbed daily by locals who can't get
enough of the *kôw man gài* (Hainanese-
style boiled chicken). Each plate comes
with soup, chilli sauce and blood pudding
and the menu also includes wok-fried
chicken and pork and *sà·đé* (grilled skewers
of pork or chicken). There's no English sign
but you'll know it when you see it.

Lert Ros Thai $
(Soi 1, Th Ratchadamnoen; mains 30-160B;
☺noon-9pm) As you enter this local-style
hole in the wall, you'll pass the main course:
delicious whole tilapia fish, grilled on coals
and served with a fiery Isan-style dipping
sauce. Eaten with sticky rice, this is one of
the great meals of Chiang Mai. The menu
also includes fermented pork grilled in
banana leaves, curries and *sôm·đam* (spicy
green papaya salad).

Blue Diamond Vegetarian $
(35/1 Soi 9, Th Moon Muang; mains 65-220B;
☺7am-9pm Mon-Sat; 🖉) Blue Diamond offers
an adventurous menu of sandwiches,
salads, curries, stir-fries and curious fusion
dishes such as *đôm yam* (Thai-style sour
soup) macaroni. Packed with fresh produce, prepackaged spice and herb mixes,
and freshly baked treats, it also feels a little
like a wholefood store.

🛈 East of the Old City

Kao Soi
Fueng Fah Thai $
(Soi 1, Th Charoen Phrathet; mains 40-60B;
☺7am-9pm) The most flavourful of the
Muslim-run *kôw soy* (wheat-and-egg
noodles in a curry broth) vendors along
Halal St, with the choice of beef or chicken
with your noodles.

Hideout Breakfast $$
(Th Sithiwongse; breakfasts 55-160B; ☺8am-
5pm closed Mon; 🅿) Hidden but found by
expats looking for Western breakfast and
coffee a cut above the rest, this place
takes great care to serve perfectly cooked
eggs, bacon fried to order, house-made
muesli and yoghurt, creative sandwiches
on fresh bread and the best banana bread

Chiang Mai's Cafe Scene

Chiang Mai adores coffee. Much of it is grown locally as a replacement crop for opium. Here are some top spots for a brew:

Akha Ama Cafe (www.akhaama.com; 175/1 Th Ratchadamnoen; ⊙8am-6pm; 🔊) Locally harvested, sustainable, direct-trade beans from the jungles north of Chiang Mai.

Ristr8to (www.ristr8to.com; Th Nimman-haemin; espresso drinks 88B; ⊙8.30am-7pm, closed Tue) From flat whites to the hyper-caffeinated doppio ristretto that uses 18g of ground coffee.

Raming Tea House (Th Tha Phae; drinks 50-120B; ⊙8.30am-5.30pm) Victorian-era cafe serving Thai mountain teas.

Ristr8to
SUPHANAT / SHUTTERSTOCK ©

we've eaten in Southeast Asia. The coffee is amazing too. Seating is very limited so arrive early for a table.

Service 1921 Southeast Asian $$$

(☎053 253333; www.chiang-mai.anantara.com; Anantara Resort, 123 Th Charoen Prathet; mains 290-2000B; ⊙6am-11pm) The pan-Asian restaurant at the Anantara Resort & Spa is elegance incarnate, with waitstaff in full 1920s garb and interior decor resembling the secret offices of MI6 – appropriate as the gorgeous teak villa housing the restaurant used to be the British Consulate. The food is made with top-notch ingredients, though some dishes have the spice dialled down to appeal to international palates.

The hotel also has an international restaurant in a similarly romantic location overlooking the river.

🔵 West of the Old City

Pun Pun Vegetarian $

(www.punpunthailand.org; Wat Suan Dok, Th Suthep; mains 40-85B; ⊙8am-4pm Thu-Tue; 🍴) 🌿 Tucked away at the back of Wat Suan Dok, this studenty cafe is a great place to sample Thai vegetarian food prepared using little-known herbs and vegetables and lots of healthy whole grains grown on its concept farm, which doubles as an education centre for sustainable living.

There's a branch called **Imm Aim Vegetarian Restaurant** (10 Th Santhitham; mains 45-90B; ⊙10am-9pm; 🍴) 🌿 near the International Hotel Chiangmai.

🍷 DRINKING & NIGHTLIFE

Good View Bar

(www.goodview.co.th; 13 Th Charoenrat/Th Fa-ham; ⊙10am-2am) Good View attracts plenty of locals, with a big menu of Thai standards and sushi platters (mains 100B to 250B) and a nightly program of bands with rotating line-ups (meaning the drummer starts playing guitar and the bass player moves behind the piano).

Kafe 1985 Bar

(127/3 Th Moon Muang; ⊙8.30am-midnight, closed Thu) Open since 1985, Kafe is none-theless a timeless place to sip a Singha and dig into classic Thai-style drinking snacks (mains 60B to 150B) such as deep-fried fermented pork ribs.

Zoe in Yellow Bar

(40/12 Th Ratwithi; ⊙11am-2am) Part of a complex of open-air bars at the corner of Th Ratchaphakhinai and Th Ratwithi, Zoe is where backpackers come to sink pitchers of cold Chang, sip cocktails from buckets, rock out to cheesy dance-floor fillers, ca-noodle and swap travel stories until the wee hours. There's also a few Indian food places between the bar joints.

Mixology   Bar

(61/6 Th Arak; ⊘3pm-midnight Tue-Fri, 11am-midnight Sat & Sun) A tiny, eclectic bar with a huge selection of microbrews, a thick menu of fruity house drinks, burgers and northern Thai eats, and a lounging dog. Even if you drink too many chilli-infused 'prick me ups', you probably won't regret it the next day.

Khun Kae's
Juice Bar   Juice Bar

(Soi 7, Th Moon Muang; ⊘10.30am-7.30pm) Our vote for Chiang Mai's best juice shack. Tonnes of fresh fruit, heaps of delicious combinations, generous serves and all this for prices that are almost comically low (drinks from 40B).

⊗ ENTERTAINMENT

North Gate Jazz Co-Op   Live Music

(www.facebook.com/northgate.jazzcoop; 95/1-2 Th Si Phum; ⊘7-11pm) This compact jazz club tends to pack in more musicians than patrons, but the music can be pretty hip.

Inter   Live Music

(271 Th Tha Phae; ⊘4pm-1am) This small wooden house packs in a lively line-up of local talent. It has that beach-shack vibe beloved by travellers everywhere and a popular pool table – though we recommend against challenging the multiple-trophy-winning lady who owns the place!

ⓘ INFORMATION

Traffic is annoying; during rush hour, expect long waits at traffic lights. Take care when crossing busy roads; drivers don't give way. In March and April, smoky haze from farmers burning off their fields causes poor air quality. But, otherwise, compared to Bangkok, Chiang Mai is a breeze.

Chiang Mai Ram Hospital (⊘053 920300; www.chiangmairam.com; 8 Th Bunreuangrit) The most modern hospital in town.

Tourism Authority of Thailand (TAT; ⊘053 248604; www.tourismthailand.org; Th Chiang Mai-Lamphun; ⊘8.30am-4.30pm) English-speaking staff provide maps, and advice on travel across Thailand.

Nightlife in Chiang Mai

ALEXANDER MAZURKEVICH / SHUTTERSTOCK ©

⇨ Mae Sa Valley

Just north of the city is Mae Sa Valley and a 100km loop that winds through fantastic high-altitude scenery. It is a beautiful ride, often done on hired motorcycles.

The first stop is **Nam Tok Mae Sa** (น้ำตกแม่สา; adult/child 100/50B, car 30B; ⊗8am-4.30pm), a chain of cascades set in the fringes of Doi Suthep-Pui National Park on Rte 1096. Further on, **Queen Sirikit Botanic Gardens** (สวน พฤกษศาสตร์สมเด็จพระนางเจ้าสิริกิติ์; www.qsbg. org; Rte 1096; adult/child 100/50B, car/ motorcycle 100/30B; ⊗8.30am-4.30pm) has gardens and greenhouses full of exotic and local flora. The road eventually climbs into a high-altitude basin, once a centre for opium poppy production. With sponsorship from the Thai royal family, local hill-tribe farmers reseeded their terraced fields with vegetables, fruits and flowers, processed under the Doi Kham label. The **Mon Cham restaurant** (Nong Hoi Mai; mains 60-180B; ⊗7am-7pm; ✍), teetering on a ridge top, cooks up tasty dishes. From the main road, turn off at Ban Pong Yaeng to the Hmong village of Nong Hoi. Above the village, you'll find the restaurant.

The rest of the route swings around the mountain ridge, passing spectacular viewpoints, and then begins its descent into Chiang Mai via Rte 1269 to Rte 121.

Queen Sirikit Botanic Gardens
PIXHOUND / SHUTTERSTOCK ©

Tourist Police (✍053 247318, 24hr emergency 1155; 608 Rimping Plaza, Th Charoenraj; ⊗6am-midnight) Volunteer staff speak a variety of languages.

ℹ GETTING THERE & AWAY

AIR

Domestic and international flights arrive and depart from **Chiang Mai International Airport** (✍05 327 0222; www.chiangmaiairportthai.com), 3km southwest of the old city.

BUS

The **Arcade Bus Terminal** (Th Kaew Nawarat), about 3km from the old city, is Chiang Mai's long-distance station.

TRAIN

Run by the State Railway of Thailand, the **Chiang Mai Train Station** (✍053 245363, nationwide 1690; Th Charoen Muang) is about 2.5km east of the old city. The train station has an ATM, a left-luggage room (5am to 8.45pm, 20B per item) and an advance-booking counter (you'll need your passport to book a ticket).

ℹ GETTING AROUND

Motorcycles cost 150B to 500B to hire. **Thai Rent a Car** (✍053 904188; www.thairentacar. com; Chiang Mai International Airport) has a good reputation for car hire. *Rót daang* (literally 'red cars') operate as shared taxis and roam the streets picking up passengers heading in the same direction. Journeys start at 20B for a short trip and 40B for a longer trip. Túk túk and *rót daang* can be chartered; negotiate a price beforehand.

Where to Stay

Make reservations far in advance if visiting during Chinese New Year, Songkran and other holiday periods.

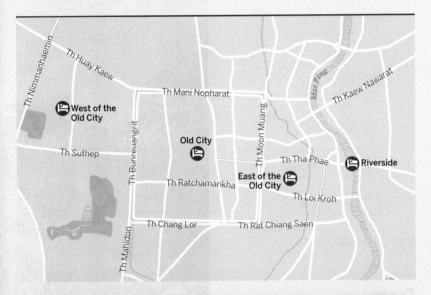

Neighbourhood	Atmosphere
Old City	Close to sights, old-school Chiang Mai feel, international dining and bars; lots of touts and tourists
East of the Old City	Lots of budget and midrange options, easy access to markets; noisy and hectic, sexpat hang-outs
West of the Old City	Less touristy, easy access to dining and nightlife; far from sights
Riverside	Lots of midrange and top-end options; lack of dining and entertainment, far from sights

Detour to Pai

Live music, fun bars and fresh-air activities have made this formerly tiny village, located three hours west of Chiang Mai, a serious backpacker destination.

Great For...

☑ Need to Know

Most of Pai's sights are found outside the city centre, making hiring a motor-cycle (100B to 250B per 24 hours) a necessity.

In a nearly picture-perfect mountain-valley setting, the popular town of Pai (ปาย) is perfect for a whole host of natural, lazy activities to keep visitors entertained. It also has a vibrant art scene. The town's Shan roots can still be seen in its temples, quiet backstreets and fun afternoon market.

Memorial Bridge

Originally built by Japanese soldiers during WWII, this **bridge** (สพานประวัติศาสตร์ท่าปาย; Rte 1095) is one of several crucial photo ops to the thousands of Thais who stop along the '762 curves' to Pai during the tourist season. It's located 9km from Pai along the road to Chiang Mai.

Ban Santichon

The cheesy photo ops, piped-in music, restaurants serving Yunnanese food, tea tastings, pony rides, tacky re-creation of the Great Wall of China and **mountaintop viewpoint** (บ้านสันติชล) can make parts of Ban Santichon seem like a theme park. But get past these and you'll find a living, breathing Chinese village, one well worth exploring. Located about 4km west of Pai.

Pai Canyon

Located 8km from Pai along the road to Chiang Mai, a paved **stairway** (กองแลนปาย; Rte 1095; ⊙daylight hours) culminates in an elevated lookout over high rock cliffs and the Pai valley. The trail lacks shade so is best tackled in the morning or afternoon.

Wat Phra That Mae Yen

This **temple** (วัดพระธาตุแม่เย็น; ⊙daylight hours) sits atop a hill and has terrific views overlooking the valley. To get here, walk 1km

Memorial Bridge

east from the main intersection in town to get to the stairs (353 steps) that lead to the top. Or, if you've got wheels, take the 400m sealed road that follows a different route.

Activities

Pai is a great place to learn a new skill. The curriculum of courses available in Pai ranges from drumming to circus arts; check listings publications such as the *Pai Events Planner*

Where to Stay

Pai's popularity, particularly among domestic tourists, has resulted in a glut of midrange and upscale places. Rooms are cheaper just outside the centre of town, which is where you should base yourself if you're coming to Pai with notions of an idyllic, rural stay.

NICOLE KWIATKOWSKI / SHUTTERSTOCK ©

(PEP) or the *Pai Explorer* (www.paiexplorer. com) to see what's on when you're in town. It's also a great place for pampering. There are plenty of traditional Thai massage places charging from around 150B an hour. Reiki, crystal healing, acupuncture, reflexology and other nonindigenous methods of healing are also available. In addition to these, a few local businesses, all of which are located approximately 1.5km northwest of **Tha Pai Hot Springs** (บ่อน้ำร้อนท่าปาย; adult/child 300/150B; ⏰7am-6pm), have made open-air hot tubs with the area's thermal waters.

If you're more of a go-getter, rafting along Mae Nam Pai during the wet season (approximately June to October) is a popular activity. The trip runs from Pai to Mae Hong Son, which, depending on the amount of water, can traverse rapids from class 1 to class 5. Trips can be arranged with **Thai Adventure Rafting** (☏053 699111; www.thai rafting.com; Th Chaisongkhram; ⏰10am-9pm).

Drinking & Nightlife

There are dozens of bars in Pai, often with a life span of a fruit fly. As a general guide to the town's drinking scene, most of the open-air and VW van–based cocktail bars are found along Th Chaisongkhram; Th Wiang Tai is where you'll find Pai's highest concentration of bars, many with a reggae vibe; Th Rangsiyanon is where most of the guesthouse-style restaurant-bars with a diverse soundtrack and a dinner menu are located; and a knot of open-air, reggae-style bars can be found at the eastern end of Th Raddamrong, just across the bridge.

ⓘ Getting There & Away

The **bus station** (Th Chaisongkhram) is the place to catch slow, fan-cooled buses as well as more frequent and efficient minivans to Chiang Mai and destinations in Mae Hong Son. **Aya Service** (☏053 699888; www.ayaservice.com; ⏰7am-10pm) and **Duan-Den** (☏053 699966; ⏰7am-9pm) also run air-con minivan buses to Chiang Mai (150B to 200B, three hours, hourly 7am to 5.30pm).

KO SAMUI

Ko Samui at a Glance...

Ko Samui is a small city by the sea, wearing a soft stole of white sand and adorned by modern conveniences. Curvaceous beaches, fast flights to Bangkok, high-end hotels, all-night parties and luxury spas cement Samui's reputation as Phuket's little sister. In places it is glitzy, brash and even slapdash, perfect for holidaymakers who prefer recreation over rest. Yet sleepy villages can still be found and beach-hopping to quieter corners delivers solitude. Samui is everyone's version of an island idyll, you just have to know where to look.

Ko Samui in Two Days

Laze around the beach, eat, sleep, drink, repeat. Supplement this itinerary with a spa treatment at **Tamarind Springs** (p120). Have dinner at a local seafood spot, such as **Bang Po Seafood** (p122). Party with the pros in Chaweng's beach bars and nightclubs.

Ko Samui in Four Days

Join a tour to **Ang Thong Marine National Park** (p116). Rent a motorcycle and tour the southern part of the island with stops at **Ban Hua Thanon** (p120) and **Hin-Ta and Hin-Yai** (p120). Enjoy a splash-out dinner at **Dining on the Rocks** (p123).

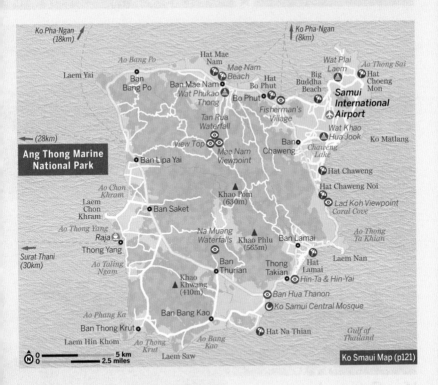

Ko Pha-Ngan (18km)

Ko Pha-Ngan (8km)

Ao Bang Po

Laem Yai

Ban Bang Po

Ban Mae Nam

Wat Phukao Thong

Hat Mae Nam

Mae Nam Beach

Bo Phut

Hat Bo Phut

Bo Phut

Fisherman's Village

Wat Plai Laem

Big Buddha Beach

Ao Thong Sai

Hat Choeng Mon

Samui International Airport

Tan Rua Waterfall

View Top

Mae Nam Viewpoint

Ban Chaweng

Wat Khao Hua Jook

Chaweng Lake

Ko Matlang

(28km)

Ang Thong Marine National Park

Ban Lipa Yai

Hat Chaweng

Hat Chaweng Noi

Ao Chon Khram

Laem Chon Khram

Ban Saket

Khao Pom (630m)

Lad Koh Viewpoint
Coral Cove

Ao Thong Yang

Raja

Na Muang Waterfalls

Khao Phlu (565m)

Ban Lamai

Ao Thong Ta Khian

Surat Thani (30km)

Thong Yang

Ao Taling Ngam

Ban Thurian

Thong Takian

Hat Lamai

Laem Nan

Khao Khwang (410m)

Hin-Ta & Hin-Yai

Ao Phang Ka

Ban Bang Kao

Ban Hua Thanon

Ko Samui Central Mosque

Ban Thong Krut

Laem Hin Khom

Ao Thong Krut

Ao Bang Kao

Hat Na Thian

Gulf of Thailand

Laem Saw

N
0   5 km
0   2.5 miles

Ko Smaui Map (p121)

Arriving on Ko Samui

Ko Samui Airport Located in the northeast of the island near Big Buddha Beach. Taxis conduct airport transfers. Boats to nearby islands depart from various piers around Samui and pier transfer is usually included in the ticket price.

Sleeping

Chaweng and Lamai have the largest range of accommodation but they are also the busiest. The north coast is quieter with pretty Choeng Mon, populated mainly by high-end hotels; Bo Phut, with artsy flash-pads; and low-key Mae Nam, which retains some backpacker spots.

For more information, see p123.

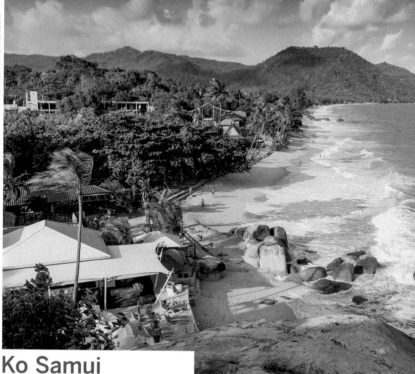

Ko Samui Beaches

East coast beaches are leggy and legendary, famed for their looks and their parties. The north coast gets quieter and more family-friendly. And the south-western beaches are perfect for a sundowner.

Great For...

☑ Don't Miss

Doing an around-the-island tour to discover your favourite stretch of sand.

Each beach on Samui has a different personality, ranging from uber-social to quiet recluse.

East Coast

Most of the beach development on Samui is on the east coast. **Chaweng** has the beach version of an hourglass figure: soft white sand that gently curves from Ko Matlang in the north to Chaweng Noi in the south. The wide centre swath is crowded. Music blares from the beach bars and vendors tirelessly trudge through the sand to deliver amusements.

Lamai is just as pretty but not as famous as flamboyant Chaweng. In fact, Lamai has an identity complex. It is the birthplace of Samui's fasting culture thanks to Spa Samui's two Lamai branches, but visitors looking for enlightenment will find hedonism

Lamai

in Lamai's commercial strip of bars. The southern end of the beach has a more old-fashioned, castaway feel.

North Coast

Samui's alternative coast, the north coast, is more subdued. Near the northeastern tip, **Choeng Mon** is a scenic bay with shallow waters and a low-key bar scene that is popular with families. Locals consider Choeng Mon's crescent-shaped beach to be the best on the island. Next in line is **Big Buddha Beach** (Bang Rak), named after the huge golden Buddha. The beach's western half is by far the best, with an empty stretch of white sand though uncomfortably close to the main road. **Bo Phut** and its **Fisherman's Village** represent the new generation of Thai beaches. Bo Phut's beach is pebbly and narrow but the village is the place to be

for an evening dinner and stroll. The village retains the ambience of an old fishing town now occupied by design-minded restaurants and hotels. **Mae Nam** offers the right balance of beach distractions with enough Thai necessities to give it a sense of place. The northwestern peninsula is carved into a few stunning bays for luxury resorts but you can spend the day soaking up the views on **Ao Thong Sai**.

South & West Coasts

The south coast is good for exploring: cruising through little village lanes, checking out different spits of land, nodding to a forlorn water buffalo. The coast is spotted with rocky headlands and smaller coves of pebble sand that are used more as parking lots for Thai fishing boats than for lounge chairs. The west coast also has views out to the Five Islands and the shadowy greens of the mainland are beguiling.

View from Ko Mae

Ang Thong Marine National Park

The 40-some jagged jungle islands of Ang Thong Marine National Park stretch across the cerulean sea like a shattered emerald necklace. This virgin territory is best explored on a guided tour from Samui.

Great For...

☑ **Don't Miss**

The islands' full-time residents are monkeys, birds, bats and crustaceans.

After an hour's boat journey from Samui, you start to see a looming landmass on the horizon. Slipping closer, the jumbled shadow separates into distinct islands, seemingly moored together. Limestone outcroppings jut skyward like ship masts creating the illusion of anchored shapes in the sapphire-coloured water. Closer still and an internal geometry is revealed: primordial figures woven together by a watery maze. The powerful ocean has whittled dramatic arches and hidden caves into the malleable rock.

Birth of a Park

Designated a park in 1980, Ang Thong (Golden Bowl) is 35km west of Samui. The parks covers a total area of 102 sq km with land comprising only 18 sq km. It used to be a training ground for the Royal Thai

Climbing the Ko Wua Talap viewpoint

JARUNG H / SHUTTERSTOCK ©

Navy. The rugged islands are devoid of human inhabitants except day-trippers. This dynamic landscape hosted the fictionalised commune in the other backpacker bible, *The Beach,* by Alex Garland.

Ko Mae

The myth-maker is Ko Mae (Mother Island) and its inner lagoon. The exterior of the island is a jagged shell of limestone and grizzled vegetation, but a steep climb up to the top reveals a sink-hole filled with a gleaming gem-coloured lake filled by underwater channels. You can look but you can't touch: the lagoon is strictly off-limits to the unclean human body.

Ko Wua Talap

Ko Wua Talap (Sleeping Cow Island) is the largest island in the chain and hosts the national park office and visitor bungalows. The island has a stunning mountain-top viewpoint, a necessary reward after clawing your way to the summit of the 450m trail, booby-trapped with sharp jagged rocks. A second trail leads to Tham Bua Bok, a cavern with lotus-shaped stalagmites and stalactites. There is a small sandy beach on the sunrise side of the island and a castaway's tranquillity.

Other Islands

The naturally occurring stone arches on Ko Samsao and Ko Tai Plo are visible during seasonal tides and certain weather conditions. Because the sea is quite shallow around the island chain, reaching a maximum depth of 10m, extensive coral reefs have not developed except in a few protected pockets on the southwest and northeast sides. There is also some diving, though the park is not as spectacular as other nearby spots. Soft powder beaches line Ko Tai Plao, Ko Wuakantang and Ko Hintap.

Mae Nam Viewpoint Trek

Take a journey from sea level up to a terrific viewpoint with ranging views over the island, via a waterfall deep in the jungle.

Start Mae Nam
Distance 5.5km
Duration 30 minutes riding or two hours walking

Laem Na
Phra Lan

Hat
Mae Nam

2 Back on the road, follow the waterfall signs and in 3km, stop for a coffee and a bite to eat at **Tarzan Restaurant**.

5 Head back to Tarzan for your scooter, and set out for **View Top** FREE, turning left at the fork in the road and left again up the switchbacks. Don't forget to rest your brakes regularly on the way back down!

Ko Samui

2

3

4

5
FINISH

4 Ten minutes from Canopy Adventures, admire gushing **Tan Rua Waterfall** FREE.

1 Ride your scooter south along Soi 4 from the Chinatown archway to quiet **Wat Phukao Thong** `FREE` and enter to explore and climb the green-dragon-lined steps.

Laem Sai

Ban Mae Nam

Chinatown
Archway
START

Classic photo
Mae Nam Viewpoint – for a view over Samui.

Take a Break
The cafe at Canopy Adventures has wi-fi, snacks and superb views.

3 Leave your scooter at Tarzan and hike 1km to **Canopy Adventures** (www.canopyadventuresthailand. com; ☏077 300340), where you can either try the zipline (2950B), or walk across (50B) to a wooden platform and viewpoint.

Ⓝ 0 _____ 2 km
0 _____ 1 miles

◉ SIGHTS

Ban Hua Thanon
Area

Just south of Hat Lamai, Hua Thanon is full of photo ops and home to a vibrant Muslim community; its anchorage of high-bowed fishing vessels by the almost deserted beach through the palm trees at the end of the community is a veritable gallery of intricate designs, though it's a shame about all the rubbish on the sand. Look out for the green, gold and white mosque in the village, along the main drag.

Hin-Ta & Hin-Yai
Landmark

At the south end of Hat Lamai, you'll find these infamous genitalia-shaped stone formations (also known as Grandfather and Grandmother Rocks) that provide endless mirth for giggling Thai tourists.

Fisherman's Village
Village

This concentration of narrow Chinese shophouses in Bo Phut has been transformed into some trendy (and often mid-range) boutique hotels, eateries, cafes and bars. The accompanying beach, particularly the eastern part, is slim and coarse but becomes whiter and lusher further west. The combination of pretty sands and gussied-up old village is a winner, but it can get busy during peak season. Off-season, it's lovely, quiet and elbow-free.

Na Muang Waterfalls
Waterfall

FREE Spilling down from the island's highest points, these two waterfalls – close to each other – are lovely when in full spate, pouring frigid water into rock pools and gushing down towards the blue sea. The larger of the two, at 30m, is the most famous waterfall on Samui and lies in the centre of the island about 12km from Na Thon. During the rainy season, the water cascades over ethereal purple rocks, and there's a superb, large pool for swimming at the base.

Wat Plai Laem
Buddhist Temple

(⊙dawn-dusk) **FREE** The most arresting statue on the island is the thousand-arm Kwan Im (the Buddhist bodhisattva of compassion), displayed here with 18 arms, in a fan arrangement at this recently built, stunning temple. Perched on an island in a lake, the colourful statue rises up next to a temple hall – similarly constructed above the water. To the north of the hall is a statue of the jovial Maitreya Buddha (the Buddha to come). The setting is highly picturesque and photogenic.

✪ ACTIVITIES

Tamarind Springs
Massage

(☏080 569 6654; www.tamarindsprings.com; off Rte 4169; spa packages from 1500B) Tucked far away from the beach within a silent coconut-palm plantation, Tamarind's small collection of villas and massage studios is seamlessly incorporated into nature: some have granite boulders built into walls and floors, while others offer private ponds or creative outdoor baths. There's also a superhealthy restaurant and packages for three-night or longer stays in the elegant villas and suites.

Absolute Sanctuary
Yoga, Spa

(☏077 601190; www.absolutesanctuary.com; Choeng Mon) Detox, spa, yoga, Pilates, fasting, lifestyle and nutrition packages, in an alluring Moroccan-inspired setting.

Samui Institute of Thai Culinary Arts
Cooking

(SITCA; ☏077 413172; www.sitca.com; Chaweng Beach Rd; courses 1850B) For Thai cooking skills, SITCA is the place to do it, with daily Thai cooking classes and courses in the aristocratic Thai art of carving fruits and vegetables into intricate floral designs. Lunchtime classes begin at 11am, while dinner starts at 4pm (both are three-hour courses with three or more dishes).

Lamai Muay Thai Camp
Health & Wellbeing

(☏087 082 6970; www.lamaimuaythaicamp.com; 82/2 Moo3, Lamai; day/week training sessions 300/1500B; ⊙7am-8pm) The island's best moo·ay tai (Thai boxing; also spelt muay Thai) training (for the seriously serious) is at this place, which caters to beginners as well as those wanting to hone their skills. There's also a well-equipped gym for boxers and nonboxers who want to up their fitness levels, plus accommodation and breakfast (and all-meals-included) packages.

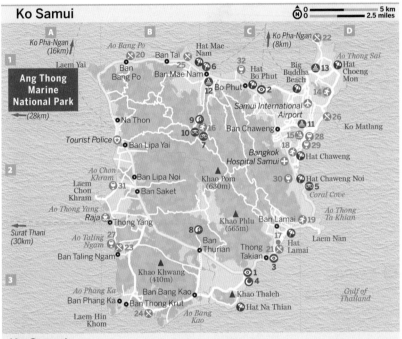

Ko Samui

 Ko Samui's Best Viewpoints

View Top (p118) Stunning views over the jungle interior, sea and Ko Pha-Ngan.

Mae Nam Viewpoint (p118) Consider a hike to this viewpoint among the trees.

Lad Koh Viewpoint (off Rte 4169) Supreme views of the Gulf of Thailand.

Wat Khao Hua Jook (Chaweng; ⊙8am-5pm) FREE Fine views from a golden pagoda.

Wat Khao Hua Jook
KRITHNARONG / GETTY IMAGES ©

EATING

Hat Chaweng

Dr Frogs Steak $$$
(☑077 448505; www.drfrogssamui.com; Rte 4169; mains from 480B; ⊙7am-11pm) Perched atop a rocky overlook, Dr Frogs combines beautiful ocean vistas with delicious international Italian grills, seafood, pasta, pizza and Thai favourites. Delectable steaks and crab cakes, and friendly owners, make it a winner. It's a romantic setting, and for harassed parents there's a kids playground in the front garden. Live guitar music on Mondays and Wednesdays at 7.30pm.

Larder European $$$
(☑077 601259; www.thelardersamui.com; Chaweng Beach Rd; mains 300-820B; ⊙noon-11pm Mon-Sat; ⊙) This restaurant/bar/gastro-pub pulls out the stops in an invigorating menu of classic fare in a relaxing and tasteful setting, supported by a strong selection of wines and zesty cocktails. It's a winning formula, with dishes ranging from slow-cooked lamb spare ribs to fish and chips.

Hat Lamai

Hua Thanon Market Market $
(Ban Hua Thanon; dishes from 30B; ⊙6am-6pm) Slip into the rhythm of this village market slightly south of Lamai; it's a window into the food ways of southern Thailand. Vendors shoo away the flies from the freshly butchered meat, and housewives load bundles of vegetables into their baby-filled motorcycle baskets. Follow the market road to the row of food shops delivering edible Muslim culture: chicken biryani, fiery curries or toasted rice with coconut, bean sprouts, lemon grass and dried shrimp.

Baobab French $$
(☑084 838 3040; Hat Lamai; mains 150-380B; ⊙8am-6pm) Grab a free beach towel and crash out on a sun lounger after a full meal at breezy Baobab, or have a massage next door, but seize one of the beach tables (if you can). You'll need two hands to turn over the hefty menu, with its all-day breakfasts, French/Thai dishes, grills, pastas and popular specials, including red tuna steak (350B).

North Coast

Bang Po Seafood Seafood $$
(Bang Po; dishes from 100B; ⊙dinner) A meal at Bang Po Seafood is a test for the taste buds. It's one of the only restaurants that serves traditional Ko Samui fare: recipes call for ingredients such as raw sea urchin roe, baby octopus, sea water, coconut and local turmeric.

Barracuda Mediterranean $$$
(☑077 430003; www.barracuda-restaurant.com; The Wharf, Fisherman's Village; mains from 575B; ⊙6-11pm) Abounding in alluring Mediterranean culinary inflections, but only open come evening, Barracuda is one of the island's best dining options. The romantic and seductive night-time environment is almost as delightful as the menu: expect to be charmed and well fed on a diet of seared scallops, yellowfin tuna, rack of lamb, Norwegian salmon, delectable pasta dishes and fine service.

Dining on
the Rocks Fusion $$$

(☎077 245678; www.sixsenses.com/resorts/
samui/dining; Choeng Mon; set menus from
2800B; ⊗5-10pm) At the isolated Six Senses
Samui, the island's ultimate dining experience takes place on nine cantilevered
verandahs yawning over the gulf. After
sunset (and wine), guests feel like they're
dining on a barge set adrift on a starlit sea.
Each dish on the set menu is the brainchild
of cooks experimenting with taste, texture
and temperature.

John's Garden
Restaurant Thai $$

(☎077 247694; www.johnsgardensamui.com;
Mae Nam; mains from 160B; ⊗1-10pm) This
delightful garden restaurant is a picture,
with tables slung out beneath bamboo
and palms and carefully cropped hedges.
It's particularly romantic when lantern-lit
at night, so reserve ahead, but pack some
mosquito repellent (which is generally
provided, but it's good to have backup). The
signature dish on the Thai and European
menu is the excellent massaman chicken.

🌀 South Coast

Hemingway's
on the Beach Thai $$

(☎088 452 4433; off Rte 4170, Ao Thong Krut;
mains from 175B; ⊗10am-8pm Sat, Mon, Tue
& Thu, 10am-6pm Sun) With appetising Thai
dishes – and popular cookery courses too
– this beachside choice on Rte 4170 as it
loops into Thong Krut is an excellent reason
to escape to the southwest corner of Ko
Samui; tuck into fresh seafood and bask
in the views, especially come sundown.
Hemingway's also arranges long-tail and
speedboat island tours, while massage is at
hand for post-meal relaxation.

Five Islands Seafood $$$

(☎077 423577; www.thefiveislandssamui.com;
Taling Ngam; dishes 250-620B; ⊗11.30am to
late) Five Islands offers a unique (yet pricey)
eating experience. First, a long-tail boat
(tours for two including meal 7500B to
9250B) will take you out into the turquoise

Where
to Stay

The most famous beaches, Chaweng
and Lamai, are crowded in the central
area but calm on the periphery. Families
opt for Choeng Mon, Bo Phut and Mae
Nam.

Chaweng Beautiful beach, variety of
accommodation; loud and crowded

Lamai Beautiful beach, variety of lodging; seedy bars

Choeng Mon Beautiful bay, kid-friendly;
high-end lodging

Bo Phut & Fisherman's Village Small,
coarse-sand beach, atmospheric village;
artsy midrange lodging

Mae Nam Pretty and quiet beach; backpacker and midrange lodging

sea to visit the haunting Five Sister Islands
where you'll learn about the ancient art of
harvesting bird nests to make bird's-nest
soup, a Chinese delicacy. When you return
a deluxe meal is waiting for you on the
beach.

🍸 DRINKING & NIGHTLIFE

A recent ruling that all bars need to close
by 1am means the island is quieter at night
than it once was. Samui's biggest party
spot is brash and noisy Hat Chaweng.
Lamai and Bo Phut come in second and
third respectively, while the rest of the
island is generally quiet, with drinking
usually focused on resort bars. For sunset
cocktails, hit the west coast, or parts of the
north coast.

Coco Tam's Bar

(Fisherman's Village; ⊗1pm-1am) Grab a swing
at the bar or plop yourself on a beanbag
on the sand, order a giant cocktail served
in a jar and take a toke on a shisha (water
pipe; 500B). It's a bit pricey, but this boho,
beach-bum-chic spot oozes relaxation,
it's lovely when the sun goes down and

the coconut milkshakes are to die for. Fire dancers perform most nights.

Air Bar
Bar

(www.samui.intercontinental.com; Intercontinental Samui Baan Taling Ngam Resort, Taling Ngam; ⏰5pm-midnight) Toast the setting sun as it sinks into the golden gulf from this magnificent outside bar perched above a cliff at the swanky Intercontinental Samui Baan Taling Ngam Resort. There's an excellent menu of tapas and snacks if you simply can't pull yourself away and want to make a meal of it. This is pretty much the top romantic choice on the island.

Woobar
Bar

(☎077 915999; Bo Phut; ⏰11am-midnight; 🛜) With serious wow factor and 270-degree panoramas, the W Retreat's signature lobby bar gives the word 'swish' a whole new meaning, with cushion-clad pods of seating plonked in the middle of an expansive infinity pool that stretches out over the infinite horizon. This is, without doubt, the best place on Samui for sunset cocktails blended with cool music mixes.

Jungle Club
Bar

(☎081 894 2327; www.jungleclubsamui.com; ⏰9am-9.30pm) With knockout views from its high-altitude perch, you'll want to head up and back sober if on a scooter as the approach is very steep, otherwise Jungle Club can arrange pick-up from Chaweng for 400B, or you can get a taxi for a similar fare.

Ark Bar
Bar

(☎7am-1am; www.ark-bar.com; Hat Chaweng) Drinks are dispensed from the multi-coloured bar to an effusive crowd, guests recline on loungers on the beach, and the party is on day and night, with fire shows lighting up the sands after sundown and DJs providing house music from the afternoon onwards.

Nikki Beach
Bar

(☎077 914500; www.nikkibeach.com/kohsamui; Lipa Noi; ⏰11am-11pm; 🛜) The acclaimed luxury brand brings international flair to the secluded west coast of Ko Samui. Think haute cuisine, chic decor, gaggles of jet-setters and killer sunsets. Themed brunch and dinner specials keep the masses com-

Bar in Hat Chaweng

ing throughout the week, and sleek villa accommodation is also on offer.

Drink Gallery
Cocktail Bar

(☏077-422767; www.thelibrary.co.th; Chaweng Beach Rd; ⊗4pm-1am) Part of the Library Hotel, this highly stylish bar has top design and some excellent cocktails. It's a place to be seen in, and a place to people-watch from or just admire the interior artwork, while nibbling on tapas-style Thai bites.

 ## INFORMATION

Always wear a helmet and drive carefully on a motorcycle; traffic fatalities are high.

Bangkok Hospital Samui (☏077 429500, emergency 077 429555; www.bangkokhospital samui.com) Your best bet for just about any medical problem.

Tourist Police (☏077 421281, emergency 1155) Based south of Na Thon.

GETTING THERE & AWAY

AIR
Samui International Airport (www.samui airportonline.com) is in the northeast of the island.

BOAT
There are almost a dozen daily departures between Ko Samui and Ko Pha-Ngan and many of these continue on to Ko Tao.

There are regular boat departures between Samui and Don Sak on the mainland. High-speed **Lomprayah** (☏077 4277 656; www.lomprayah. com) departs from Na Thon; there's also the slower but regular **Raja** (☏022 768211-2, 092 274 3423-5; www.rajaferryport.com; adult 130B) car ferry, which departs from Thong Yang.

 ### Ko Samui's 'Walking Street' Night Markets

Ko Samui's 'Walking Streets' are a fun dining experience. These food-filled markets occur at least once per week, offering you the chance to sample local delicacies, shop for gifts and mingle with tourists and locals. They start at around 4pm and run till around midnight.

This was the schedule at the time of research, but some are considering opening more frequently:

Ban Chaweng Monday to Thursday and Saturday

Ban Lamai Sunday

Ban Meanam Thursday

Bo Phut (Fisherman's Village) Friday

Ban Choeng Mon Friday

Ban Chaweng
POSZTOS / SHUTTERSTOCK ©

GETTING AROUND

You can hire motorcycles (and bicycles) on the island for 150B to 200B per day. *Sŏrng·tăa·ou* (pick-up trucks) run regular routes around the island during daylight hours. It's about 50B to travel between beaches. These vehicles can also be chartered for private transport. Taxis have high but standardised prices.

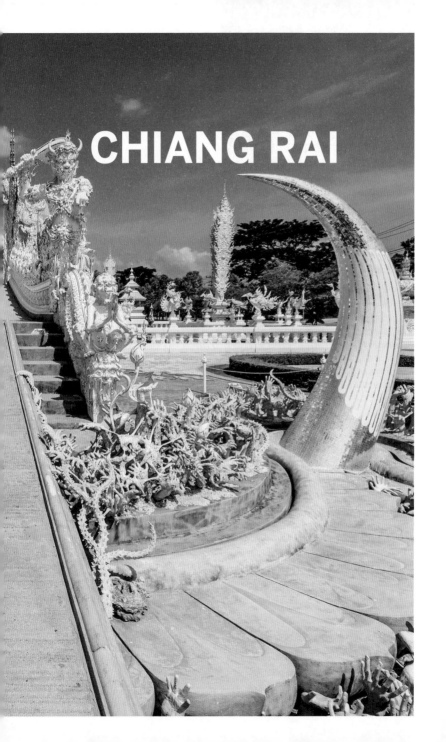

CHIANG RAI

Chiang Rai at a Glance...

Rising from the fertile plains to a rugged mountain range, Thailand's northernmost province, Chiang Rai, belts the border between Southeast Asia and China. The charming provincial capital of Chiang Rai is used as a base to explore this intersection of cultures and dramatic mountain scenery. The province is home to many minority hill tribes, Shan and other Tai groups, and more recently Chinese immigrants, all struggling to maintain their cultural identity and traditional lifestyle in the modern age.

Chiang Rai in Two Days

Dip into local culture at **Mae Fah Luang Art & Culture Park** (p136). Devote the evening to shopping at the **Walking Street** (p138). The next day visit **Wat Rong Khun** (p132) and enjoy dinner at **Lung Eed** (p138).

Chiang Rai in Four Days

Head out of town for a **multiday trek** (p131), the proceeds of which go to aid local hill-tribe villages with infrastructure and education projects. Or do an overnight trip to **Doi Mae Salong** (p134), an ethnic Chinese village that balances on a mountain ridge cultivated with tea plantations.

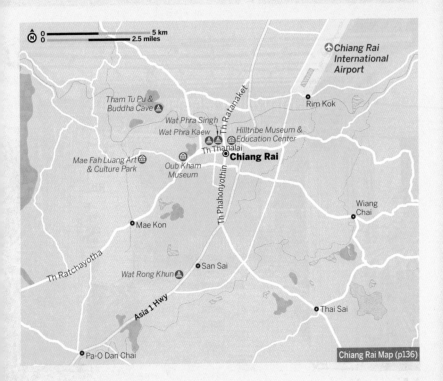

Chiang Rai International Airport

Tham Tu Pu & Buddha Cave

Wat Phra Singh
Wat Phra Kaew

Th Ratanaket

Hilltribe Museum & Education Center

Th Thanalai
Chiang Rai

Rim Kok

Mae Fah Luang Art & Culture Park

Oub Kham Museum

Th Phahonyothin

Wiang Chai

Mae Kon

Th Ratchayotha

Wat Rong Khun
San Sai

Asia 1 Hwy

Thai Sai

Pa-O Dan Chai

Chiang Rai Map (p136)

Arriving in Chiang Rai

Chiang Rai International Airport
Located approximately 8km north of the city. Taxis make the run into town.

Bus station Located 5km away from 'downtown' Chiang Rai. Frequent *sŏrng·tăa·ou* (pick-up minibuses) link it with town from 6am to 5.30pm.

Interprovincial bus station Located right in the centre of town.

Sleeping

Chiang Rai has a great selection of places to stay, and price increases have been incremental over recent years, making accommodation in town good value. Most budget places are in the centre, clustered around Th Jetyod; the majority of midrange places are a brief walk from 'downtown'. Chiang Rai's upscale accommodation is generally located outside the centre of town in country-style resorts.

SAKOJP / SHUTTERSTOCK ©

Minority Cultures

Thailand's ethnic minorities who inhabit the mountainous region of Chiang Rai Province are often called 'hill tribes', or chow kǒw (mountain people). Hill-tribe villages host trekking groups from the provincial capital to showcase their unique culture.

Great For...

☑ **Don't Miss**

Sharing a meal with a village family is a treasured cultural exchange.

Hill-Tribe History

Most of the hill-tribe communities are of semi-nomadic origin, having come from Tibet, Myanmar, China and Laos during the past 200 years or so. The Tribal Research Institute in Chiang Mai recognises 10 different hill tribes, but there may be up to 20. Hill tribes are increasingly integrating into the Thai mainstream and many of the old ways and traditional customs are disappearing.

Hilltribe Museum

This **museum and education centre** (พิพิธภัณฑ์และศูนย์การศึกษาชาวเขา; www.pdacr. org; 3rd fl, 620/25 Th Thanalai; 50B; ⊙8.30am-6pm Mon-Fri, 10am-6pm Sat & Sun) is a good place to visit before undertaking any hill-tribe trek. Run by the nonprofit Population

Akha woman

ⓘ Need to Know

Two-day treks range from 2300B to 6000B and include meals, jungle walking, overnight village accommodation and hotel transfer.

✕ Take a Break

Once you return to Chiang Rai, relax at one of the city's cafes, such as BaanChivitMai Bakery (p139).

★ Top Tip

Ask your guide about the village's dos and don'ts so that you're a respectful guest.

& Community Development Association (PDA), the displays are a bit dated, but contain a wealth of information.

A visit begins with a 20-minute slide show on Thailand's hill tribes, followed by self-guided exploration through exhibits on traditional clothing, tools and implements, and other anthropological objects. The curator is passionate about his museum and, if present, will talk about the different hill tribes and the community projects that the museum funds. The PDA also run highly recommended treks.

Trekking

Nearly every guesthouse and hotel in Chiang Rai offers hill-tribe hiking excursions. The following have a grassroots, sustainable or nonprofit emphasis:

○ **Rai Pian Karuna** (☏062 246 1897; www. facebook.com/raipiankaruna) A new, community-based enterprise conducting one- and multiday treks and homestays at Akha, Lahu and Lua villages in Mae Chan, north of Chiang Rai.

○ **PDA Tours & Travel** (☏053 740088; Hilltribe Museum & Education Center, 3rd fl, 620/25 Th Thanalai; ◷8.30am-6pm Mon-Fri, 10am-6pm Sat & Sun) A well-established NGO offering one- to three-day treks. Profits go back into community projects such as HIV/AIDS education, mobile health clinics, education scholarships and the establishment of village-owned banks.

○ **Mirror Foundation** (☏053 737616; www. thailandecotour.org) Higher rates than most but this NGO helps support the training of its local guides. Treks range from one to three days and traverse the Akha, Karen and Lahu villages of Mae Yao District, north of Chiang Rai.

Wat Rong Khun

RADHARANI / SHUTTERSTOCK ©

Day Trips from Chiang Rai

Dabble in the bizarre and the foreign with these day trips. Wat Rong Khun is an elaborate and fantastic hybrid of modern and religious art, while Doi Mae Salong is a sleepy ethnic Chinese village perched on a mountain spine.

Great For...

☑ **Don't Miss**

Strawberries and other more familiar fruits can grow in the cooler, northern climate. Pick up from roadside stands.

Wat Rong Khun

Looking like a supersized confection, **Wat Rong Khun** (วัดร่องขุ่น, White Temple; off Rte 1/AH2; ⏰8am-5pm Mon-Fri, to 5.30pm Sat & Sun) **FREE** is Thailand's most eclectic and avant-garde temple. It was built in 1997 by noted Thai painter turned architect Chalermchai Kositpipat and mixes modern motifs and pop-culture references with traditional religious iconography.

The exterior of the temple is covered in whitewash and clear-mirrored chips. Walk over a bridge and sculpture of reaching arms (symbolising desire) to enter the sanctity of the wát where the artist has painted contemporary scenes representing *samsara* (the realm of rebirth and delusion). Images such as a plane smashing into the Twin Towers and, oddly enough, Keanu Reeves as Neo from *The Matrix*

Four Buddha Pavilion, Baandam

VALOGA / SHUTTERSTOCK ©

dominate the one wall. If you like what you see, an adjacent gallery sells reproductions of Chalermchai Kositpipat's rather New Age–looking works.

The temple is 13km south of Chiang Rai. Take a regular bus bound for Chiang Mai or Phayao and ask to get off at Wat Rong Khun.

Baandam

The bizarre brainchild of Thai National Artist Thawan Duchanee, and a rather sinister counterpoint to Wat Rong Khun, **Baandam** (บ้านดำ, Black House; off Rte 1/AH2; adult/child 80B/free; ⊙9am-5pm) unites several structures, most of which are stained black and ominously decked out with animal pelts and bones.

The centrepiece is a black, cavernous, temple-like building holding a long wooden dining table and chairs made from deer antlers – a virtual Satan's dining room. Other buildings include white, breast-shaped bedrooms, dark phallus-decked bathrooms, and a bone- and fur-lined 'chapel'. The structures have undeniably discernible northern Thai influences, but the dark tones, flagrant flourishes and all those dead animals coalesce in a way that is more fantasy than reality.

It's located 13km north of Chiang Rai in Nang Lae; any Mae Sai–bound bus will drop you off here for around 20B.

Ban Ruam Mit & Around

Ruam Mit means 'mixed', an accurate description of this riverside village, a convenient jumping-off point for the surrounding hilly area that's home to ethnic groups including Thai, Karen, Lisu and Akha.

Most visitors come to Ban Ruam Mit to ride elephants (which we don't recommend as it's been proven to be harmful to the animals). But a better, not to mention more sustainable, reason is hiking among the surrounding area's numerous villages and to visit **Pha Soet Hot Spring** (บ่อน้ำพุร้อนผา เสริฐ; Ban Pha Soet; adult/child 30/10B; ⊘8am-6pm) or **Lamnamkok National Park** (อุทยาน แห่งชาติลำน้ำกก; ⊘8am-4.30pm).

There are a couple of riverside Thai-style 'resort' hotels in Ban Ruam Mit. Alternatively, both basic hotels and homestay-style accommodation can be found in the surrounding villages. One of the best options is **Bamboo Nest de Chiang Rai** (☑095 686 4755, 089 953 2330; www.bamboonest-chiang rai.com; bungalows incl breakfast 800-1600B), which takes the form of simple but spa

cious bamboo huts perched on a hill overlooking tiered rice fields. There are a few basic eateries in Ban Ruam Mit, and each of the hotels has its own restaurant.

From Chiang Rai, the easiest way to get to Ban Ruam Mit is via boat. A daily passenger boat departs from **CR Pier** (☑053 750009; ⊘7am-4pm), 2km northwest of Chiang Rai, at 10.30am (100B, about one hour); a charter will run about 800B. In the opposite direction, boats stop in Ban Ruam Mit around 2pm.

Doi Mae Salong

For a taste of China without crossing any international borders, head to this hilltop village.

Doi Mae Salong was originally settled by the 93rd Regiment of the Kuomintang

Tea plantation, Doi Mae Salong

(KMT), who had fled to Myanmar from China after the establishment of communist rule in 1949. The KMT were forced to leave Myanmar in 1961. Crossing into northern Thailand with their pony caravans, they settled into mountain villages and re-created a society like the one they had left behind in Yunnan. Generations later, this unique community still persists and is a domestic tourist attraction.

A tiny but busy and vibrant **morning market** (ตลาดเช้าดอยแม่สลอง; ⊘6-8am) convenes at the T-intersection near Shin

PEERAPONG W AUSSAWA / SHUTTERSTOCK ©

Sane Guest House. The market attracts town residents and tribespeople from the surrounding districts and is worth waking up early for.

Shin Sane Guest House (☑053 765026; www.maesalong-shinsane.blogspot.com; r 200-400B, bungalows 400-500B; @⊚) and **Little Home Guesthouse** (☑053 765389; www.maesalonglittlehome.com; Rte 1130; r & bungalows 500-800B; @⊚) both have free maps with hiking routes to hilltribe villages. The best hikes are north of Mae Salong between Ban Thoet Thai and the Myanmar border. Ask first about political conditions before heading off in this direction; Shan and Wa armies competing for control over this section of the Thailand–Myanmar border do occasionally clash in the area.

Many Thai tourists come to Doi Mae Salong simply to eat Yunnanese dishes such as *màn·tǒh* (steamed Chinese buns) served with braised pork belly and pickled vegetables, or black chicken braised with Chinese-style herbs. Homemade wheat and egg noodles are another speciality of Doi Mae Salong, and are served with a local broth that combines pork and a spicy chilli paste. They're available at several places in town. Places to dig into the local cuisine include the morning market, **Sue Hai** (Rte 1130; mains 80-300B; ⊘7am-9pm; ☑) and **Salima Restaurant** (Rte 1130; mains 60-220B; ⊘7am-8pm).

To Doi Mae Salong from Chiang Rai, take a bus to Mae Chan, from where there are frequent green *sǒrng·tǎa·ou* to Doi Mae Salong (60B, one hour, four departures daily). In the reverse direction, you can flag down *sǒrng·tǎa·ou* near Doi Mae Salong's 7-Eleven.

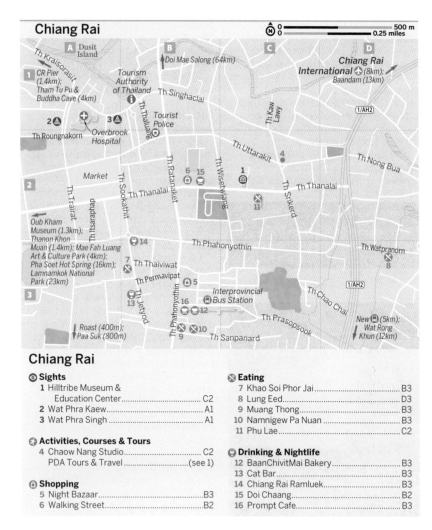

Chiang Rai

◉ SIGHTS

Mae Fah Luang Art & Culture Park   Museum

(ไร่แม่ฟ้าหลวง; www.maefahluang.org/rmfl;
313 Mu 7, Ban Pa Ngiw; adult/child 200B/free;
⊗8.30am-4.30pm Tue-Sun) In addition to a
museum that houses one of Thailand's
biggest collections of Lanna artefacts, this
vast, meticulously landscaped compound
includes antique and contemporary art,

Buddhist temples and other structures. It's
located about 4km west of the centre of
Chiang Rai; a túk-túk or taxi here will run to
around 100B.

Oub Kham Museum   Museum

(พิพิธภัณฑ์อูบคำ; www.oubkhammuseum.com;
Th Nakhai; adult/child incl tour 300/200B;
⊗8am-5pm) This slightly zany private
museum houses an impressive collection

of paraphernalia from virtually every corner of the former Lanna kingdom. The items, some of which truly are one of a kind, range from a monkey-bone food taster used by Lanna royalty to an impressive carved throne from Chiang Tung, Myanmar.

It's located 2km west of the town centre and can be a bit tricky to find; túk-túk will go here for about 60B.

Wat Phra Kaew
Buddhist Temple

(วัดพระแก้ว; Th Trairat; donations appreciated; ⊙temple 7am-7pm, museum 9am-5pm) Originally called Wat Pa Yia (Bamboo Forest Monastery) in the local dialect, this is the city's most revered Buddhist temple. The main prayer hall is a medium-sized, well-preserved wooden structure. The octagonal *chedi* (stupa) behind it dates from the late 14th century and is in typical Lanna style. The adjacent two-storey wooden building is a museum housing various Lanna artefacts.

Wat Phra Singh
Buddhist Temple

(วัดพระสิงห์; Th Singhaclai; donations appreciated; ⊙daylight hours) This temple dates back to the late 14th century, and its oldest surviving original buildings are typical northern Thai-style wooden structures with low, sweeping roofs. The main *wí·hǎhn* (sanctuary) houses impressive wooden doors thought to have been carved by local artists, as well as a copy of Chiang Mai's sacred Phra Singh Buddha.

Tham Tu Pu & Buddha Cave
Buddhist Temple

(ถ้ำตุ๊ปู่/ถ้ำพระ; Th Ka Salong; ⊙daylight hours) FREE Cross the Mae Fah Luang Bridge (located just northwest of the city centre) to the northern side of Mae Nam Kok and you'll come to a turn-off for both Tham Tu Pu and the Buddha Cave. Neither attraction is particularly amazing on its own, but the surrounding country is beautiful and would make an ideal destination for a lazy bike or motorcycle ride.

Follow the road for 1km, then turn off onto a dirt path for 200m to the base of a limestone cliff, where there is a steep set of stairs leading to a main chamber holding a dusty Buddha statue; this is Tham Tu Pu.

Continue along the same road for 3km more (the sign says 'Buddha Images Cave') and you'll reach Buddha Cave, a cavern by Mae Nam Kok containing a tiny but active Buddhist temple, a lone monk and numerous cats. The temple was one of several destinations on a visit to the region by King Rama V in the early 20th century.

🅒 ACTIVITIES

Hiking excursions through hill-tribe country are popular in Chiang Rai, and can be organised through local guesthouses and hotels. Prices depend on the type of activities and the number of days and participants, and generally includes everything from accommodation to transport and food. See p131 for further information.

Suwannee
Cooking

(📞084 740 7119; www.suwanneethaicooking classchiangrai.blogspot.com; lessons 1250B; ⊙courses 9.30am-2pm) Suwannee's cooking courses involve a visit to a local market and instruction in cooking four dishes. Her house is about 3km outside the city centre, but she can pick you up at most centrally located hotels and guesthouses.

Chiang Rai Bicycle Tours
Cycling

(📞053 774506, 085 662 4347; www.chiangrai bicycletour.com; tours from 1450B) Offers a variety of two-wheeled excursions in the areas surrounding Chiang Rai.

Chaow Nang Studio
Cultural

(645/7 Th Uttarakit; ⊙10am-7pm) Dress up like a member of Lanna royalty and have your portrait (from 1000B) taken for posterity – a must-do activity for Thai visitors to Chiang Mai and Chiang Rai. It has a huge array of costumes and backdrops.

🔒 SHOPPING

Thanon Khon Muan   Market
(Th Sankhongnoi; ⊘6-9pm Sun) Come Sunday
evening, the stretch of Th Sankhongnoi
from Soi 2 heading west is closed to traffic
and in its place are vendors selling clothes,
handicrafts and local food. Th Sankhongnoi is called Th Sathanpayabarn where
it intersects with the southern end of Th
Phahonyothin.

Walking Street   Market
(Th Thanalai; ⊘4-10pm Sat) If you're in town
on a Saturday evening, be sure not to miss
the open-air Walking Street, an expansive
street market focusing on all things Chiang
Rai, from handicrafts to local dishes. The
market spans Th Thanalai from the Hilltribe
Museum to the morning market.

Night Bazaar   Market
(off Th Phahonyothin; ⊘6-11pm) Adjacent
to the bus station off Th Phahonyothin
is Chiang Rai's night market. On a much
smaller scale than the one in Chiang Mai,
it is nevertheless an OK place to find an

assortment of handicrafts and touristy
souvenirs.

✕ EATING

Come mealtime, you'll inevitably be pointed
in the direction of Chiang Rai's night bazaar,
but the food there is generally pretty dire
– you've been warned. Instead, if you're in
town on a weekend, hit the vendors at Chiang Rai's open-air markets, Thanon Khon
Muan and the Walking Street, which feature
a good selection of local dishes.

Lung Eed   Thai $
(Th Watpranorn; mains 40-100B; ⊘11.30am-
9pm Mon-Sat, 3-7pm Sun) One of Chiang Rai's
most delicious dishes is available at this
simple shophouse restaurant. There's an
English-language menu on the wall, but
don't miss the sublime *lâhp gài* (minced
chicken fried with local spices and topped
with crispy deep-fried chicken skin, shallots
and garlic).

The restaurant is about 150m east of
Rte 1/AH2.

Night Bazaar

CHIRADECH CHOTCHUANG / SHUTTERSTOCK ©

Paa Suk   Thai $
(Th Sankhongnoi, no Roman-script sign; mains
10-25B; ☺8.30am-3pm) Paa Suk does big,
rich bowls of *kà·nŏm jeen nám ngée·o*
(a broth of pork or beef and tomatoes
served over fresh rice noodles).

The restaurant is between Soi 4 and Soi
5 of Th Sankhongnoi (the street is called
Th Sathanpayabarn where it intersects
with the southern end Th Phahonyothin).
There's no Roman-script sign; look for the
yellow sign.

Khao Soi
Phor Jai   Thai $
(Th Jetyod; mains 40-50B; ☺7am-4pm) Phor
Jai serves mild but tasty bowls of the
eponymous curry noodle dish, as well as a
few other northern Thai staples. There's no
Roman-script sign, but look for the open-air
shophouse with the white-and-blue interior.

Phu Lae   Thai $
(673/1 Th Thanalai; mains 80-320B; ☺11.30am-
3pm & 5.30-11pm; ❄) This air-conditioned
restaurant is popular with Thai tourists for
its tasty but somewhat gentrified northern
Thai fare. Recommended local dishes
include the *gaang hang·lair* (pork belly in
a rich Burmese-style curry) served with
cloves of pickled garlic, and *sâi òo·a* (herb-
packed pork sausages).

Namnigew
Pa Nuan   Vietnamese, Thai $
(Th Sanpanard; mains 10-120B; ☺9am-5pm)
This semi-concealed place (there's no
Roman-script sign) serves a unique mix
of Vietnamese and northern Thai dishes.
Tasty food, friendly service and a fun, barn-
like atmosphere make us wish it was open
for dinner as well.

Muang Thong   Chinese, Thai $
(cnr Th Sanpanard & Th Phahonyothin; mains
30-100B; ☺24hr) Comfort food for Thais and
travellers alike: this long-standing open-air
place serves the usual repertoire of satisfy-
ingly salty and spicy Chinese-Thai dishes.

 **Chiang Rai's
Cafe Scene**

For a relatively small town, Chiang Rai
has an enviable spread of high-quality,
Western-style cafes. This is largely due
to the fact many of Thailand's best coffee beans are grown in the more remote
corners of the province.

BaanChivitMai Bakery (www.bcmthai.
com; Th Prasopsook; ☺8am-7pm Mon-Fri, to
6pm Sat & Sun; 🛜) In addition to a proper
cup of joe made from local beans, you
can snack on surprisingly authentic
Swedish-style sweets and Western-style
meals and sandwiches at this popular
bakery. All the profits go to BaanChivit-
Mai, an organisation that runs homes
and education projects for vulnerable,
orphaned or AIDS-affected children.

Doi Chaang (Th Thanalai; ☺8am-8pm; 🛜)
Doi Chaang is the leading brand among
Chiang Rai coffees, and its beans are
now sold as far abroad as Canada and
Europe. The flagship cafe is a comfortable place to sip and offers a short
menu of snacks and light meals.

Prompt Cafe (www.facebook.com/prompt
cafedripcoffee; 417/4 Th Phahonyothin;
☺7.30am-5.30pm) This closet sized cafe,
probably the city's most sophisticated,
serves single-origin drip coffees (with
locally sourced beans) and espresso
drinks.

Roast (Th Sankhongluang; ☺7.30am-5pm)
This 'drip bar' treats local beans with the
utmost respect.

Western-style cafe
SIRINTRA PUMSOPA / SHUTTERSTOCK ©

Motorcycle Touring in Northern Thailand

A good introduction to motorcycle touring in northern Thailand is the 100km **Samoeng loop**, which can be tackled in half a day. The route extends north from Chiang Mai and follows Rtes 107, 1096 and 1269, passing through excellent scenery and with plenty of curves and providing a taste of what a longer ride up north will be like.

The 470km **Chiang Rai loop**, which passes through scenic Fang and Tha Ton along Rtes 107, 1089 and 118, is another popular ride that can be broken up with a stay in Chiang Rai.

The classic northern route is the **Mae Hong Son loop**, a 600km ride that begins in Chiang Mai and takes in 1864 curves along Rte 1095 with possible stays in Pai, Mae Hong Son and Mae Sariang, before looping back to Chiang Mai via Rte 108.

A lesser known but equally fun ride is to follow Rtes 1155 and 1093 from Chiang Khong in Chiang Rai Province to the little-visited city of Phayao, a day trip that passes through some of the most dramatic mountain scenery in the country.

The best source of information on motorcycle touring in the north is **Golden Triangle Rider** (GT Rider; www.gt-rider.com). Publishers of a series of terrific motorcycle touring-based maps, its website includes heaps of information on hiring bikes (including recommended hire shops in Chiang Mai and Chiang Rai) plus a variety of suggested tours with maps and an interactive forum.

Motorcycling in Chiang Rai
YOUYUENYONG BUDSAWONGKOD / SHUTTERSTOCK ©

🍷 DRINKING & NIGHTLIFE

Chiang Rai
Ramluek Bar
(Th Phahonyothin; ⊗4pm-midnight) For a Thai-style night out on the town, consider this popular place. There's no English-language sign, but follow the live music and look for the knot of outdoor tables. Food is also available.

Cat Bar Bar
(1013/1 Th Jetyod; ⊗5pm-1am) Long-standing Cat Bar has a pool table and, on some nights, live music from 10.30pm.

ℹ️ INFORMATION

There are several banks with foreign exchange and ATMs on both Th Phahonyothin and Th Thanalai.

Overbrook Hospital (📞053 711 366; www.overbrook-hospital.com; Th Singhaclai) English is spoken at this modern hospital.

Tourism Authority of Thailand (TAT; 📞053 744674, nationwide 1672; tatchrai@tat.or.th; Th Singhaclai; ⊗8.30am-4.30pm) English is limited, but staff here do their best to give advice and can provide a small selection of maps and brochures.

Tourist Police (📞053 740 249, nationwide 1155; Th Uttarakit; ⊗24hr) English is spoken and police are on standby around the clock.

ℹ️ GETTING THERE & AWAY

AIR

Chiang Rai International Airport (Mae Fah Luang International Airport; 📞053 798 000; www.chiangraiairportthai.com) is approximately 8km north of the city. Taxis run into town from the airport for 200B.

BUS

Buses bound for destinations within Chiang Rai Province depart from the **interprovincial bus station** (📞053 715952; Th Prasopsook) in the centre of town. If you're heading beyond

Market stall

Chiang Rai (or are in a hurry), you'll have to go to the **New Bus Station** (053 773989; Rte 1/AH2), 5km south of town on Rte 1/AH2; frequent *sŏrng·tăa·ou* linking it and the interprovincial station run from 6am to 5.30pm.

❶ GETTING AROUND

Chiang Rai Taxi (053 773477) operates inexpensive metered taxis in and around town. A túk-túk ride anywhere in central Chiang Rai should cost around 60B. In addition to most guesthouses, several places along Th Jetyod hire motorcycles, with rates starting at 200B for 24 hours.

RAILAY

Railay at a Glance...

The Andaman's fairy-tale limestone crags come to a dramatic climax at Railay (also spelt Rai Leh), a mountainous peninsula of Krabi Province that is only reached by boat, giving the illusion of being a far-flung island. Rock climbers scramble up huge limestone towers for amazing clifftop views while kayakers and snorkellers take an amphibious assault on the landscape. The wind-down scene has a Thai-Rasta vibe that enthusiastically toasts the sunsets and welcomes new acolytes.

Railay in Two Days

Take a two-day **rock-climbing course** (p147) to master the vertical cliffs and embrace endless sea views. Carbo load for your day at **Mama's Chicken** (p149), a favourite for healthy eats.

Railay in Four Days

Find a cosy patch of sand and nap through the day, or hire a long-tail boat to take you out for snorkelling at the nearby islands. Break up the routine with a sweaty hike to **Sa Phra Nang** (p148) and **Tham Phra Nang** (p148); remember your bug spray. Reward breaking a sweat with a cocktail at **Last Bar** (p150) and dinner at **Sunset Restaurant** (p149).

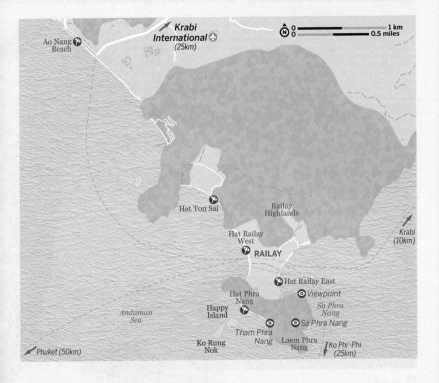

Arriving in Railay

Long-tail boats run from Krabi's Tha Khong Kha (45 minutes). There's also a year-round ferry from Phuket (2¼ hours). All boats arrive/depart at Hat Railay West.

Sleeping

There aren't a lot of lodging options on Railay because it is so small but the options do cover the budget spectrum. Railay Highlands and Hat Ton Sai favour backpackers while Railay East and Railay West have midrange and top-end options. Book in advance in December and January as vacancies become slim.

Overnight trips to deserted islands can be arranged with local boat owners, but you'll need your own camping gear and food.

For more information on the best area to stay in, see p151.

HENN PHOTOGRAPHY / GETTY IMAGES ©

Rock Climbing

Railay is one of Southeast Asia's top climbing spots and continues to gain in popularity. The routes are varied in technical challenge and have rewarding sea views.

Great For...

☑ **Don't Miss**

Try deep-water soloing, where if you fall you'll probably just get wet.

With over 1000 bolted routes, ranging from beginner to advanced, all with unparalleled clifftop vistas, you could spend months climbing and exploring. Deep-water soloing, where free-climbers scramble up ledges over deep water, is incredibly popular.

Climbing Routes

Most climbers start off at **Muay Thai Wall** and **One, Two, Three Wall**, at the southern end of **Hat Railay East** (Hat Sunrise), where there are at least 40 routes graded from 4b to 8b on the French system. The mighty **Thaiwand Wall** sits at the southern end of Hat Railay West, offering a sheer limestone cliff with some of the most challenging climbing routes, graded from 6a to 7c+.

Other top climbs include **Hidden World**, with its classic intermediate routes;

SOMPORN SUEBHAIT / SHUTTERSTOCK ©

Ao Nang Tower

Wee's Present Wall

Diamond Cave

Thaiwand Wall

RAILAY Hat Railay East

One, Two, Three Wall

Muay Thai Wall

Hidden World

Andaman Sea

ℹ️ Need to Know

Climbing courses cost 1000B for a half-day and 1800B for a full day.

✕ Take a Break

Talk bolts and ropes at Highland Rock Climbing (p150), a popular climbing school hang-out.

★ Top Tip

Chalk is obligatory for avoiding sweaty palms in this tropical climate.

Wee's Present Wall, an overlooked 7c+ winner; **Diamond Cave**, a busy beginner–intermediate favourite; and **Ao Nang Tower**, a three-pitch climbing wall reached only by boat.

There's excellent climbing information at www.railay.com. *Rock Climbing in Thailand and Laos* (2014; Elke Schmitz) is an up-to-date guide to the area.

Courses & Gear

Beginners can start with a half- or full-day session. Private sessions are also available. Three-day courses involve lead climbing, where you clip into bolts on the rock face. Experienced climbers can rent gear sets for two people from the climbing schools for around 1200B per day (quality varies); the standard set consists of a 60m rope, two climbing harnesses and climbing shoes.

If climbing independently, you're best off bringing your own gear, including nuts and cams as backup for thinly protected routes. Some climbing schools sell a limited range of imported gear.

Climbing Outfitters

Recommended companies include the following:

○ **Basecamp Tonsai** (📱081 149 9745; www.tonsaibasecamp.com; Hat Ton Sai; half/full day 800/1500B, 3-day course 6000B; ⊗8am-5pm & 7-9pm)

○ **Hot Rock** (📱085 641 9842; www.railayadventure.com; Hat Railay East; half/full day 1000/1800B, 3-day course 6000B; ⊗9am-8pm)

○ **King Climbers** (📱081 797 8923; www.railay.com; Walking St; half/full day 1000/1800B, 3-day course 6000B; ⊗8.30am-9pm Mon-Fri, to 6pm Sat & Sun)

◎ SIGHTS

Sa Phra Nang
Lagoon

(Holy Princess Pool) Halfway along the trail linking Hat Railay East to Hat Tham Phra Nang, a sharp 'path' leads up the jungle-cloaked cliff wall to this hidden lagoon. The first section is a steep 10-minute uphill climb (with ropes for assistance). Fork right for the lagoon, reached by sheer downhill climbing. If you fork left, you'll quickly reach a dramatic cliff-side viewpoint; this is a strenuous but generally manageable, brief hike.

Tham Phra Nang
Cave

(ถ้ำพระนาง, Princess Cave; Hat Tham Phra Nang) At the eastern end of Hat Tham Phra Nang is this important shrine for local fishermen (Muslim and Buddhist), who make offerings of carved wooden phalluses in the hope that the inhabiting spirit of a drowned Indian princess will provide a good catch. According to legend, a royal barge carrying the princess foundered here in a storm during the 3rd century BC. Her spirit took over the cave, granting favours to all who paid their respects.

Viewpoint
Viewpoint

A steep, rough trail leads to this viewpoint, which offers fine vistas over the peninsula. The trail is halfway along the path linking Hat Railay East to Hat Phra Nang. Note that the first section involves a 10-minute uphill climb (with ropes for assistance). Turn left at the fork for the viewpoint.

⊕ ACTIVITIES

Dive operations in Railay run trips out to local dive sites, including Ko Poda. Two dives cost 3700B; an Open Water dive course is 14,500B. There are also dive trips to Ko Phi-Phi and King Cruiser Wreck for 4900B. Most Ao Nang–based dive operators (where there's more choice) will pick up from Railay.

Full-day, multi-island snorkelling trips to Ko Poda, Ko Hong, Ko Kai and beyond can be arranged through resorts and agencies from 1200B, or you can charter a long-tail (half-/full-day 1800/2800B) from Hat Railay West. One-day snorkelling tours to Ko Phi-Phi cost 2400B. If you're just snor-

From left: Tham Phra Nang; Thai-style seafood; Sa Phra Nang

kelling off Railay, most resorts rent mask sets and fins for around 150B each.

Rent kayaks on Hat Railay West or Hat Ton Sai (200/800B per hour/day).

EATING

The beachfront resort restaurants at Hat Railay West are the best, and the most expensive, on Railay. You'll find more affordable Thai and Western options inland. Don't expect fine dining at Hat Ton Sai, where cheap eats abound.

Sunset Restaurant   Seafood $$

(☎075 819463; www.krabisandsea.com; Hat Railay West; mains 180-400B; ☺11am-9pm; 🛜) Attached to the Sand Sea Resort and with a fine beachfront location, this is a popular place to sample fresh seafood while gazing out to sea. It also does the full range of Thai classics: curries, stir-fries and salads.

Mama's Chicken   Thai $

(Hat Ton Sai; mains 70-100B; ☺7am-10pm; 🍴) Relocated to the jungle path leading inland to Hat Railay East and West, Mama's

remains one of Ton Sai's favourite food stops for its international breakfasts, fruit smoothies and extensive range of cheap Thai dishes, including a rare massaman tofu and other vegetarian-friendly adaptations.

Mangrove Restaurant   Thai $$

(Walking St; mains 80-350B; ☺10am-10pm) This humble, heaving, local-style place, set beneath a stilted thatched roof between east and west beaches, turns out all the Thai favourites, from glass-noodle salad and cashew-nut stir-fry to curries, *sôm·đam* (spicy green papaya salad) and the wonderful creation that is egg-grilled sticky rice. Praise goes to the kitchen's matriarch.

The Grotto   International, Thai $$$

(☎075 620740; www.rayavadee.com; Hat Phra Nang; mains 400-690B; ☺noon-8pm) Part of the exclusive Rayavadee resort complex, the Grotto plates up a menu of Thai and Mediterranean treats half inside an illuminated cave fronting Hat Phra Nang,

The Terrace   Thai $$$

(Hat Phra Nang; mains 450-1890B; ☺11am-11pm; 🍴) An upscale pan-Asian menu –

Japanese, Vietnamese, Indian and Thai dishes – on a terrace overlooking Hat Phra Nang. Decent cocktails too.

⊖ DRINKING & NIGHTLIFE

Last Bar   Bar

(Hat Railay East; ⊙11am-late) A reliably packed-out multilevel tiki bar that rambles to the edge of the mangroves, with bunting, balloons and cushioned seats on one deck, candlelit dining tables on another, live music at the back and waterside fire shows.

Chill Out   Bar

(Hat Ton Sai; ⊙11am-late; 🛜) Kick back over cold beers, live music, DJ beats and frenzied fire shows at Ton Sai's top jungle reggae bar.

Highland Rock Climbing   Cafe

(Railay Highlands; 📞084 443 9539; ⊙8am-8pm) Part climbing school, part cafe, this driftwood-clad place sources beans from sustainable farms in Chiang Rai and serves some of the peninsula's best coffee.

❶ GETTING THERE & AROUND

Long-tail boats run to Railay from Krabi's Tha Khong Kha and from the seafront at Ao Nang and Ao Nam Mao. To Krabi, long-tails leave from Hat Railay East. Boats in both directions leave between 7.45am and 6pm when they have eight people (150B, 45 minutes).

A year-round ferry runs to Ko Phi-Phi (400B, 1¼ hours) and Phuket (650B, 2¼ hours).

Where to Stay

There are four beaches around Railay, or you can sleep up on the headland. It's a five-minute walk between Hat Railay East, Hat Railay West, Hat Tham Phra Nang and the highlands.

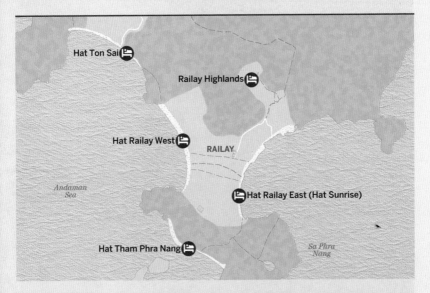

Area	Atmosphere
Hat Railay East (Hat Sunrise)	This shallow, steamy, muddy bay is lined with affordable hotels, guesthouses and restaurants and is only a five-minute walk to better beaches.
Hat Railay West	A near flawless white wonder and the best place to swim or watch a fiery sunset. It's all tasteful midrange and top-end resorts here. Long-tail boats to/from Ao Nang.
Hat Tham Phra Nang	One of the world's most beautiful beaches; there's only one place to stay here – the peninsula's most exclusive resort, Rayavadee. Anyone can drop a beach towel.
Hat Ton Sai	The grittier climbers' and budgeteers' retreat. Bars and bungalows are nestled further back in the jungle and it's a lively, fun scene. To get to the other beaches you'll need to take a long-tail (50B), scramble over rocks at low tide, or hike 30 minutes through the jungle.
Railay Highlands	About 500m inland from Hat Railay West or East, sea breezes cool the jungle canopy and lodgings are good value.

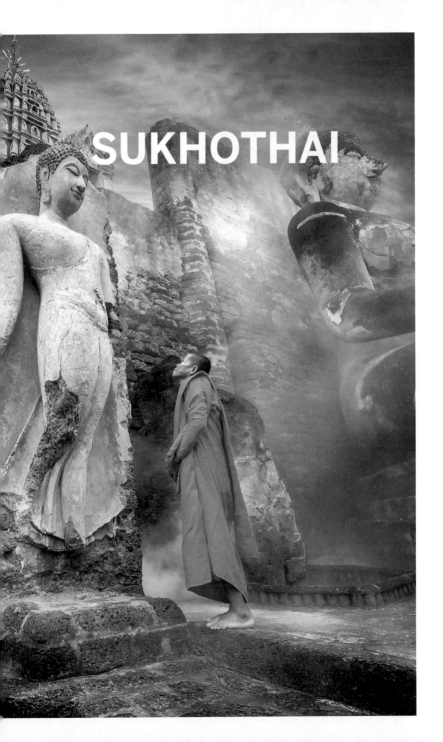

SUKHOTHAI

Sukhothai at a Glance...

Sukhothai is widely regarded as the first capital of Siam. After breaking away from the Khmer kingdom in 1238, the newly founded state established itself as a regional power and a cultural leader. Beautiful temples mixing Khmer and unique Sukhothai styles were built to honour the newly adopted Theravada Buddhism and the new dynasty. Today the old city is sheltered in a quiet park-like setting that creates a meditative calm, perfect for enjoying the gravity of the majestic monuments. Sukhothai never feels crowded but there are off-the-beaten-path corners such as Si Satchanalai-Chaliang, where you can be a solo adventurer.

Sukhothai in Two Days

Explore **Sukhothai Historical Park** (p156). The central and northern zones are easily visited by bicycle. The next day hire a motorcycle to explore the western and southern zones.

Sukhothai in Four Days

Spend day three at **Si Satchanalai-Chaliang Historical Park** (p160). On your last day sign up for a **cycling tour** (p165) of Sukhothai for a guided adventure to unexplored corners of the park and environs.

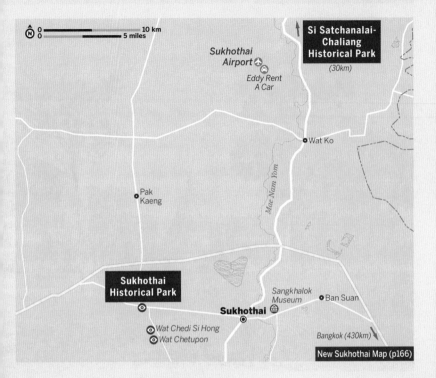

 10 km
5 miles

Sukhothai
Airport

Eddy Rent
A Car

**Si Satchanalai-
Chaliang
Historical Park**
(30km)

Wat Ko

Mae Nam Yom

Pak
Kaeng

**Sukhothai
Historical Park**

Sangkhalok
Museum

Ban Suan

Sukhothai

Wat Chedi Si Hong
Wat Chetupon

Bangkok (430km)

New Sukhothai Map (p166)

Arriving in Sukhothai

Sukhothai Airport Most visitors arrive
by bus from Bangkok though Sukhothai
does have an airport (located 27km
north) and there's another in nearby
Phitsanulok. Minivan services link
both airports to accommodation in
Sukhothai.

Bus station Located 1km northwest
of New Sukhothai; motorcycle taxis
do the run between here and central
New Sukhothai, or you can hop on any
sŏrng·tăa·ou (pick-up minibus) bound
for Sukhothai Historical Park.

Sleeping

Most accommodation is in New
Sukhothai, which is home to some of
the best-value budget accommodation
in northern Thailand. Clean, cheerful
hotels and guesthouses abound, with
many places offering attractive banga-
lows, free pick-up from the bus station
and free use of bicycles. There are an
increasing number of options near
the park, many of them in the upscale
bracket.

Sukhothai Historical Park

Crumbling temple ruins and serene Buddha statues provide a meditative journey through this ancient Thai capital, designated a Unesco World Heritage Site. The central leafy compound is one of the country's most impressive and peaceful historical parks.

Great For...

☑ Don't Miss

Hiring a bicycle and cycling around the ruins is the best way to explore the central zone.

The Sukhothai kingdom ('Sukhothai' means 'rising happiness') flourished from the mid-13th century to the late 14th century, as the imperial Angkor kingdom in Cambodia was losing its grip on its western frontier. This period is often viewed as the golden age of Thai civilisation. Sukhothai's dynasty lasted 200 years and spanned nine kings. By 1438 Sukhothai was absorbed by Ayuthaya.

Central Zone

The pockmarked ruins of the kingdom, believed to be the administrative centre, are concentrated in the **central zone** (อุทยานประวัติศาสตร์สุโขทัย โซนกลาง; 100B, plus per bicycle/motorcycle/car 10/20/50B; ⏰6.30am-6pm Sun-Fri, to 9pm Sat), in an area known as *meuang·gòw* (old city), a 45-sq-km compound.

Detail, Wat Mahathat

PAKIN SONGMOR / GETTY IMAGES ©

Sukhothai Historical Park ⊙

ⓘ Need to Know

On Saturday night much of the central zone is illuminated and remains open until 9pm.

✕ Take a Break

Coffee Cup (Rte 12; dishes 30-150B; ⊙8am-10pm; 🛜) serves fresh breads, drinks and other cafe fare.

★ Top Tip

The soft light and cooler temperatures of evening make it a perfect time to visit the central zone.

Ramkhamhaeng National Museum

A good starting point for exploring the historical park is this **museum** (พิพิธภัณฑสถาน แห่งชาติรามคำแหง; 150B; ⊙9am-4pm), named for the third Sukhothai king. King Ramkhamhaeng is considered to be the founding father of the nation. He is credited with creating the Thai script and establishing Theravada Buddhism as the kingdom's primary religion. A replica of the famous Ramkhamhaeng inscription, said to be the earliest example of Thai writing, is kept here among an impressive collection of Sukhothai artefacts.

Religious art and architecture of the era are considered to be the most classic of Thai styles, influenced by the preceding Khmer period but adapted with graceful elements found in the features and gestures of the Buddha sculptures of the time.

Other hallmarks are the shape of the *chedi* (stupa) and stucco relief work. The temple ruins of the historic park are viewed by historians as a transition between Khmer and Thai art.

Admission to the museum is not included in the ticket to the central zone.

Wat Mahathat

The largest temple in the historic park, **Wat Mahathat** (วัดมหาธาตุ) was completed in the 13th century and is considered to be the former spiritual and administrative centre of the old capital. It is a hybrid of Khmer and Sukhothai artistic styles. The temple is surrounded by brick walls (206m long and 200m wide) and a moat that is believed to represent the outer wall of the universe and the cosmic ocean, a common theme in Khmer architecture. Multiple *chedi* feature the famous lotus-bud motif, considered a distinctive Sukhothai artistic feature adapted from the Sri Lankan bell-shaped *chedi*. Some of the original stately Buddha figures still sit among the ruined columns of the old *wí·hǎhn* (sanctuary). There are 198 *chedi* within the monastery walls and many photogenic specimens.

Wat Si Sawai

Just south of Wat Mahathat, this Buddhist **shrine** (วัดศรีสวาย) dating from the 12th and 13th centuries features three Khmer-style towers and a picturesque moat. It was originally built by the Khmers as a Hindu temple. Sukhothai craftspeople added stucco reliefs depicting mythical creatures, such as *apsara* (heavenly maidens) and *naga* (serpents).

Wat Sa Si

Wat Sa Si (วัดสระศรี, Sacred Pond Monastery) sits on an island west of the bronze monument of King Ramkhamhaeng. It's a simple, classic Sukhothai-style wát containing a

large Buddha, one bell-shaped *chedi* and the columns of the ruined *wí·hǎhn.* Bell-shaped *chedi,* an artistic inheritance from Sri Lanka, migrated to Sukhothai thanks to the adoption of Buddhism.

Wat Trapang Thong

Next to the Ramkhamhaeng National Museum, this small, still-inhabited **wát** (วัดตระพัง ทอง; off Rte 12; ⊙daylight hours) with fine stucco reliefs is reached by a footbridge across the large lotus-filled pond that surrounds it. This reservoir, the original site of Thailand's Loi Krathong festival, supplies the Sukhothai community with most of its water.

Northern Zone

The **northern zone** (อุทยานประวัติศาสตร์ สุโขทัย โซนเหนือ; 100B, plus per bicycle/motorcycle/car 10/20/50B; ⊙7.30am-5.30pm) is

Wat Sa Si

500m north of the old city walls and is easily reached by bicycle. It rivals the central zone with important architectural ruins.

Wat Si Chum

Beloved by shutterbugs, this **temple** (วัดศรี ชุม) is northwest of the old city and contains an impressive *mon·dòp* (a chedi-like spire) with a 15m, brick-and-stucco seated Buddha. The Buddha's elegant, tapered fingers are much photographed and larger than life. Archaeologists theorise that this image

---

★ Did You Know?

The park includes the remains of 21 historical sites and four large ponds within the old walls, with an additional 70 sites within a 5km radius.

BOONSOM / GETTY IMAGES ©

is the 'Phra Atchana' mentioned in the famous Ramkhamhaeng inscription. A passage in the *mon·dòp* wall that leads to the top has been blocked so that it's no longer possible to view the *Jataka* inscriptions that line the tunnel ceiling.

Wat Phra Phai Luang

Often viewed as an architectural companion to Wat Si Sawai in the central zone, this somewhat isolated **temple** (วัดพระพายหลวง) featured three 12th-century Khmer-style towers. All but one tower has collapsed and the remaining structure is decorated with time-worn stucco relief indicative of Sukhothai style. This may have been the centre of Sukhothai when it was ruled by the Khmers of Angkor prior to the 13th century.

Western Zone

The **western zone** (อุทยานประวัติศาสตร์สุโขทัย โซนตะวันตก; 100B, plus per bicycle/motorcycle/ car 10/20/50B; ⊘8am-4.30pm) is about 2km from the old city and is rarely crowded. The road here leads past scenic countryside.

Wat Saphan Hin

The name of this **wát** (วัดสะพานหิน), located on the crest of a hill that rises about 200m above the plain, means 'stone bridge', a reference to the slate path and staircase that lead up to the temple and are still in place. All that remains of the original temple are a few *chedi* and the ruined *wí·hǎhn,* consisting of two rows of laterite columns flanking a 12.5m-high standing Buddha image on a brick terrace. The site is 3km west of the former city wall and gives a good view of the Sukhothai ruins to the southeast and the mountains to the north and south.

★ Did You Know?

The establishment of Sukhothai in 1238 is often described as the first Thai kingdom; however, the kingdom of Chiang Saen had already been established 500 years earlier, so this is technically incorrect.

SOMRAK JENDEE / SHUTTERSTOCK ©

Si Satchanalai-Chaliang Historical Park

Picturesque countryside and forests frame the ruins of this satellite city of the Sukhothai kingdom, dating to the 13th to 15th centuries. You're likely to encounter fewer visitors here.

Great For...

☑ **Don't Miss**

Climbing the stairs to the hilltop temple of Wat Khao Phanom Phloeng is a sightseeing workout.

As Sukhothai's influence grew, it expanded to this strategic position on the banks of the Mae Nam Yom between two lookout hills. Si Satchanalai hosted many of the Sukhothai kingdom's monasteries and temples as well as ceramics factories that exported to neighbouring countries. After the fall of Sukhothai, this area continued to be used by the rival forces of Lanna and Ayuthaya. Si Satchanalai, along with Sukhothai, was recognised as a Unesco World Heritage Site. The park covers roughly 720 hectares and is surrounded by a 12m-wide moat.

Wat Phra Si Ratana Mahathat

Si Satchanalai's main attraction, **Wat Phra Si Ratana Mahathat** (วัดพระศรีรัตน มหาธาตุ; 20B) sits outside the entrance to the historical park on the banks of Mae Nam Yom. The impressive central tower

Wat Khao Phanom Phloeng — Wat Chang Lom — Wat Chedi Jet Thaew — Wat Phra Si Ratana Mahathat — Mae Nam Yom — Wat Nang Phaya — Wat Chao Chan

Si Satchanalai-Chaliang Historical Park

❶ Need to Know

อุทยานประวัติศาสตร์ศรีสัชนาลัย-เชลียง; off Rte 101; 100B; ⊗8.30am-4.30pm

✗ Take a Break

Roadside vendors line the main road and sell simple meals and drinks.

poses peacefully among the surrounding greenery and is framed by a large seated Sukhothai Buddha and pillars. Nearby is a smaller standing image and a bas-relief of the famous walking Buddha, exemplary of the flowing, boneless Sukhothai style. The tower is a corn-cob shape, suggestive of Khmer style, but it is actually an Ayuthaya style because it has a smooth curvature rather than the Khmer 'steps'. Near the main entrance, look for a pillar topped by a Khmer-style four-faced figure, evocative of temples in Angkor. The figure depicts the Hindu god Brahma.

Wat Chang Lom

This fine **temple** (วัดช้างล้อม; 100B), marking the centre of the old city of Si Satchanalai, is encircled by elephant statues and a towering bell-shaped chedi that is somewhat

better preserved than its counterpart in Sukhothai. The elephants' entire bodies are intact giving the visual appearance of the structure being carried on the backs of the elephants. In Buddhist iconography, elephants are often regarded as guardians and were a common motif in Sukhothai temples. An inscription states that the temple was built by King Ramkhamhaeng between 1285 and 1291.

Wat Khao Phanom Phloeng

On the hill overlooking Wat Chang Lom are the remains of **Wat Khao Phanom Phloeng** (วัดเขาพนมเพลิง; 100B), meaning Holy Fire Mountain Temple. The forest closes in among a chedi, a large seated Buddha and stone columns that once supported the roof of the wí·hǎhn. From here you can make out the general design of the once great city. It is a sweaty walk up the 44 steps made of laterite blocks to the top, but the surrounding forest adds a mystique of adventure. A small shrine to a local goddess receives supplications of dresses from devotees. The hilltop is also a nesting site for waterbirds, including egrets and cranes; locals often carry umbrellas to protect themselves from bird droppings.

Wat Chedi Jet Thaew

A strong contender for Si Satchanalai's best, **Wat Chedi Jet Thaew** (วัดเจดีย์เจ็ด แถว; 100B), next to Wat Chang Lom, is so named because of its seven rows of *chedi*, the largest of which is a copy of one at Wat Mahathat in Sukhothai. An interesting brick-and-plaster *wí·hăhn* features barred windows designed to look like lathed wood (an ancient Indian technique used all over Southeast Asia). The temple dates back to the 14th century and contains a mix of styles: Khmer, Lanna and Sukhothai.

Wat Nang Phaya

One of the youngest temples in the collection, **Wat Nang Phaya** (วัดนางพญา; 100B), south of Wat Chedi Jet Thaew, has a bell-shaped Sinhalese *chedi* and was built in the 15th or 16th century. Stucco reliefs on the large laterite *wí·hăhn* in front of the *chedi* – now sheltered by a tin roof – date from the Ayuthaya period when Si Satchanalai was known as Sawankhalok. Goldsmiths in the district still craft a design known as *nahng pá·yah*, modelled after these reliefs.

Wat Chao Chan

Sheltered by woods, **Wat Chao Chan** (วัดเจ้า จันทร์; 100B, combined entry with Si Satchanalai & Si Satchanalai Centre for Study & Preservation of Sangkalok Kilns 250B; ⏰8am-5pm) is a large Khmer-style tower similar to later towers

Wat Chang Lom (p161)

built in Lopburi and probably constructed during the reign of Khmer king Jayavarman VII (1181–1217). The tower has been restored and is in fairly good shape. The roofless *wí·hǎhn* on the right contains the laterite outlines of a large standing Buddha that has all but melted away from exposure and weathering.

Si Satchanalai Centre for Study & Preservation of Sangkalok Kilns

At one time, more than 200 huge pottery kilns lined the banks of the Mae Nam Yom

> ☑ **Don't Miss**
>
> When visiting the park, make sure to check out the excavated kilns along Mae Nam Yom.

in the area around Si Satchanalai. The kilns produced glazed ceramics that were exported to other Asian countries. In China – the biggest importer of Thai pottery during the Sukhothai and Ayuthaya periods – the pieces produced here came to be called Sangkalok, a mispronunciation of Sawankhalok, the original name of the region.

Excavated kilns can be visited at the **Si Satchanalai Centre for Study & Preservation of Sangkalok Kilns** (ศูนย์ ศึกษาและอนุรักษ์เตาสังคโลก; 100B, combined ticket with Si Satchanalai & Wat Chao Chan 250B; ⊙8am-4.30pm), located 5km northwest of the Si Satchanalai ruins. There are also many intact pottery samples and interesting displays despite the lack of English labels. Ceramics are still made in the area, and a local ceramic artist even continues to fire his pieces in an underground wood-burning oven.

CHIRAWAN THAIPRASANSAP / SHUTTERSTOCK ©

★ **Did You Know?**

Wat Phra Si Ratana Mahathat is one of the largest, oldest and most historically important in the park and received the status of royal property after a visit by the previous king.

◉ SIGHTS

Sangkhalok Museum   Museum

(พิพิธภัณฑ์สังคโลก; Rte 1293; adult/child 100/50B; ⊗8am-5pm) This small but comprehensive museum is an excellent introduction to ancient Sukhothai's most famous product and export, its ceramics. The ground floor displays an impressive collection of original Thai pottery found in the area, plus some pieces traded from Vietnam, Myanmar and China. The 2nd floor features examples of non-utilitarian pottery made as art, including some beautiful and rare ceramic Buddha statues. The museum is about 2.5km east of the centre of New Sukhothai; a túk-túk here is about 100B.

Wat Chetupon   Historic Site

(วัดเชตุพน; off Rte 1272, Southern Zone, Sukhothai Historical Park; ⊗24hr) FREE Located 1.4km south of the old city walls, this temple once held a four-sided mon·dòp (a chedi-like spire) featuring the four classic poses of the Buddha (sitting, reclining, standing and walking). The graceful lines of the walking Buddha can still be made out today.

Wat Chedi Si Hong   Historic Site

(วัดเจดีย์สี่ห้อง; off Rte 1293, Southern Zone, Sukhothai Historical Park; ⊗24hr) FREE Directly across from Wat Chetupon, the main chedi here has retained much of its original stucco relief work, which shows still vivid depictions of elephants, lions and humans.

◉ ACTIVITIES

Organic Agriculture Project   Cooking

(☑055 647290; off Rte 1195; half-day incl lunch 900B; ⊗8am-5pm Thu-Tue) Sukhothai's Organic Agriculture Project allows visitors to take part in traditional Thai farm activities.

Taking place at Sukhothai Airport's organic farm, the half-day begins by donning the outfit of a Thai rice farmer and riding an ee dǎan (a traditional utility vehicle) to gather duck eggs. This is followed by riding a buffalo, checking into an orchid farm, witnessing the stages of rice production and, ultimately, planting or gathering rice. The session ends with an informal cooking lesson and meal using organic produce

From left: Sukhothai-style noodles; Sukhothai Historical Park (p160); Wat Chetupon

NAME THOMYA / SHUTTERSTOCK ©

MATTHEW MICAH WRIGHT / GETTY IMAGES ©

from the farm. Book in advance for an English-speaking guide.

The compound is also home to a restaurant serving dishes made from the farm's organic produce (mains 50B to 120B, open 8am to 5pm Thursday to Tuesday).

The project is located on the same road as Sukhothai's airport, 27km from New Sukhothai off Rte 1195, and is not accessible by public transport. If you don't have your own wheels, you can arrange a ride with the Sukhothai Airport's minivan service (p167).

Cycling Sukhothai   Cycling

(☏085 083 1864, 055 612519; www.cycling -sukhothai.com; off Th Jarodvithithong; half/full day 800/990B, sunset tour 450B) A resident of Sukhothai for nearly 20 years, Belgian cycling enthusiast Ronny Hanquart offers themed bike tours, such as the Historical Park Tour, which also includes stops at lesser-seen wát and villages.

The office is about 1.2km west of Mae Nam Yom, off Th Jarodvithithong in New Sukhothai; free transport can be arranged.

ⵏ◎⵿ Sukhothai-Style Noodles

Sukhothai's signature dish is *gŏo·ay đĕe·o sù·kŏh·tai* (Sukhothai-style noodles), featuring a slightly sweet broth with different preparations of pork, ground peanuts and thinly sliced green beans. The best places to try the dish:

Jayhae (Th Jarodvithithong; dishes 30-120B; ⊗8am-4pm) You haven't been to Sukhothai if you haven't tried the noodles at Jayhae, an extremely popular restaurant that serves Sukhothai-style noodles, *pàt tai* and tasty coffee drinks. Located about 1.3km west of Mae Nam Yom, off Th Jarodvithithong.

Tapui (off Th Jarodvithithong; dishes 30-50B; ⊗7am-3pm) Consisting of little more than a brick floor with a tin roof over it, Tapui claims to be the first shop in Sukhothai to have sold the city's namesake dish. Located about 1.3km west of Mae Nam Yom, off Th Jarodvithithong; there's no roman-script sign.

New Sukhothai

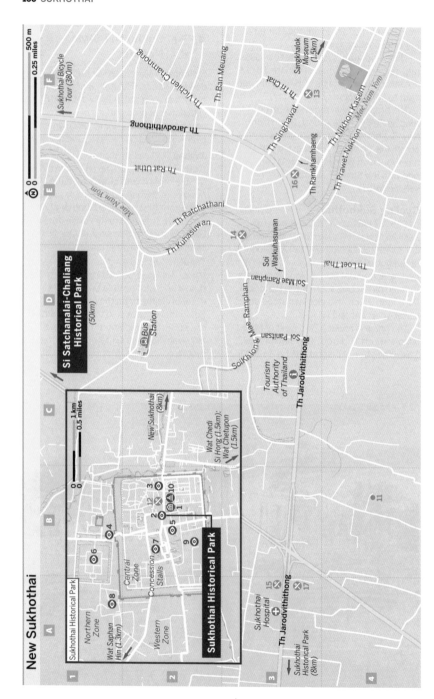

New Sukhothai

Sukhothai Bicycle Tour   Cycling

(☏086 931 6242; www.sukhothaibicycletour.com; 34/1 Th Jarodvithithong; half day 750B, full day 1050-1150B) A bicycle-based tour outfit that gets overwhelmingly positive feedback.

EATING

Dream Café   Thai $$

(86/1 Th Singhawat; mains 120-350B; ◷5-11pm; ❄🍸) A meal at Dream Café is like dining in an antique shop. Eclectic but tasteful furnishings abound, staff members are competent and friendly and, most importantly of all, the food is good. Try one of the well-executed *yam* (Thai-style 'salads').

Night Market   Market $

(Th Ramkhamhaeng; mains 30-60B; ◷6-11pm) A wise choice for cheap eats is New Sukhothai's tiny night market. Most vendors here are accustomed to accommodating foreigners and even provide bilingual menus.

Fueang Fah   Thai $$

(107/2 Th Khuhasuwan; dishes 50-350B; ◷10am-10pm) Pretend you're a local in the know and head to this long-standing riverside restaurant. The speciality is freshwater fish dishes, such as the tasty 'fried fish', the first item on the barely comprehensible English-language menu. There's no Roman-script sign; it's just after the bridge on Th Khuhasuwan.

ⓘ INFORMATION

Sukhothai Hospital (☏055 610280; Th Jarodvithithong) Located just west of New Sukhothai.

Tourism Authority of Thailand (TAT; ☏055 6162 28, nationwide 1672; www.tourismthailand.org; Th Jarodvithithong; ◷8.30am-4.30pm) About 750m west of the bridge in New Sukhothai, this office has a good selection of maps and brochures.

ⓘ GETTING THERE & AWAY

AIR

Sukhothai's airport is a whopping 27km north of town off Rte 1195. There is a **minivan service** (☏055 647220; Sukhothai Airport; ◷7am-7pm) between the airport and New Sukhothai or Sukhothai Historical Park. Alternatively, Air Asia and Nok Air offer minivan transfers to/from both old and new Sukhothai via the airport in Phitsanulok, less than an hour away.

BUS

Sukhothai's **minivan and bus station** (☏055 614529; Rte 101) is almost 1km northwest of the centre of New Sukhothai; a motorcycle taxi between here and central New Sukhothai should cost around 50B, or you can hop on any *sŏrng·tăa·ou* (pick-up minibus) bound for Sukhothai Historical Park – they stop at the bus station on their way out of town between 6am and 5.30pm.

ⓘ GETTING AROUND

Frequent *sŏrng·tăa·ou* run between New Sukhothai and Sukhothai Historical Park from 6am to 6pm, leaving from a stop on Th Jarodvithithong. The best way to get around the historical park is by bicycle, which can be rented at shops outside the park entrance for 30B per day. Motorbike rental starts at about 250B per day.

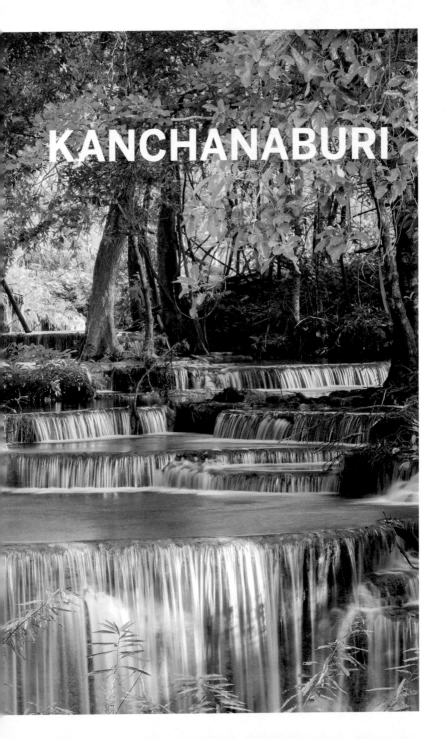

KANCHANABURI

Kanchanaburi at a Glance...

Kanchanaburi is home to an array of lush riverside resorts, and is a gateway to national parks in Thailand's wild west. But the biggest draw to this central Thai town is its history.

During WWII, Japanese forces used Allied prisoners of war and conscripted Asian labourers to build a rail route between Thailand and Myanmar. The harrowing story became famous after the publication of Pierre Boulle's book The Bridge Over the River Kwai, and the 1957 movie that followed. War cemeteries, museums and the chance to ride a section of the so-called 'Death Railway' serve as reminders of this time.

Kanchanaburi in Two Days

Travel back in time at Kanchanaburi's **Death Railway Bridge** (p172) and its various WWII museums. On day two, take the train to **Hellfire Pass Memorial** (p175). Take in the river with dinner at **Blue Rice** (p177).

Kanchanaburi in Four Days

With more time, you can explore the sights outside of the city centre such as the cave temples of **Wat Tham Khao Pun** (p176) and **Wat Tham Seua** (p176), or the waterfalls at **Erawan National Park** (p176). Take a cooking course at **Apple & Noi Thai Cooking** (p176).

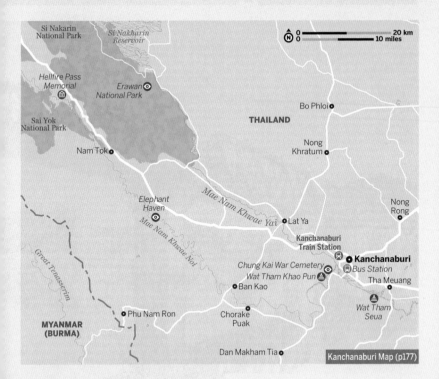

Kanchanaburi Map (p177)

Arriving in Kanchanaburi

Bus station Located in the centre of town just off Th Saengchuto.

Train station Located in the middle of town is this terminal for 3rd-class, fan-cooled trains to/from Bangkok.

Sleeping

Travellers flock to the plentiful accommodation options along Th Mae Nam Khwae. Budget and midrange digs sit alongside (or literally on) the river. A few high-end resorts exist in town but the best are in the surrounding countryside (where it's a good idea to have a car). Many Bangkokians arrive for the weekend; reserve well ahead.

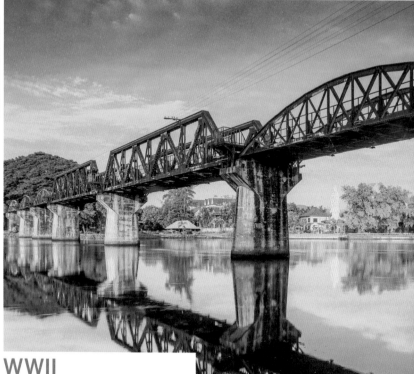

BULE SKY STUDIO / SHUTTERSTOCK ©

WWII History

Beyond its hectic modern centre and river views, Kanchanaburi has a dark history, paid tribute to at excellent memorials and museums.

Great For...

☑ Don't Miss

For Thais, a photo on the so-called Death Railway Bridge is a must-do.

Death Railway Bridge

This 300m-long **bridge** (สะพานข้ามแม่น้ำ แคว, Bridge Over the River Kwai; ⊙24hr) **FREE**, made famous by the movie *The Bridge on the River Kwai* (1957), is heavy with the history of the Thailand–Burma Railway, the construction of which cost thousands of imprisoned labourers their lives.

The 415km railway was built by hard labour during the WWII Japanese occupation of Thailand (1941–45). Japan's Allied prisoners of war (POWs) and conscripted workers were armed only with basic tools and dynamite as they toiled. Well over 12,000 POWs and as many as 90,000 recruited and forced labourers (many of them Malay, Chinese and Indian) died due to disease, poor hygiene, lack of medical equipment and brutal treatment by camp guards. Many Thais risked their lives to aid

Death Railway Bridge

the bridge, so the site can have a jarring, funfair-like atmosphere; come early or late to avoid the scrum.

If you'd like to see more, it's possible to take a train to Hellfire Pass Memorial (p175), a poignant museum and memorial trail that pay tribute to those who died building the railway.

Thailand–Burma Railway Centre

This excellent **museum** (ศูนย์รถไฟไทย-พม่า; 034 512721; www.tbrconline.com; 73 Th Jaokannun; adult/child 140/60B; 9am-5pm) balances statistics and historical context with personal accounts of the conditions endured by POWs and other imprisoned labourers forced to build the railway. Kanchanaburi's role in WWII is thoroughly explained, but most of the museum traces the journey of railway workers from transport in cramped boxcars to disease-ridden labour camps in the jungle, as well as survivors' fates after the war. Allow time for the poignant video with testimony from both POWs and Japanese soldiers.

Galleries upstairs display wartime artefacts, and there's a 3m-deep diorama showing how Hellfire Pass got its name. Allow at least an hour for your visit.

the POWs, most of whom were Australian, American, British and Dutch, but they could offer only limited help.

The objective of the railway was to secure an overland supply route to Burma (Myanmar) for the Japanese conquest of other Asian countries. Because of the mountainous landscape, 688 bridges were built along the route. Most were wooden trestle bridges, such as those at the oft-visited Tham Krasae. The Death Railway Bridge was the only steel bridge built in Thailand; Burma had seven. It was bombed several times by the Allies, but the POWs were sent to rebuild it. When the war's tide turned, the railway became an escape path for Japanese troops.

You're free to roam over the bridge; stand in a safety point if a train appears. Food and souvenir hawkers surround

Kanchanaburi War Cemetery

Immaculately maintained by the Commonwealth War Graves Commission, this **cemetery** (สุสานทหารพันธมิตรดอนรัก, Allied War Cemetery; Th Saengchuto; ⏰24hr) is right in town. Of the 6982 soldiers buried here, nearly half were British; the rest came mainly from Australia and the Netherlands. As you stand at the cemetery entrance, the entire right-hand side contains British victims, the front-left area contains Australian graves, the rear left honours Dutch and unknown soldiers, and those who were cremated lie at the furthest spot to the left.

Chung Kai War Cemetery

Smaller and less visited than the war cemetery in town (but just as well maintained),

Chung Kai War Cemetery (สุสานทหารพันธมิตรช่องไก่; Nong Ya; ⏰7am-6pm) **FREE** honours 1400 Commonwealth and 300 Dutch soldiers. This was the site of one of the biggest Allied POW camps. Prisoners built their own hospital and church close by and the majority of those buried here died at the hospital.

The cemetery is near the river, 2.5km southwest of the Wat Neua bridge. It's easily reached by bicycle.

JEATH War Museum

This small, open-air **museum** (พิพิธภัณฑ์สงคราม; cnr Th Wisuttharangsi & Th Pak Phraek; 50B; ⏰8.30am-4.30pm) displays correspondence and artwork from former POWs involved in the building of the Death Railway.

JEATH War Museum

Their harsh living conditions are evident in the many photos on display alongside personal effects and war relics, including an unexploded Allied bomb dropped to destroy the bridge. One of the three galleries is built from bamboo in the style of the shelters (called *attap*) the POWs lived in; another has a 10-minute video presentation.

JEATH is an acronym of the warring countries involved in the railway: Japan, England, Australia/USA, Thailand and the Netherlands. The museum is run by the monks of the adjacent **Wat Chaichum-**

> ★ Top Tip
> For in-depth wartime and railway history, the Thailand–Burma Railway Centre (p173) can organise tours.

HOLGER LEUE / GETTY IMAGES ©

phon (วัดไชยชุมพลชนะ; Th Pak Phraek), which is worth a wander to see its many interesting statues and shrines, including one fashioned from a WWII-era boat dredged out of the river.

WWII Museum

Though well-intentioned, the dispersed (and usually context-free) displays at this **museum** (พิพิธภัณฑ์สงครามโลกครั้งที่สอง; Th Mae Nam Khwae; 40B; ⊗8am-6pm) have limited educational value. Still, you'll see trains, Japanese motorcycles, anchors and old helmets, plus the museum has a great view of the bridge (the tower in the northwest corner has the best viewpoint).

Life-sized statues of soldiers re-create the harsh conditions endured by prisoners building the Thailand–Burma Railway, though the overall impression is of a museum of horrors rather than a historical display. For reasons known only to the museum owners, other exhibits include jade carvings and a display case warning of the dangers of alcohol.

The museum complex adjoins a temple. Between the two buildings is a stupa with coloured bowls decorating its exterior.

Hellfire Pass Memorial

A poignant museum and **memorial** (พิพิธภัณฑ์ช่องเขาขาด; ☑034 919605; Hwy 323; ⊗museum 9am-4pm, grounds 7.30am-6pm; P) FREE trail pay tribute to those who died building the railway. Begin at the museum and ask for the free audio guide, which provides historical detail and fascinating first-person accounts from survivors. Then descend behind the museum to a trail following the original rail bed. The infamous cutting known as Hellfire Pass was the largest along the railway's length and the most deadly for the labourers forced to construct it.

The museum is 80km northwest of Kanchanaburi on Hwy 323 and can be reached by Sangkhlaburi and Thong Pha Phum buses (45B to 65B, two hours, every 30 minutes). The last bus back to Kanchanaburi passes here around 5pm.

⊙ SIGHTS

Heritage Walking Street   Area
(ถนนป่ากแพรก; Th Pakprak) A stroll along this enchanting street offers a glimpse of a bygone Kanchanaburi. Many buildings date to the interwar period. Though worn by the passage of time, their Sino-Portuguese, Thai, Vietnamese and Chinese styles have been preserved; yellow signs reveal their history, architecture and current owners. The walk begins at the restored **City Gate** (ประตูเมือง; Th Lak Meuang).

Wat Tham Khao Pun   Buddhist Temple
(วัดถ้ำเขาปูน; Nong Ya; 30B; ⊙6am-6pm) The nearest cave temple to Kanchanaburi town is a spellbinding labyrinth of stone passageways. The marked trail can be slippery (and a bit of a squeeze) in places, but ducking beneath limestone protrusions to discover these subterranean shrines is an otherworldly experience; it's pin-drop silent (aside from fluttering bats) down here. The temple is 4km southwest of the town centre, beyond Chung Kai War Cemetery (p174).

Wat Tham Seua   Buddhist Temple
(วัดถ้ำเสือ; Muang Chum; ⊙daylight hours; P) **FREE** The centrepiece of this hilltop temple is a striking 18m-high Buddha covered in golden mosaics. One of the merit-making ceremonies for devotees is to place coins in small trays on a conveyor belt that drops donations into a central bowl with a resounding clang. It's fun to ride the steep cable car (20B per person) to the top of the temple, but you can also climb the stairs.

Erawan National Park   National Park
(อุทยานแห่งชาติเอราวัณ; ☏034 574222; adult/child 300/200B, car/motorbike 30/20B; ⊙8am-4.30pm; P) Splashing in cerulean pools under Erawan Falls is the highlight of this 550-sq-km park. Seven tiers of waterfall tumble through the forest, and bathing beneath these crystalline cascades is equally popular with locals and visitors. Reaching the first three tiers is easy; beyond here, walking shoes and some endurance are needed to complete the steep 2km hike (it's worth it to avoid the crowds in the first two pools). There are hourly buses from Kanchanaburi (50B, 1½ hours).

⊙ ACTIVITIES

Apple & Noi Thai Cooking   Cooking
(☏034 512017; www.applenoikanchanaburi.com/apple-noi-cooking; Apple's Retreat; per person 1990B; ⊙by arrangment) If you don't know your *sôm·đam* from your *đôm yam*, Khun Noi can assist. Her very popular one-day course has an emphasis on local recipes and seasonal produce, beginning at the local market and ending, four dishes later, at the dining table. Book well ahead.

Half-day or multi-day courses are also available, but enquire well in advance.

River Kwai Canoe Travel Services   Kayaking
(☏087 001 9137, 086 168 5995; riverkwaicanoe@yahoo.com; 11 Th Mae Nam Khwae; ⊙hours vary) Takes you out of town and lets you paddle back. The three-hour, 15km trip (500B per person) is the most popular option, but longer and shorter trips are also available.

Elephant Haven   Elephant Interaction
(☏053 272855; www.elephantnaturepark.org; Sai Yok; half-day/full-day 1500/2500B; ⊙by arrangement) ✔ Cruel elephant rides remain tragically common in central Thailand, but Elephant Haven, a satellite of Chiang Mai's renowned Elephant Nature Park (p87), offers a gentler, educational alternative. Visitors can observe elephants up close, feed them tasty rice and millet balls, and listen to the echoing crunch as they devour greenery. Staff treat these gentle beasts with affection and care, and elephants – most of them rescued or retired from elephant riding outfits – can enjoy their natural stamping grounds of forest and river. Prices include lunch, refreshments and an optional transfer to and from Kanchanaburi. It's 30km west of Kanchanaburi and 20km southeast of Nam Tok.

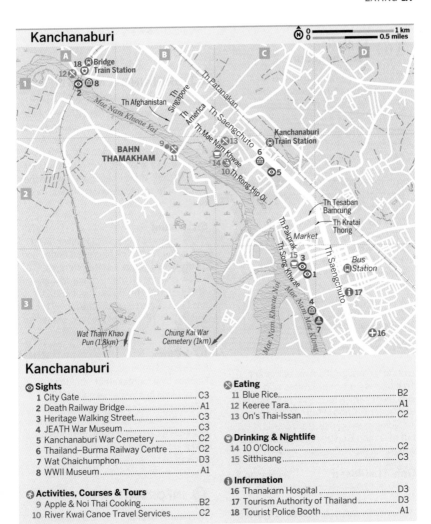

Kanchanaburi

⊗ EATING

Blue Rice   Thai $

(www.applenoikanchanaburi.com; 153/4 Mu 4, Ban Tamakahm; mains from 135B; ⊙noon-2pm & 6-10pm; P🛈📶🌶) Masterful spice blends, a creative menu and peaceful river views make this one of the most irresistible restaurants in Kanchanaburi. The signature massaman curry is perfectly balanced, and the menu is packed with reinvented Thai classics such as *yam sôm oh* (pomelo salad) and chicken-coconut soup with banana plant. The eponymous rice is stained with pea-flower petals, if you're wondering.

Keeree Tara   Thai $$

(📞034 513855; www.facebook.com/keereetara; 431/1 Th Mae Nam Khwae; mains 150-400B; ⊙11am-11pm) This refined riverside eatery is ever so slightly upriver from the melee

ⓘ Exploring Kanchanaburi

Tours are a convenient way to see the main sights outside the city, though if you have a small group it may be cheaper to hire a driver and plan your movements independently. Day trips generally cost 800B to 1100B per person, usually including admission fees and lunch. Kanchanaburi is rich in natural wonders, and many standard tours include bamboo rafting and short jungle treks.

Many companies offer similar itineraries. One of the most popular programs is a day to Erawan Falls, Hellfire Pass Memorial and the Death Railway's 'wooden bridge' at Tham Krasae. But more adventurous options – such as cycling tours and overnight jungle trekking, usually staying in a Karen village – are available if enough people are interested.

around the bridge. It serves upmarket Thai dishes from duck stuffed with lily to succulent catfish heaped with red curry. Still hungry? Choose from Thai desserts including *đa·go peu·ak* (taro pearls in coconut milk) and French-inspired gateaux and white chocolate mousse.

On's Thai-Issan   Vegetarian $

(☏087 364 2264; www.onsthaiissan.com; Th Mae Nam Khwae; mains from 70B; ☉noon-10pm; ❄️🍽️) At this casual restaurant, vegetarian and vegan recipes borrow Isan flavours and reinvent classic Thai dishes from entirely plant-based ingredients, with other healthy flourishes such as brown rice. Banana flower salad, ginger tofu and 'morning glory' (pan-seared greens) are cooked before your eyes on fryers outside and served in generous portions.

Friendly On will even teach you how to make your favourite dishes. A two-hour,

three-dish **cookery course** costs 600B (book a few days ahead).

🍸 DRINKING & NIGHTLIFE

Tourists and expats spend their evenings along bar-lined Th Mae Nam Khwae. Many venues have pool tables and screen sports matches (particularly the numerous Australian and British-themed bars). For the brave, street-side bars here offer shots for 10B. Th Song Khwae, along the river in the centre of town, has a variety of bars; most don't get started until late.

Sitthisang   Cafe

(Th Pakprak; ☉8am-6pm; 🛜) Hunker down with a bit of history – plus great coffee and dainty baked goods – in this primrose-yellow building on the Heritage Walking Street (p176). This house (built in 1920) has been owned by the same family for generations; it's one of the best-preserved buildings along this storied street.

10 O'Clock   Cafe

(off Th Mae Nam Khwae; ☉10am-10pm; 🛜) Flanked by a fountain that wouldn't look out of place in a Viennese palace, 10 O'Clock (guess the opening hours) has outdoor tables under shady trees. Within the clock-bedecked cafe, passionfruit frappés and good coffee are served to the clickety-clack of patrons using the free wi-fi.

ⓘ INFORMATION

Thanakarn Hospital (☏034 622366; off Th Saengchuto) The best-equipped hospital to deal with foreign visitors.

Tourism Authority of Thailand (TAT; ☏034 511200; www.tourismthailand.org/Kanchanaburi; Th Saengchuto; ☉8.30am-4.30pm) Provides free maps of the town and province, along with bus timetables.

Tourist Police Booth (☉9am-4pm) Near Death Railway Bridge (p172).

Buddha statue, Wat Tham Seua (p176)

ℹ️ GETTING THERE & AWAY

BUS

Kanchanaburi's **bus station** (034 515907; Th Lak Meuang) is in the centre of town just off Th Saengchuto, and minivans outnumber buses. Minivans to Bangkok depart until around 10pm (100B to 150B, 2½ hours).

TRAIN

Kanchanaburi's **train station** (034 511285) is in the middle of town. It's on the Bangkok Noi–Nam Tok rail line, which includes a portion of the Death Railway. The SRT promotes this as a historic route, and so charges foreigners 100B for any one-way journey along the line, regardless of the distance. The trains are 3rd class, meaning wooden benches and no air-con, and you should not expect them to run on time. If you are planning a day trip to Kanchanaburi and time is tight, take a bus.

ℹ️ GETTING AROUND

Motorcycles can be rented at guesthouses and shops along Th Mae Nam Khwae for around 200B per day. Bicycle rentals cost from 50B per day.

KO PHA-NGAN

Ko Pha-Ngan at a Glance...

Hippie-at-heart Ko Pha-Ngan has become so synonymous with the wild Full Moon Party that the rest of the island gets eclipsed. After the werewolves of the Full Moon leave, Ko Pha-Ngan returns to its hammock hanging.

The island is carved into sandy coves with offshore reefs and a thick jungle crown in the interior. The gentle coral-fringed bays make it perfect for families. And a diversity of accommodation – from cheapish bungalows on party beaches to sophisticated resorts on the remote east coast – makes this tropical island a well-rounded holiday companion.

Ko Pha-Ngan in Two Days

Savour the great diversity of the ocean's blues and greens from one of Ko Pha-Ngan's many beautiful beaches. Go for a beach snorkel or dive. Check out the punters on **Hat Rin** (p184) for a sundowner, or more.

Ko Pha-Ngan in Four Days

Start day three exploring the eastern side of the island for castaway fantasies. Then do a full-day **dive tour** (p186) of the Gulf's famous dive spots. Lounge around and do nothing on your last day.

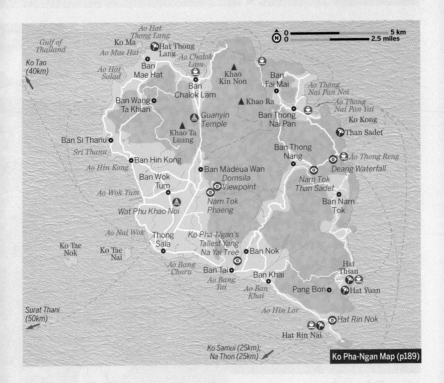

Ko Pha-Ngan Map (p189)

Arriving on Ko Pha-Ngan

Thong Sala Boats connect Ko Pha-Ngan with Ko Samui, Chumphon and Surat Thani. *Sŏrng·tăa·ou* (pick-up minibuses) meet passengers for hotel transfers.

Sleeping

Hat Rin is the busy party beach with a huge selection of accommodation. The west coast is a nice hybrid, with enough amenities to avoid feeling stranded and a diverse range of accommodation. There's limited lodging and transport is expensive at the north coast beaches but there's also dramatic scenery and secluded beaches. The east coast beaches are deliciously secluded and have minimal development; transport is limited.

Ko Pha-Ngan
Party Scene

Throngs of whisky-bucket sippers and fire twirlers gather on Hat Rin Nok (Sunrise Beach) for the infamous Full Moon Parties. Full-on debauchery rages until the sun replaces the moon in the sky.

Great For...

☑ **Don't Miss**

Transforming yourself into a walking day-glo stick – it is *the* thing to do.

No one knows exactly when or how these crazy parties started – most believe they began in 1988, but accounts of the first party range from an Australian backpacker's going-away bash to a group of hippies escaping Samui's 'electric parties'. None of that is relevant now: today thousands of bodies converge for an epic trance-a-thon. Crowds can swell to an outrageous 40,000 partiers during high season, while the low season still sees a respectable 5000 pilgrims.

Party Tips

If your trip doesn't coincide with a full moon, fear not. Enterprising locals have organised a slew of other reasons to get sloshed. There are Black Moon Parties,

Full Moon Party, Hat Rin

Half Moon Parties and Moon-set Parties to name a few. Some critics claim the party has lost its carefree flavour after increasing violence (assaults, thefts and injuries). Precautions should be followed to ensure personal and property safety.

● Secure all valuables, especially when staying in budget bungalows.

● Wear protective shoes during the sandy celebration, unless you want a tetanus shot.

● Don't sample the drug buffet, nor swim in the ocean under the influence of alcohol.

● Stay in a group of two or more people, especially if you're a woman, and especially when returning home at the end of the evening.

Party Places

The Full Moon Party unfolds on the soft sands of **Hat Rin** (Sunrise Beach). Surrounding bars also have their own periphery parties.

● **Rock** (📞093 725 7989; Hat Rin Nok; ⊙8am-late) Superb views of the party from the elevated terrace on the far southern side of the beach are matched by the best cocktails in town.

● **Sunrise** (📞077 375144; Hat Rin Nok) Claims a spot on the sand where trance beats shake the graffitied walls, with drum 'n' bass coming into its own at Full Moon.

● **Tommy** (Hat Rin Nok) Hat Rin's largest venue with blaring Full Moon trance music. Drinks are dispensed from a large ark-like bar.

Diving on Ko Pha-Ngan

Everyone will tell you to go to nearby Ko Tao to learn to dive. But Ko Pha-Ngan enjoys a much quieter, more laid-back diving scene focused on fun diving.

Great For...

☑ **Don't Miss**

Wake up and hit the near-shore snorkelling spots – better than a cup of coffee.

Dive Sites

A major perk of diving from Ko Pha-Ngan is the proximity to Sail Rock (Hin Bai) and Chumphon Pinnacle, the premier dive sites in the Gulf of Thailand.

Chumphon Pinnacle (36m maximum depth) has a colourful assortment of sea anemones along the four interconnected pinnacles. The site plays host to schools of giant trevally, tuna and large grey reef sharks. Whale sharks are known to pop up once in a while.

Sail Rock (40m maximum depth) features a massive rock chimney with a vertical swim-through, and large pelagics like barracuda and kingfish. This is one of the top spots in Southeast Asia to see whale sharks; in the past few years they have been seen year-round, so there's no

ℹ Need to Know

Three dives cost 3650B to 4000B and include a full lunch. Two dives cost around 2500B to 2800B.

✗ Take a Break

After a day of diving, grab a sundowner at Amsterdam (p192) with tourists and locals alike.

★ Top Tip

Ko Pha-Ngan is now competitive with Ko Tao for Open Water certification prices.

clear season. An abundance of corals and large tropical fish can be seen at depths of 10m to 30m.

Like the other islands in the Samui Archipelago, Pha-Ngan has several small reefs dispersed around the island. The clear favourite is **Ko Ma**, a small island in the northwest connected to Ko Pha-Ngan by a sandbar. There are also some rock reefs of interest on the eastern side of the island. Hiking and snorkelling day trips to Ang Thong Marine National Park (p116) generally depart from Ko Samui, but recently tour operators are starting to shuttle tourists from Ko Pha-Ngan as well. Ask at your accommodation for details about boat trips as companies often come and go due to unstable petrol prices.

Dive Companies

Group sizes tend to be smaller on Ko Pha-Ngan than on Ko Tao since the island has fewer divers in general. But be warned that demand goes up before and after the Full Moon Parties because there are more tourists.

The most popular trips departing from Ko Pha-Ngan are three-site day trips, stopping at Chumphon Pinnacle, Sail Rock and one of the other premier sites in the area.

Lotus Diving (☏077 374142; www.lotus diving.com; Ban Chalok Lam; ⊘7am-6pm) and **Haad Yao Divers** (☏086 279 3085; www. haadyaodivers.com; from 1400B) are the main operators on the island with a solid reputation.

◎ SIGHTS

This large island has many jungle attractions in addition to its spectacular beaches. Explore the isolated beaches on the east coast: Than Sadet, Hat Yuan, Hat Thian and the teeny Ao Thong Reng. Note that most of the waterfalls (p192) slow to a trickle during the dry season, so aim to visit from October to January.

Domsila
Viewpoint   Viewpoint

The terrific Domsila Viewpoint – offering a rocky perch with superb, ranging views – is a 15-minute, root-choked climb up from Nam Tok Phaeng waterfall (p192). Then you can then either backtrack or continue on the two- to three-hour trail through the jungle in a loop, past other waterfalls before bringing you back. Take water and good shoes.

Ko Pha-Ngan's Tallest
Yang Na Yai Tree   Landmark

Thrusting into the heavens near Wat Pho, Ko Pha-Ngan's tallest Yang Na Yai (*Dipterocarpus alatus*; ยางนา) is an astonishing sight as you veer round the bend for the diminutive Wat Nok, a small shrine tucked away in the greenery beyond. These giants grow to over 50m in height and, for tree lovers, are real beauties. This imposing specimen is often garlanded with colourful ribbons.

Guanyin
Temple   Buddhist Temple

(40B; ⊙7am-6pm) Signposted as the 'Goddess of Mercy Shrine Joss House', this fascinating Chinese temple is dedicated to Guanyin, the Buddhist Goddess of Mercy. The temple's Chinese name (普岳山) on the entrance gate refers to the island in China that is the legendary home of the goddess. The main hall – the Great Treasure Hall – is a highly colourful confection, containing several bodhisattvas, including Puxian (seated on an elephant) and Wenshu (sitting on a lion).

Wat Phu Khao Noi   Buddhist Temple

(⊙dawn-dusk) FREE The oldest temple on the island is Wat Phu Khao Noi, near the hospital in Thong Sala. While the site is open to visitors throughout the day, the monks are only around in the morning.

🔒 SHOPPING

Thong Sala
Walking Street   Market

(Taladkao Rd, Thong Sala; ⊙4-10pm Sat) Thong Sala's Walking Street market kicks off every Saturday from around 4pm, with a terrific choice of street food, souvenirs, gifts, handicrafts and clothes. It's the best time to see Thong Sala at its liveliest.

Lilawadee   Clothing

(☑630 920327; Thong Sala; ⊙10.30am-1.30pm & 5-9pm Fri-Wed) This neat and idiosyncratic shop stocks a sparkling range of customised, head-turning glitter motorbike helmets, stacked temptingly on shelves at the rear, fashion, art and clothing. If it's raining, expect hours to be reduced to noon to 8pm.

✖ EATING

Most visitors quickly adopt the lazy lifestyle and wind up eating at their accommodation, which is a shame as Ko Pha-Ngan has some excellent restaurants scattered around the island; at the very least, it's another reason to get exploring.

✖ Hat Rin

Lazy House   International $$

(Hat Rin Nai; dishes 90-270B; ⊙lunch & dinner) Back in the day, this joint was the owner's apartment – everyone liked his cooking so much that he decided to turn the place into a restaurant and hang-out spot. Today, Lazy House is one of Hat Rin's best places to veg out in front of a movie with a scrumptious shepherd's pie.

Monna Lisa   Italian $$

(☑084 441 5871; Hat Rin Nai; pizza & pasta from 200B; ⊙3-11pm) Travellers still rave about the pizza here, and the pasta gets

Ko Pha-Ngan

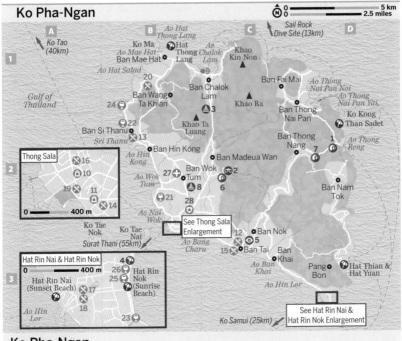

Ko Pha-Ngan

a thumbs-up as well. It's run by a team of friendly Italians and has a basic, open-air atmosphere. There's another branch in Thong Sala.

⊗ Southern Beaches
Bubba's Coffee Bar Cafe $
(Ban Tai; mains 120-220B; ⏰7am-5pm; 🕾)
Bubba's is a superb caffeination choice on

the north side of the road between Thong Sala and Hat Rin. Pull in, find a seat and enjoy some fine coffee and the easy-going atmosphere (despite attracting legions of customers from the nearby hostels). The wholesome menu is lovely too, as is the cool interior.

Fisherman's Restaurant
Seafood $$

(☏084 454 7240; Ban Tai; dishes 50-600B; ⏲1.30-10pm) Sit in a long-tail boat looking out over the sunset and a rocky pier. Lit up at night, it's one of the island's nicest settings, and the food, from the addictive yellow-curry crab to the massive seafood platter to share, is as wonderful as the ambience. Reserve ahead, especially when the island is hopping during party time.

⊗ Other Beaches

Crave
Burgers $$

(☏098 838 7268; www.cravekohphangan.com; Sri Thanu; mains from 200B; ⏲6-10pm Wed-Mon; 🛜) Attractively bedecked with glowing lanterns at night, this excellent, very pop-ular and atmospheric choice in Sri Thanu puts together some fine burgers in a cosy and charming setting. Cocktails are great too, starting at 170B. Shame it's only open evenings.

Dots
Cafe $

(Thong Sala; snacks from 60B; ⏲8.30am-9pm Mon-Sat, 9am-6pm Sun; 🛜) Light, bright and spacious, Dots is a welcome addition to Thong Sala's cafe culture, with a modern and chilled vibe. Pretty much right next to the Food Market, it's a sharp-looking spot for a slice of carrot cake, frappé, full-flavoured coffee, hot choc or a croissant for brekkie.

Fat Cat
Cafe $

(Thong Sala; breakfast from 70B, mains 90-195B; ⏲9am-3pm Mon-Sat; 🛜) This small, charming, colourful and busy – with staff rather run off their feet – Portuguese-run cafe does wholesome breakfasts and lovely coffees through the day. It's a very enjoyable place for a wake-up meal first thing in the morning, or any other time.

Guanyin Temple (p188)

Thai-style noodle dish

Food Market   Market $

(Thong Sala; dishes 25-180B; ⊙1-11pm) A heady
mix of steam and snacking locals, Thong
Sala's terrific food market is a must for
those looking for doses of culture while
nibbling on low-priced snacks. Wander the
stalls for a galaxy of Thai street food, from
vegetable curry puffs to corn on the cob,
spicy sausages, kebabs, spring rolls, Hain-
anese chicken rice or coconut ice cream.

There's a sit-down section at the rear,
served by a number of Thai kitchens,
including a few Italian ones as well and a
vegetarian option.

Nira's   Bakery $

(Thong Sala; snacks from 80B; ⊙7am-7pm; 🛜)
With lots of busy staff offering outstanding
service, a big and bright interconnected
two-room interior, scrummy baked goodies,
tip-top coffee (and exotic rarities such as
Marmite and Vegemite) and trendy furniture,
Nira's is second to none in Thong Sala, and
perhaps the entire island. This is *the* place
for breakfast. Music is cool, jazzy chill-out.
There's another (small) branch in Hat Rin.

Peppercorn   Steak $$

(📞087 896 4363; www.peppercornphangan.com;
Hat Salad; mains 160-400B; ⊙4-10pm Mon-Sat;
🖋) Escargot, succulent steaks and schnit-
zel in a rickety jungle cottage? You bet!
Peppercorn may be tucked in the brush
away from the sea, but that shouldn't dis-
suade foodies from seeking out some of Ko
Pha-Ngan's best international cuisine, with
a fine selection of good vegetarian dishes
to boot, and mango cake for dessert. No
MSG or artificial ingredients.

🍸 DRINKING & NIGHTLIFE

For something mellower, the west coast has
several excellent bars, where you can raise
a loaded cocktail glass to a blood-orange
sunset from a hilltop or over mangrove
trees at the water's edge. Thong Sala has a
couple of decent bars too.

Belgian Beer Bar   Bar

(www.seetanu.com; Ban Sri Thanu; ⊙8am-10pm)
Run by the affable Quentin, this enjoyable
bar defies Surat Thani's appropriation by

Ko Pha-Ngan's Waterfalls

Nam Tok Phaeng

Protected by a national park, this waterfall is a pleasant reward after a short, but rough, hike. After the waterfall (dry out of season), it's a further exhilarating 15-minute climb up a root-choked path (along the Phaeng-Domsila Nature Trail) to the fantastic Domsila Viewpoint, with superb, ranging views. The two- to three-hour trail then continues on through the jungle in a loop, past other waterfalls before bringing you back. Take water and good shoes.

Nam Tok Than Sadet

These falls feature boulders carved with the royal insignia of Rama V, Rama VII and Rama IX. King Rama V enjoyed this hidden spot so much that he returned over a dozen times between 1888 and 1909. The river waters of Khlong Than Sadet are now considered sacred and used in royal ceremonies.

Deang Waterfall

Than Sadet has a string of waterfalls down to the beach at Ao Thong Reng, and this is the best. Deang features a sequence of falls, a pool for swimming in and lots of rock-clambering opportunities. You may even find someone slumped in the main flow, cooling off on the rocks in the gush of the water. Look for the signs.

Deang Waterfall
VASIT BUASAMUI / SHUTTERSTOCK ©

yogis and the chakra-balancing crowd with a heady range of Belgian beer, the most potent of which (Amber Bush) delivers a dizzying 12.5% punch. If the yogic flying doesn't give you wings, this might.

Amsterdam   Bar

(☏089 072 2233; Ao Plaay Laem; ☉noon-midnight) Near Ao Wok Tum on the west coast, hillside Amsterdam attracts tourists and locals from all over the island, seeking a superchilled spot to catch a Ko Pha-Ngan sunset and totally zone out.

Secret Beach Bar   Bar

(Hat Son; ☉9am-7pm) There are few ways better to unwind at the end of a Ko Pha-Ngan day than watching the sun slide into an azure sea from this bar on the northwest sands of the island. Grab a table, order a mojito and take in the sunset through the palm fronds.

ⓘ INFORMATION

Ko Pha-Ngan Hospital (☏077 377034; Thong Sala; ☉24hr) About 2.5km north of Thong Sala, this government hospital offers 24-hour emergency services.

Main Police Station (☏191, 077 377114; Thong Sala) Located about 2km north of Thong Sala. Come here to file a report. You might be charged between 110B and 200B to file the report, which is for insurance and refusing to pay may lead to complications. If you are arrested you have the right to an embassy phone call; you don't have to accept the 'interpreter' you are offered.

ⓘ GETTING THERE & AWAY

AIR

Ko Pha-Ngan's airport was under construction at the time of writing; its opening date has not been released.

BOAT

Rough waves cancel ferries during the monsoon (October and December). Boats connect to Ko Samui (20 minutes to one hour, 200B to 300B), and bus-boat combinations provide overland transport to Bangkok (10 to 17 hours, 1000B to 1300B).

PETER UNGER / GETTY IMAGES ©

Hat Rin (p185)

ℹ️ GETTING AROUND

You can rent motorcycles all over the island (200B to 250B). Ko Pha-Ngan has many motorcycle accidents; always wear a helmet.

Sŏrng·tăa·ou (pick-up minibuses) chug along the island's major roads and the riding rates double after sunset. The trip from Thong Sala to Hat Rin is 100B; further beaches will set you back around 150B to 200B.

Long-tail boats connect the southern piers (Thong Sala and Hat Rin) to the north and east coast beaches (Chalok Lam and Hat Khuat); expect to pay anywhere from 50B for a short trip, and up to 300B for a lengthier journey.

KO PHI-PHI

Ko Phi-Phi at a Glance...

With its curvy, bleach-blonde beaches and bodacious jungles, it's no wonder Phi-Phi has become the darling of the Andaman Coast. And like any good starlet, this island can party hard all night and still look great the next morning.

Ko Phi-Phi is actually two islands: Ko Phi-Phi Don is a car-less island crisscrossed by footpaths leading to small-scale bungalows and resorts, while uninhabited Ko Phi-Phi Leh is a protected park only allowing visitors on day trips.

Ko Phi-Phi in Two Days

Bliss out on the beaches. Party until late at **Sunflower Bar** (p203) or **Banana Bar** (p203). The next day, temper that hangover with a spicy Thai lunch at **Esan Ganeang** (p202) or a splurge at **Jasmin** (p202). Repeat.

Ko Phi-Phi in Four Days

Dive and snorkel (p198) the spectacular underwater gardens of Ko Phi-Phi. Take a tour of Phi-Phi Don's virgin sister, **Phi-Phi Leh** (p200). Or make it a **dinner or cocktail cruise** (p201) if you prefer scenery with an adult beverage.

Arriving on Ko Phi-Phi

Most boats from Phuket and Railay moor at Ao Ton Sai on Phi-Phi Don. There are no roads. Transport is by foot, or long-tail boat charter.

Sleeping

Phi-Phi's reputation as a party island makes it very difficult to sleep peacefully. The island's small size also means that room shortages are a problem during the high season and rates increase excessively. Budget options huddle around the village of Ton Sai and Ao Lo Dalam. The island gets quieter on the east coast where there are top-end resorts and low-key bungalows.

For more information on the best area to stay in, see p205.

Clownfish in coral

PLACEBO365 / GETTY IMAGES ©

Ko Phi-Phi Diving & Snorkelling

Crystalline water and abundant marine life make the perfect recipe for top-notch diving. Leopard sharks and hawksbill turtles are common on Ko Phi-Phi's dive sites. Whale sharks sometimes make cameo appearances in February and March.

Great For...

☑ **Don't Miss**

Ko Mai Phai is a popular shallow snorkelling spot where you may see small sharks.

Dive Sites

Popular dive spots include **Anemone Reef**, which is a hard coral reef with plentiful anemones and clownfish at a depth of 17m to 26m. **Hin Bida Phi-Phi** is a submerged pinnacle with hard coral, turtles, leopard sharks and occasional mantas and whale sharks, at 5m to 30m. **King Cruiser Wreck** is a 1997 sunken passenger ferry; underwater creatures to keep an eye out for include snappers, leopard sharks, barracudas, scorpionfish, lionfish and turtles.

Kledkaeo Wreck is a decommissioned Thai navy ship that was deliberately sunk as an artificial dive site in March 2014. Underwater inhabitants include lionfish, snappers, groupers and barracudas. **Ko Bida Nok** is a karst massif with gorgonians, leopard sharks, barracudas and occasional whale sharks and mantas (18m to 22m).

Snorkelling over jellyfish

GOODOLGA / GETTY IMAGES ©

ⓘ Need to Know

Phi-Phi dive prices are fixed across the board. Open Water certification costs 13,800B, while standard two-dive trips cost 2500B to 3500B.

✕ Take a Break

Lunch is usually provided on full-day dive trips.

★ Top Tip

November to February boasts the best visibility.

Ko Phi-Phi Leh (p206) is rimmed with coral and swim-throughs visited by moray eels, octopuses and seahorses.

Snorkelling Sites

Ko Mai Phai, 6km north of Phi-Phi Don, is a popular shallow snorkelling spot where you may see small sharks. There's good snorkelling along the east coast of **Ko Nok**, along the east coast of **Ko Nai**, and off **Hat Yao**. Most resorts rent out snorkel, mask and fins sets (200B per day).

Snorkelling trips cost 600B to 1500B, depending on whether you travel by long-tail or motorboat. You can tag along with dive trips, and many dive operators also offer specialised snorkelling tours. Those with the Adventure Club come highly recommended.

Dive Companies

Recommended dive companies include the following:

◦ Adventure Club (☏081 895 1334; www.diving-in-thailand.net; 125/19 Mu 7, Ton Sai Village, Ko Phi-Phi Don; 2 dives 2500B; ⊙7am-10pm) ✿

◦ Blue View Divers (☏094 592 0184; www.blueviewdivers.com; Phi Phi Viewpoint Resort, Ao Lo Dalam, Ko Phi-Phi Don; 2 dives 2500B; ⊙10am-8pm) ✿

◦ Princess Divers (☏088 768 0984; www.princessdivers.com; Ton Sai Village, Ko Phi-Phi Don; ⊙9.30am-10pm)

◦ Sea Frog Diving (☏087 920 0680, 075 601073; www.ppseafrog.com; Ton Sai Village, Ko Phi-Phi Don; 2 dives 2500B; ⊙7am-10pm)

Viking Cave

KSL / SHUTTERSTOCK ©

Ko Phi-Phi Leh

Rugged Phi-Phi Leh is the smaller of the two Phi-Phi Islands, protected on all sides by soaring, jagged cliffs. Coral reefs crawling with marine life lie beneath the crystal-clear waters and are hugely popular with day-trippers.

Great For...

☑ **Don't Miss**

Kayaking around the bay gives a glimpse into the remarkable marine life that resides at the high-water mark.

Ever since Leo (DiCaprio) smoked a spliff in the film rendition of Alex Garland's *The Beach*, Phi-Phi Leh has been something of a pilgrimage site. Aside from long-tail boat trips to Phi-Phi Leh, tour agencies organise sunset tours around the island that include Monkey Bay and the beach at Wang Long.

Viking Cave

On the northeastern tip of the island, Viking Cave is a major collection point for valuable swifts' nests, the key component of Chinese speciality bird's-nest soup. Nimble collectors scamper up fragile bamboo scaffolding to the roof of the cave to gather the nests. Before ascending, they pray and make offerings of tobacco, incense and liquor. The cave gets its misleading moniker from the 400-year-old boat graffiti created by crews of passing Chinese fishing junks.

Ao Maya

GLENN VAN DER KNUFF / GETTY IMAGES ©

Ko Nai
Tha Ao Ton Sai
Ko Nok
*Andaman
Sea*
Ko Phi-Phi Leh

ℹ Need to Know

Long-tail trips cost 600B to 800B; by motorboat you'll pay 2500B. The national park day-use fee (adult/child 400/200B) is payable upon landing.

✕ Take a Break

Tour operators provide meals and refreshments as there are no eating options on the island.

★ Top Tip

Be a good ecocitizen by avoiding littering and smoking. These are fragile environments.

At research time, visitors were not allowed inside the cave, but most tour boats slow down for a good glimpse.

Ao Pileh

Of the two gorgeous emerald lagoons that await in Phi-Phi Leh's interior, Pileh lies on the east coast. It's predictably busy, but the thrill of kayaking between these towering limestone walls never gets old.

Ao Maya

Dramatically flanked by green-clad cliffs, majestic Ao Maya sits on Phi-Phi Leh's western shoreline. In 1999, its beautiful sands were controversially used as a set for *The Beach*, based on Alex Garland's cult novel. Natural sand dunes were flattened and extra palm trees planted to increase the paradisaical backdrop and, although

the production's team restored things, many claim the damage to the ecosystem has been permanent. The level of boat traffic here nowadays somewhat detracts from the serenity, but the setting is still spectacular.

Tour Operators

You'll have to join a tour to gain access to Ko Phi-Phi Leh's territory.

○ PP Original Sunset Tour (Ton Sai Village, Ko Phi-Phi Don; per person 900B; ⊘tours 1pm) A sensational sunset cruise with snorkelling and kayaking, followed by dinner.

○ Maya Bay Sleepaboard (www.mayabay tours.com; Ton Sai Village, Ko Phi-Phi Don; per person 3500B) Camping is no longer allowed in Maya Bay so this sleepaboard is the next best thing.

○ Captain Bob's Booze Cruise (✆094 464 9146; www.phiphiboozecruise.com; Ko Phi-Phi Don; women/men 2500/3000B; ⊘tours 1-7pm) Cruise the sea with an adult beverage in hand.

⊙ SIGHTS

Phi-Phi Viewpoint   Viewpoint
(จุดชมวิวเกาะพีพีดอน; Ko Phi-Phi Don; 30B) The strenuous Phi-Phi viewpoint climb is a steep, rewarding 20- to 30-minute hike up hundreds of steps and narrow twisting paths. Follow the signs on the road heading northeast from Ton Sai Village; most people will need to stop for a break (don't forget your water bottle). The views from the top are exquisite: Phi-Phi's lush mountain butterfly brilliance in full bloom.

⊗ EATING

On Ko Phi-Phi Don, most resorts and bungalows have restaurants and on the east coast you're more or less bound to them. Restaurants in Ao Ton Sai have improved in quality in recent years and there are tons of options, whether it's seafood, Thai or international you're after, but don't expect fine dining.

Esan Ganeang   Thai $
(Ton Sai Village, Ko Phi-Phi Don; mains 70-150B; ◷10am-midnight) On an alley jammed with hole-in-the-wall places favoured by the locals, family-run Esan Ganeang has fantastic and authentic dishes from the Isan region in northeast Thailand. Come here for fiery salads and soups, as well as more mild curries and noodle dishes packed with flavour. Make sure to order sticky rice to accompany your meal.

Jasmin   Seafood $$
(Hat Laem Thong, Ko Phi-Phi Don; mains 150-500B; ◷10am-10pm) Break out of your posh resort to eat at this fine and relaxed, semi-open-air seafood place right in the middle of idyllic Laem Thong beach. The fresh fish (pay by the weight), lovingly grilled, is the draw, but it also whips up all your Thai classics, Western standards, sandwiches and breakfasts. Also does a reasonable cocktail.

Efe   Turkish $$
(Map p667; ☏095 150 4434; Ton Sai Village, Ko Phi-Phi Don; mains 170-640B; ◷noon-10.30pm; ☈) This Mediterranean newcomer has swiftly become the restaurant of choice for discerning travellers and expats, thanks to its super selection of kebabs served on

From left: Ko Phi-Phi Don nightlife; street food; view over Ko Phi-Phi

sizzling plates, salads and wraps. Also does fine burgers and pizzas. It's a cosy place, with a few tables inside and a tiny patio, so expect to wait for a table during the dinner rush.

🍺 DRINKING & NIGHTLIFE

A rowdy party scene saturates Phi-Phi. Buckets of cheap whisky and Red Bull and sickly sweet cocktails make this the domain of gap-year craziness and really bad hangovers. If you're crashing within earshot of the party, you might as well enjoy it.

Sunflower Bar   Bar

(Ao Lo Dalam, Ko Phi-Phi Don; ⊙11am-2am; 🛜)
This ramshackle driftwood gem is one of Phi-Phi's most chilled-out bars and excellent for nursing a beer while the sun dips into the sea. Destroyed in the 2004 tsunami, it was rebuilt with reclaimed wood. The long-tail booths are named for the four loved ones the owner lost in the deluge.

Banana Bar   Bar

(Ton Sai Village, Ko Phi-Phi Don; ⊙11am-2pm; 🛜)
The 'alt' bar destination in Ton Sai Village,

inland for those seeking to escape the house and techno barrage on the beach, Banana is spread over multiple levels. Climb to the rooftop, or lounge on cushions on the raised decks around the bar. Solid sounds and popular with people who like to roll their own cigarettes.

Also does Mexican food.

☆ ENTERTAINMENT

Kong Siam   Live Music

(Map p667; Ton Sai Village, Ko Phi-Phi Don; ⊙6pm-2am) Live music nightly at this popular place that draws Thais and *fa·ràng* (Westerners). The owner is a talented guitarist, and his mates and the other acts who play here aren't too shabby either.

ℹ️ INFORMATION

ATMs are spread throughout the Tourist Village but not on the eastern beaches. Wi-fi is everywhere.

Break-ins are a problem: lock the door while you sleep and close all windows when you go out.

APIGUIDE / SHUTTERSTOCK ©

Long-tail boats, Ton Sai

Be wary of anyone offering you drugs on the beaches: they may be setting you up for a visit from the local coppers.

Emergency care at **Phi-Phi Island Hospital** (☎075 622151; Ao Ton Sai, Ko Phi-Phi Don) is on the west end of Ao Ton Sai. For anything serious, get on the boat to Krabi or, better still, Phuket.

🛈 GETTING THERE & AWAY

There are also combined boat and minivan tickets to destinations across Thailand, including Bangkok (850B, 11 hours, 3.30pm), Ko Samui (500B, 6½ hours, 10.30am) and Ko Pha-Ngan (600B, seven hours, 10.30am).

Most boats moor at **Tha Ao Ton Sai** (Ton Sai Village, Ko Phi-Phi Don), though a few from Phuket use isolated, northern **Tha Laem Thong** (Ko Phi-Phi Don). Ferries operate year-round, although not always every day.

🛈 GETTING AROUND

There are no roads on Ko Phi-Phi Don. Transport is mostly by foot and chartered long-tails.

Where to Stay

Noise pollution on Ko Phi-Phi Don can be extreme. Expect serious room shortages and extortionate rates at peak holiday times.

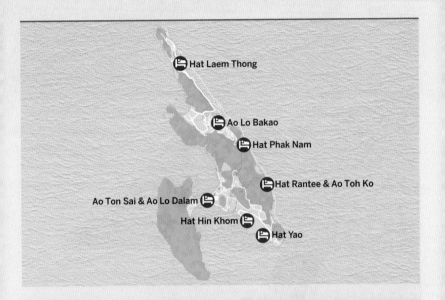

Beach	Atmosphere
Ao Ton Sai & Ao Lo Dalam	Crowded, touristy, loud; cheap lodging
Hat Hin Khom	Noisy, white-sand beach, rocky cove
Hat Laem Thong	Busy, upmarket options
Hat Phak Nam	Beautiful, low-key beach
Hat Rantee & Ao Toh Ko	Low-key, remote; family bungalows
Hat Yao	Great swimming; less busy than Ao Ton Sai
Ao Lo Bakao	Beautiful beach; upmarket lodging

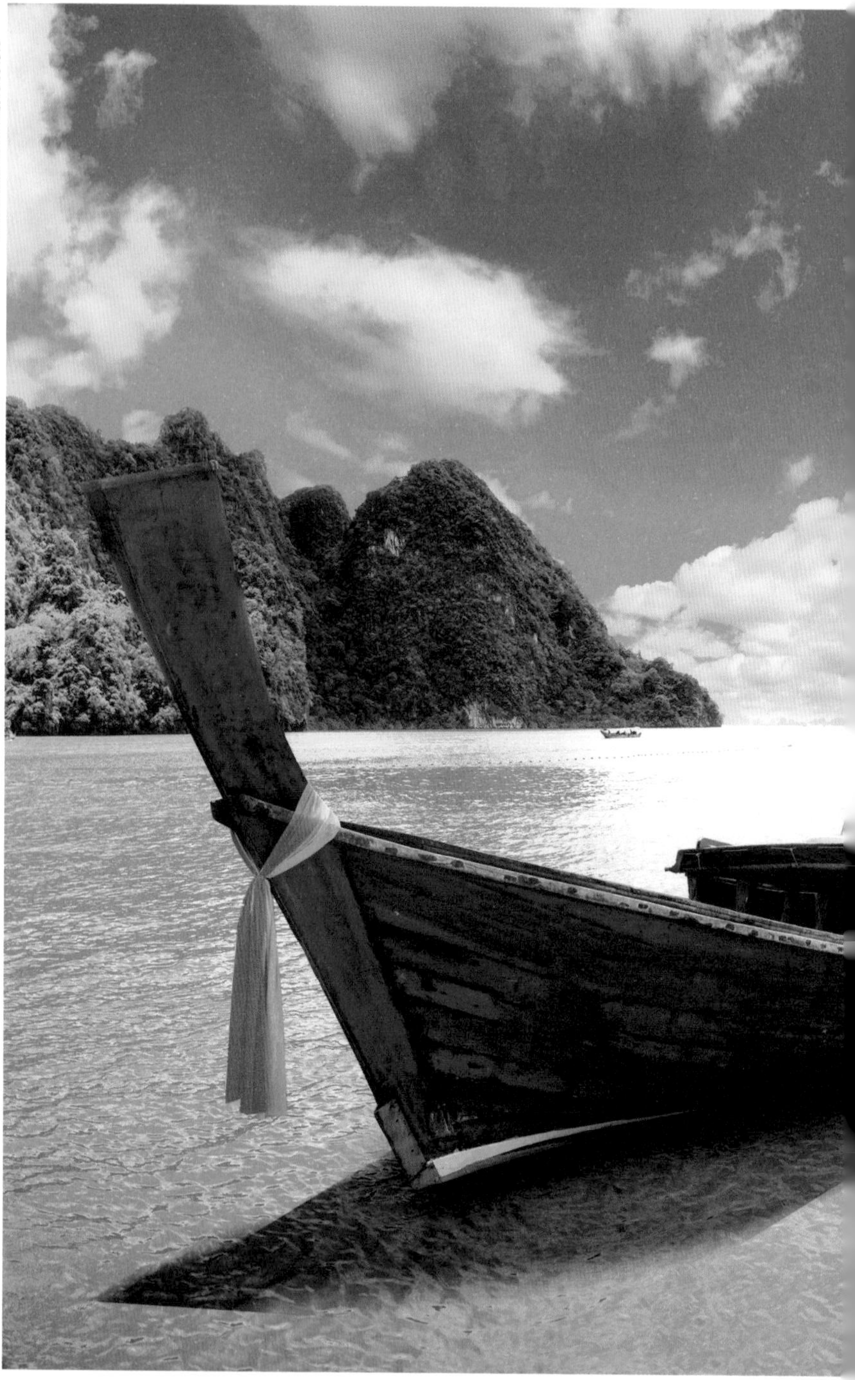

CARLOS CASTILLA / SHUTTERSTOCK ©

PHUKET

Phuket at a Glance...

Branded the 'pearl of the Andaman', Phuket doesn't feel like an island at all. It's so huge (49km long, the biggest in Thailand) that the sea feels secondary to the city accoutrements that have made Phuket the country's premier international resort and expat retirement destination. The beach town of Patong is the ultimate gong show of beach-aholics and go-go bars. Other beaches are more refined and luxury hotels, restaurants and spas dominate the island's attractions.

Phuket in Two Days

Break up the beach routine with a **walking tour** (p222) through Phuket Town's old Sino-Portuguese architecture. Enjoy fabulous fusion cuisine at **Suay** (p214). Party hard in Patong with a stop at good old **Nicky's Handlebar** (p231). Or drink up the cocktails and quirkiness at **Art Space Cafe & Gallery** (p230).

Phuket in Four Days

Devote one day to **Ao Phang-Nga National Park** (p218), a protected bay cluttered with more than 40 peaked karst islands. Spend the night on **Ko Yao** (p219) for a small sip of backwater island living.

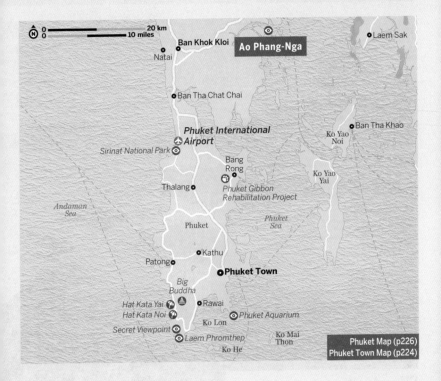

Ao Phang-Nga

Laem Sak

Ban Khok Kloi

Natai

Ban Tha Chat Chai

Ban Tha Khao

Phuket International Airport

Ko Yao Noi

Sirinat National Park

Bang Rong

Ko Yao Yai

Thalang

Phuket Gibbon Rehabilitation Project

Andaman Sea

Phuket

Phuket Sea

Phuket Town

Kathu

Patongo

Big Buddha

Hat Kata Yai

Rawai

Hat Kata Noi

Phuket Aquarium

Ko Lon

Secret Viewpoint

Ko Mai Thon

Laem Phromthep

Ko He

20 km
10 miles

Phuket Map (p226)
Phuket Town Map (p224)

Arriving in Phuket

Phuket International Airport Located 30km northwest of Phuket Town; it takes 45 minutes to an hour to reach the southern beaches from here.

Phuket Bus Terminal 2 Located 4km north of Phuket Town.

Tha Rassada The main pier for boats to Ko Phi-Phi and Krabi (Railay); 3km southeast of Phuket Town.

Sleeping

Phuket is where you splash out for lodging. The island is packed with fashionable resorts and boutique hotels. Save your penny-pinching for other locations. Book hotels well in advance during the busy high season (November to April) and hunt the online booking sites for hotel discounts.

For more information on the best area to stay in, see p233.

Patong

JOHN WALKER / GETTY IMAGES / ISTOCKPHOTO ©

Phuket Beaches

Phuket's beaches are stunning stretches of sand with emerald waters. Like a big family, each beach has its own personality. And the island's modern roads make it easy to explore the island looking for your best match.

Great For...

☑ Don't Miss

Sampling the beaches until you've found a favourite – it's a Phuket tradition.

Patong

Patong is *not* the poster child of sophistication. In fact it makes its bread and butter from the whims of the every man: knock-off T-shirts, girly bars for those in midlife crisis and slapdash commercialism of mediocre quality but immense quantity.

But past the brash beach village is a breathtaking crescent bay. In Thailand, the pretty beaches get all of the attention, for better or worse.

Karon

The next beach south of Patong is Hat Karon, which is a spillover for Patong's hyperactive commercialism. The beach village is a harmless mess of local food, Russian signage, low-key girly bars, T-shirt vendors and pretty Karon Park, with its artificial lake

Laem Singh (p212), Kamala

JETHITA / SHUTTERSTOCK ©

and mountain backdrop. Southern Karon takes on more sophistication.

On the beach, Karon has a broad golden beach that culminates at the northernmost edge (accessible from a rutted road past the roundabout) with glass-like turquoise waters. Megaresorts dominate the beach and there's still more sand space per capita here than at Patong or Kata.

Kata

The classiest of the popular west coast beaches, Kata attracts travellers of all ages and walks of life. While you won't bag a secluded strip of sand, you'll still find lots to do.

Kata has surfing in the shoulder and wet seasons (a rarity in Thailand), terrific day spas, fantastic food and a top-notch yoga studio. The gold-sand beach is carved in

two by a rocky headland. **Hat Kata Yai** (หาด กะตะ ใหญ่; Map p226) lies on the northern side; more secluded **Hat Kata Noi** (หาดกะ ตะน้อย; Map p226) unfurls to the south. The road between them is home to Phuket's original millionaire's row.

Rawai

Now this is a place to live, which is exactly why Phuket's rapidly developing south coast is teeming with retirees, artists, Thai and expat entrepreneurs, and a service sector that, for the most part, moved here from somewhere else.

The region is defined not just by its beaches but also by its lush coastal hills that rise steeply and tumble into the Andaman Sea, forming Laem Phromthep (p225), Phuket's beautiful southernmost point. For a more secluded sunset spot, seek out the **secret viewpoint** (มุมมอง; Map p226; Rte 4233) 1.5km north. These hills are home to neighbourhoods knitted together by just a few roads – though more are being carved into the hills each year and you can almost envision real-estate money chasing away all the seafood grills and tiki bars. Even with the growth you can still feel nature, especially when you hit the beach.

Ask a Phuket local or expat about their favourite beach and everyone's answer is Hat Nai Han, one of Rawai's great swimming spots (be careful of rips in low season).

Kamala

A chilled-out beach hybrid, Kamala lures in a mix of long-term, low-key visitors, families and young couples. The bay is magnificent and serene. Palms and pines mingle on the rocky northern end, where the water is a rich emerald green and the snorkelling around the rock reef is halfway

decent. Flashy new resorts are carved into the southern bluffs and jet skis make an appearance, but Kamala is quiet and laid-back, by Phuket standards.

Laem Singh, 1km north of Kamala, conceals one of the island's most beautiful beaches. Park on the headland and clamber down a steep jungle-frilled path, or charter a long-tail from Hat Kamala. It gets crowded.

Surin

With a wide, blonde beach, water that blends from pale turquoise in the shallows to a deep blue on the horizon, and lush, boulder-strewn headlands, Surin could easily attract visitors on looks alone. Day passes are available at **Catch Beach Club** (Map p226; ☎065 348 2017; www.catchbeach club.com; Hat Bang Thao; day pass low/high

Hat Nai Han, Rawai

season 1000/2000B; ☺9am-late), one of Surin's swishest resorts.

Ao Bang Thao

Stunning, and we mean 'stunning', 8km-long, white-sand Bang Thao is the glue that binds this area's disparate elements. The southern half of the region is dotted with three-star bungalow resorts. Further inland is an old fishing village laced with canals, upstart villa subdivisions and some stellar restaurants. If you see a herd of water buffalo grazing beside a gigantic construction

> ★ Top Tip
> Jamie's Phuket (www.jamiesphuket blog.com) is a fun, intelligent insider's blog written by a long-time Phuket expat.

INGOLF POMPE / LOOK-FOTO / GETTY IMAGES ©

site...well, that's how fast Bang Thao has developed.

Smack in the centre of it all is the somewhat bizarre Laguna Phuket complex, a network of five four- and five-star resorts tied together by an artificial lake (patrolled by tourist shuttle boats) and a paved nature trail. At the northern end, Mother Nature reasserts herself, and a lonely stretch of powder-white sand and tropical blue sea extends past the bustle into the peaceful bliss you originally had in mind.

Sirinat National Park

Comprising the exceptional beaches of Nai Thon, Nai Yang and Mai Khao, along with the former Nai Yang National Park and Mai Khao wildlife reserve, **Sirinat National Park** (อุทยานแห่งชาติสิรินาถ; Map p226; ☎076 328226, 076 327152; www.dnp.go.th; 89/1 Mu 1, Hat Nai Yang; adult/child 200/100B; ☺6am-6pm) encompasses 22 sq km of coastline and 68 sq km of sea, stretching from the northern end of Ao Bang Thao to Phuket's northernmost tip. This is one of the sweetest slices of the island. The whole area is 15 minutes from Phuket International Airport.

> ★ Did You Know?
> Phuket Yacht Haven Marina, on Phuket's northeasterly tip, boasts 320 high-tech berths with deep-water access, available to boats up to 60m in size.

WORRAWOUT VARINTHMANUTKUN / SHUTTERSTOCK ©

Phuket Dining

A melange of cultures come together in the cuisine of this internationally spiced island. Southern Thai food hangs out in the markets, while the high-end resorts do international gastronomy.

Great For...

☑ Don't Miss

You don't need fancy decor to have a fabulous meal. Be sure to check out the street stalls and markets.

Phuket Town

The cultural centre of the island provides authentic dining experiences, from simple market meals to formal dining.

○ Abdul's Roti Shop (Map p224; Th Thalang; mains from 40B; ☺7am-4pm Mon-Sat, to noon Sun) Sticky banana or plain *roti* served with a spicy curry.

○ One Chun (Map p224; ☎076 355909; 48/1 Th Thepkasattri; mains 90-350B; ☺10am-10pm; ☜) Good-value local dishes in an atmospheric shophouse setting.

○ Suay (Map p224; ☎081 797 4135; www.suay restaurant.com; 50/2 Th Takua Pa; mains 300-1000B; ☺5pm-midnight) Fabulous fusion at this converted house, just south of old town.

○ **Walking Street** (Map p224; Th Thalang; ⏰4-10pm Sun) Unfolds along Th Thalang for southern Thai food.

○ **Weekend Market** (p228) A massive market for cheap eats and cheap souvenirs.

○ **Thanon Ranong Day Market** (Map p224; Th Ranong; mains from 35B; ⏰5am-noon) Traces its history back to the port-town days.

Around Phuket

The restaurants on the west coast include a side order of sea view.

○ **Bampot** (Map p226; 📞093 586 9828; www.bampot.co; 19/1 Mu 1, Th Laguna; mains 500-1200B; ⏰6pm-midnight) A modern, urban edge for ambitious European-inspired meals.

○ **Blue Manao** (Map p226; 📞076 385783; 93/13 Mu 3, Th Hat Kamala; mains 130-530B; ⏰noon-11pm; 📶) Relaxed, French-run eatery with heaps of atmosphere.

○ **Boathouse Wine & Grill** (Map p226; 📞076 330015; www.boathousephuket.com; 182 Th Koktanod, Hat Kata; mains 470-1750B, tasting menus 1800-2200B; ⏰11am-10.30pm) Old-school ambience and top-notch Thai and Mediterranean.

○ **Home Kitchen** (Map p226; 📞093 764 6753; www.facebook.com/home.kitchen.bar.bed; 314 Th Phra Barami, Hat Kalim; mains 195-695B; ⏰4-11pm, closed Sun; 📶) A quirky-chic restaurant-bar with creative Thai-Mediterranean food.

○ **Rum Jungle** (Map p226; 📞076 388153; www.facebook.com/rumjungle.rawai.phuket; 69/8 Mu 1, Th Sai Yuan; mains 280-620B; ⏰3-11pm Mon-Sat; 🖊) A family affair spearheaded by a terrific Aussie chef.

○ **Breeze Restaurant** (Map p226; 📞081 271 2320; www.breezecapeyamu.com; Laem Yamu; mains from 700B, tasting menus 2000-2150B; ⏰noon-10pm Wed-Sun; 📶🖊) Inventive European-style dishes infused with local produce.

REINHARD DIRSCHERL / GETTY IMAGES ©

Phuket Water Sports

Ride the waves, the winds or the underwater currents in Phuket's ocean playground. The island has access to some of the Andaman's most famous dive sites. Monsoon weather turns surfing and kiteboarding into adrenalin sports.

Great For...

☑ **Don't Miss**

Take this opportunity to learn a new sport, if you've never mastered the waves.

Diving

Phuket enjoys an enviable location central to the Andaman's top diving destinations.

Most Phuket operators take divers to the nine decent sites near the island, including **Ko Raya Noi** and **Ko Raya Yai** (Ko Racha Noi and Ko Racha Yai), but these spots rank lower on the wow-o-meter. The reef off the southern tip of Raya Noi is the best spot, with soft corals and pelagic fish species, though it's usually reserved for experienced divers. Manta and marble rays are frequently glimpsed here and occasionally a whale shark. Snorkelling here is better than elsewhere on the island.

From Phuket, you can join a huge range of liveaboard diving expeditions to the Similan Islands and Myanmar's Mergui Archipelago. Recommended dive schools:

Diving in the Andaman Sea

❶ Need to Know

The months for water sports depend on the monsoons. Diving is good from November to April, surfing from June to September and kitesurfing nearly all year.

✕ Take a Break

Nikita's (Map p226; ☎076 288703; www. nikitas-phuket.com; Hat Rawai; mains 220-800B; ⏱10am-midnight; 🛜) offers Rawai sea views if you are a better spectator than athlete.

★ Top Tip

Be aware of the monsoon rip tides and undertows that cause drowning. Red flags usually indicate hazardous conditions.

○ **Sea Fun Divers** (Map p226; ☎076 340480; www.seafundivers.com; 29 Soi Karon Nui; 2/3-dive trip 3900/4400B, Open Water Diver certification 18,400B; ⏱9am-6pm)

○ **Rumblefish Adventure** (Map p226; ☎095 441 8665; www.rumblefishadventure.com; 98/79 Beach Centre, Th Kata, Hat Kata; 2/3-dive day trip 3500/3900B; ⏱10am-7pm)

○ **Sunrise Divers** (Map p226; ☎084 626 4646, 076 398040; www.sunrise-divers. com; 269/24 Th Patak East, Hat Karon; 3-dive trip 3700-3900B, liveaboard from 12,900B; ⏱9am-5pm)

Kitesurfing

The best kitesurfing spots are Hat Nai Yang from April to October and Rawai from mid-October to March. **Kite Zone** (Map p226; ☎083 395 2005; www.kitesurfthailand. com; Hat Friendship; 1hr lesson 1100B, 3-day course 10,000B) has all the gear and classes to get you started.

Surfing

With the monsoon's mid-year swell, glassy seas fold into barrels. **Phuket Surf** (Map p226; ☎063 870280; www.phuketsurfing.com; Hat Kata Yai; lessons 1500B, board rental per hour/day 150/500B; ⏱8am-7pm Apr-late Oct) is a good spot for break information and gear rental.

Kata Yai and Hat Nai Han both have surf spots but beware of the vicious undertows. Hat Kalim is sheltered and has a consistent 3m break, considered one of the best breaks on the island. Other spots can be found at Hat Kamala and Laem Singh. Hat Nai Yang has a consistent (if soft) wave that breaks more than 200m offshore. Hat Nai Thon gets better shape.

Ko Khao Phing Kan

MUSTANG_79 /GETTY IMAGES / ISTOCKPHOTO ©

Ao Phang-Nga

Between turquoise bays peppered with craggy limestone towers, brilliant-white beaches and tumbledown fishing villages, Ao Phang-Nga is one of the Andaman's most spectacular landscapes. It can be visited on a day trip from Phuket or with an overnight at Ko Yao.

Great For...

☑ **Don't Miss**

Keep an eye out for the monitor lizard, a small dinosaur lookalike.

Ao Phang-Nga National Park

Established in 1981, 400-sq-km Ao Phang-Nga National Park is famous for its classic karst scenery. Huge vertical cliffs frame 42 islands, some with caves accessible only at low tide and leading into hidden *hôrng* (semi-submerged island caves). The bay is composed of large and small tidal channels, which run north to south through vast mangroves functioning as aquatic highways for fisherfolk and island inhabitants. These are Thailand's largest remaining primary mangrove forests.

In high season (November to April), the bay becomes a clogged package-tourist superhighway. But if you explore in the early morning (ideally from Ko Yao) or stay out later, you'll have more opportunity to enjoy the curious formations and natural splendour.

Ao Phang-Nga National Park

UDOMPETER / SHUTTERSTOCK ©

ⓘ Need to Know

อุทยานแห่งชาติอ่าวพังงา; ☎076 481188; www.
dnp.go.th; adult/child 300/100B; ☺8am-4pm

✕ Take a Break

If you're headed to Ko Yao, the pier
at Bang Rong has vendors for quick
snacks. Just watch out for the monkeys.

★ Top Tip

The best way to explore the bay is by
kayak.

Ko Khao Ping Kan ('Leaning on Itself
Island') is the bay's top tourist draw.
The Thai name efficiently describes the
massive rock formation surrounded by a
small spit of sand but it is Hollywood that
made it famous. In the James Bond film
The Man with the Golden Gun, this rocky
island starred as Scaramanga's hidden
lair. Most tour guides refer to the island as
'James Bond Island' and photo-snapping
visitors and souvenir-hawking vendors have
turned the impressive natural feature into
something of a circus.

A stilted Muslim village clings to Ko
Panyi, a popular lunch stop for tour groups.
It's busy, but several Phang-Nga town tours
enable you to stay overnight and soak up
the scenery without the crowds.

Keep an eye out in the mangroves for
Ao Phang-Nga's marine animals including
monitor lizards, two-banded monitors
(reminiscent of crocodiles when swimming), flying lizards, banded sea snakes,
shore pit vipers and Malayan pit vipers.
Mammals include serows, crab-eating
macaques, white-handed gibbons and
dusky langurs.

Although it's nice to create your own Ao
Phang-Nga itinerary by chartering a boat,
it's easier (and cheaper) to join a tour from
either Phuket or Ko Yao. From Phuket, John
Gray's Seacanoe (p227) is the top choice
for kayakers.

Ko Yao

Soak up island living with a quick escape
from Phuket to the Yao Islands. With mountainous backbones, unspoilt shorelines,
varied bird life and a population of friendly
Muslim fisherfolk, Ko Yao (Ko Yao Yai and
Ko Yao Noi) are laid-back vantage points
for soaking up Ao Phang-Nga's beautiful
karst scenery. The islands are part of Ao
Phang-Nga National Park, but most easily
accessed from Phuket (30km away).

The relative pipsqueak, **Ko Yao Noi** is the main population centre, with fishing, coconut farming and tourism sustaining its small, year-round population. Most resorts occupy the bays on the east coast that recede to mud flats at low tides but the views of the otherworldly rock formations are incredible.

Scenic beaches include gorgeous Hat Pasai, on the southeast coast, and Hat Paradise, on the northeast coast. Hat Tha Khao, on the east coast, has its own dishevelled charm. Hat Khlong Jark is a beautiful sweep of sand with good sleeping options.

Ko Yao Yai is wilder, more remote and less developed; it's twice the size of Yao Noi with a fraction of the infrastructure. The most accessible beaches are slightly developed Hat Lo Pared, on the southwest coast, and powder-white Hat Chonglard on the northeast coast.

Ko Yao can be reached from Phuket's Tha Bang Rong (30 minutes, nine daily departures).

Activities

Touring around the sandy trails is a great way to get to know the island. You can rent bicycles from resorts and guesthouses. And if you don't have time to overnight here, Amazing Bike Tours (p227) runs popular small-group day trips to Ko Yao Noi from Phuket. And you can tackle the water with a kayak, widely available on Ko Yao Noi.

There are over 150 rock-climbing routes in the area. **Mountain Shop Adventures** (☑083 969 2023; www.facebook.com/mountain shopadventures; Tha Khao, Ko Yao Noi; half-day 3200B; ⊘9am-7pm) arranges beginner to

Sunrise off the Phuket coast

advanced outings that involve boat travel to remote limestone cliffs.

Ko Yao is so serene, you will want to harness that energy with a yoga class. **Island Yoga** (087 387 9475; www.thailandyoga retreats.com; 4/10 Mu 4, Hat Tha Khao, Ko Yao Noi; classes 600B) has popular drop-in classes.

Eating

There are several options in Ao Phang-Nga that combine accommodation with restaurants. Some of the best include the following:

○ **Rice Paddy** (076 454255, 082 331 6581; Hat Pasai, Ko Yao Noi; mains 180-890B;

> ★ **Top Tip**
> Respect local beliefs and dress modestly away from the beaches.

noon-10pm & 6-10pm May-Oct;) The flash-fried *sôm·đam* (spicy green papaya salad), falafel and hummus, and spicy, fruit-enhanced curries at this German-owned kitchen are all delcious.

○ **Sabai Corner Restaurant** (076 597497; Hat Khlong Jark, Ko Yao Noi; mains 95-300B; 8am-10pm;) This chilled-out waterside restaurant is a bubbly place to hang out over cocktails, and the Thai and Italian dishes are good (if small) too.

○ **Ko Yao Island Resort** (076 597474; www.koyao.com; 24/2 Mu 5, Hat Khlong Jark, Ko Yao Noi;) There's a snazzy bar-restaurant area and service is stellar.

○ **Chaba Café** (087 887 0625; Hat Khlong Jark, Ko Yao Noi; mains 80-220B; 9am-5pm Mon-Sat;) Rustic-cute with pastel-painted prettiness, driftwood walls, mellow music and a small gallery. Organic-oriented offerings include juices, shakes, tea and home-baked paninis, cookies and cakes, and Thai dishes.

Rock Art in Ao Phang-Nga

Many of Ao Phang-Nga's limestone islands have prehistoric rock art painted on or carved into cave walls and ceilings, rock shelters, cliffs and rock massifs. You can see rock art at Khao Khian, Ko Panyi, Ko Raya, Tham Nak and Ko Phra At Thao. Images at Khao Khian (the most visited cave-art site) contain human figures, fish, crabs, prawns, bats, birds and elephants, as well as boats, weapons and fishing equipment, seemingly referencing some communal effort tied to the all-important sea harvest. Most rock paintings are monochrome, though some have been traced in orange-yellow, blue, grey and black.

JAROMIR CHALABALA / SHUTTERSTOCK ©

> ★ **Did You Know?**
> The national park can be visited on two- to three-hour tours.

Phuket Town Walking Tour

A walk through Phuket Town's core will lead you past the mid-19th-century architectural legacies, grand mansions and narrow shop-houses of the Baba (also known as Peranakan or Straits-Chinese) people.

Start Memory at On On Hotel
Distance 2km
Duration Two hours

6 The early 20th-century **Phra Phitak Chyn Pracha Mansion** has been immaculately restored.

7 The **Chyn Pracha House** (บ้าน ชินประชา, Baan Chyn Pracha; ☎076 211167; 98 Th Krabi; 100B; ⊙9am-4.30pm Mon-Sat), built in 1903 on tin-mining wealth, is now a private home/museum.

5 Dating from 1934, the **Phuket Thaihua Museum** (p225) was the oldest Chinese school in Thailand.

Th Satun

Th Yaowarat

Th Krabi

7 **6** **5** **FINISH**

Fountain Circle

Take a Break

Stop in for local eats at Kopitiam by Wilai (☎083 606 9776; www.facebook.com/kopitiambywilai; 18 Th Thalang; mains 95-180B; ⊙11am-10pm Mon-Sat).

N 0 —————— 500 m
0 —————— 0.25 miles

Classic Photo
Grab a selfie in front of the sun-yellow Thai police building (p231).

4 Soi Romanee is home to restored Sino-Portuguese shop-houses turned boutique hotels.

Th Dibuk

Th Thephasattri

Th Thalang

Th Montri

4

1 START

2 Thai Royal Police

3

Th Phang-Nga

Th Takua Pa

Th Rassada

Th Phuket

Ao Phuket

3 The **Phuket Philatelic Museum** (☎076 211020; Th Montri; ☺9am-4.30pm Mon-Fri, to noon Sat) is a magnificent (if flaking) example of Sino-Portuguese architecture.

2 The former home of the **Standard Chartered Bank** (Th Phang-Nga) is now a museum showcasing Phuket's Baba history.

โรงแรมออนออน
ON ON HOTEL

1 Phuket's first hotel, **Memory at On On** (☎076 363700; www.the memoryhotel.com; 19 Th Phang-Nga), sprawls behind its gleaming-white Sino-Portuguese facade.

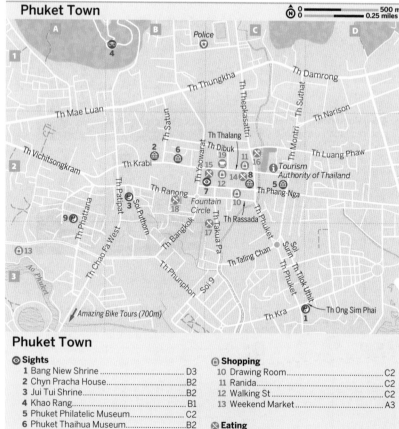

Phuket Town

Sights

Activities, Courses & Tours

Shopping

Eating

Drinking & Nightlife

◎ SIGHTS

◎ Phuket Town

Shrine of the Serene Light
Shrine

(ศาลเจ้าแสงธรรม, Saan Jao Sang Tham; Map p224; Th Phang-Nga; ⊙8.30am-noon & 1.30-5.30pm) **FREE** A handful of Chinese temples pump colour into Phuket Town, but this restored shrine, tucked away up a 50m alley, is particularly atmospheric, with its Taoist etchings on the walls and the vaulted ceiling stained from incense plumes. The altar is always fresh with flowers and burning candles. The shrine is said to have been built by a local family in the 1890s.

Phuket Thaihua Museum
Museum

(พิพิธภัณฑ์ภูเก็ตไทยหัว; Map p224; ☏076 211224; 28 Th Krabi; 200B; ☺9am-5pm) Formerly a Chinese language school, this flashy museum is filled with photos and English-language exhibits on Phuket's history, from the Chinese migration (many influential Phuketian families are of Chinese origin) and the tin-mining era to local cuisine, fashion and literature. There's an overview of the building's history, which is a stunning combination of Chinese and European architectural styles, including art deco, Palladianism and a Chinese gable roof and stucco.

Khao Rang
Viewpoint

(เขารัง, Phuket Hill; 🅿) For a bird's-eye view of the city, climb (or drive) up Khao Rang, 3km northwest of the town centre. A new viewing platform has opened up the commanding panoramas across Phuket Town and all the way to Chalong Bay, Laem Phanwa and Big Buddha. It's at its best during the week, when the summit is relatively peaceful. There are a few restaurants up here. It's about an hour's walk, but don't try it at night. A taxi up costs 700B.

◎ Around Phuket

Big Buddha
Buddhist Site

(พระใหญ่; Map p226; www.mingmongkolphuket. com; off Rte 4021; ☺6am-7pm; 🅿) **FREE** High atop the Nakkerd Hills, northwest of Chalong circle, and visible from half the island, the 45m-high Big Buddha sits grandly on Phuket's finest viewpoint. It's a tad touristy, but tinkling bells and flapping flags mean there's an energetic pulse. Pay your respects at the tented golden shrine, then step up to the glorious plateau, where you can peer into Kata's perfect bay, glimpse the shimmering Karon strand and, to the southeast, survey the pebble-sized channel islands of Chalong Bay.

Laem Phromthep
Viewpoint

(แหลมพรหมเทพ; Map p226; Rte 4233) If you want to see the luscious Andaman Sea bend around Phuket, then come here, to the island's southernmost point. The cape is crowned by a mod lighthouse shaped like a concrete crab, and an evocative elephant shrine, so you'll want to stay a while. At sunset the hordes descend in luxury buses; if you crave privacy, take the faint fisherman's trail downhill to the rocky peninsula that reaches into the ocean and watch the sun drop in peace.

⭐ ACTIVITIES

Phuket Elephant Sanctuary
Wildlife, Volunteering

(Map p226; ☏094 990 3649; www.phuket elephantsanctuary.org; 100 Mu 2, Pa Klok, on 4027 Hwy; adult/child 3000/1500B; ☺9.30am-1pm & 2-5.30pm; 🚼) Phuket's only genuine elephant sanctuary is a refuge for animals who were mistreated for decades while working in the logging and tourism industries. During the morning tour, you get to feed them, before tagging along a few metres away as the aged pachyderms wander the forest, bathe and hang out. It's a rare opportunity that almost all visitors rave about.

Suay Cooking School
Cooking

(Map p224; ☏081 797 4135; www.suay restaurant.com; 50/2 Th Takua Pa; classes per person 2500B) Learn from one of Phuket's top chefs at the most laid-back, soulful and fun cooking school around. Noy Tammasak leads visitors through the local market and teaches how to make three dishes, before cracking open a bottle of wine to enjoy with your culinary creations. Highly recommended; minimum three people.

Cool Spa
Spa

(Map p226; ☏076 371000; www.coolspaphuket. com; Sri Panwa, 88 Mu 8, Th Sakdidej; treatments from 4500B; ☺10am-9pm) One of the best spas on Phuket, this is an elegant

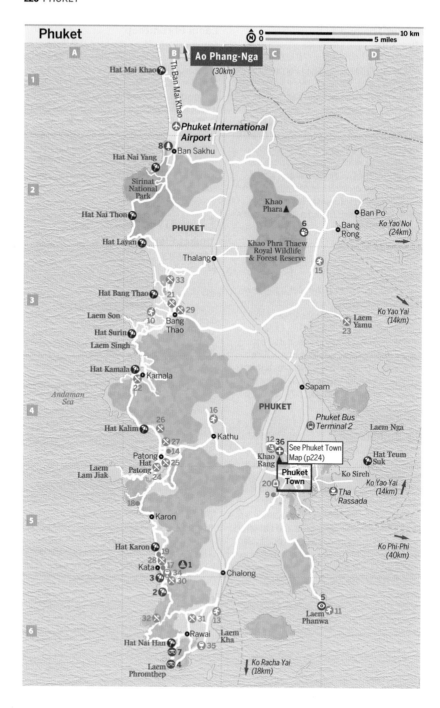

Phuket

0 — 10 km
0 — 5 miles

Ao Phang-Nga
(30km)

Hat Mai Khao

Th Ban Mai Khao

Phuket International Airport
8 Ban Sakhu

Hat Nai Yang

Sirinat National Park

PHUKET

Khao Phara

6

Ban Po

Bang Rong

Ko Yao Noi
(24km)

Hat Nai Thon

Khao Phra Thaew Royal Wildlife & Forest Reserve

Hat Layan

Thalang

15

Ko Yao Yai
(14km)

33

Hat Bang Thao
21

Laem Son
10

29

Bang Thao

Hat Surin

Laem Singh

Laem Yamu
23

Hat Kamala
22

Kamala

Andaman Sea

Sapam

PHUKET

16

Phuket Bus Terminal 2

Laem Nga

Hat Kalim
26

Kathu

12 36

Khao Rang

See Phuket Town Map (p224)

Hat Teum Suk

Patong
27

14

Hat Patong
25

24

Phuket Town

Ko Sireh

20

Ko Yao Yai
(14km)

9

Tha Rassada

Laem Lam Jiak

18

Karon

Ko Phi-Phi
(40km)

Hat Karon
19

28

17

Kata
34

3

1

Chalong

30

2

5

Laem Phanwa

11

32

31

13

Rawai
35

Laem Kha

Ko Racha Yai
(18km)

Hat Nai Han
7

4

Laem Phromthep

Phuket

wonderland of fruit-infused wraps, facials and scrubs, and hilltop ocean-view pools. Oh, and then there's the dreamy setting, on the southernmost tip of Phuket's Laem Phanwa.

TOURS

John Gray's Seacanoe   Kayaking
(Map p226; ☑076 254505; www.johngray-sea canoe.com; 86 Soi 2/3, Th Yaowarat; adult/child from 3950/1975B) ✔ The original, the most reputable and by far the most ecologically sensitive kayaking company on Phuket. The 'Hong by Starlight' trip dodges the crowds, involves sunset paddling and will introduce you to Ao Phang-Nga's famed after-dark bioluminescence. Like any good brand in Thailand, John Gray's 'Seacanoe' name and itineraries have been frequently copied. Located 3.5km north of Phuket Town.

Amazing Bike Tours   Cycling
(Map p226; ☑087 263 2031, 076 283436; www. amazingbiketoursthailand.asia; 32/4 Th Chaofa;

half/full-day trip 1900/3200B) This highly popular adventure outfitter leads small groups on half-day bicycle tours through the villages of northeast Phuket, as well as on terrific full-day trips around Ko Yao Noi and more challenging three-day adventure rides around Khao Sok National Park (14,900B) and Krabi Province (15,900B). Prices include bikes, helmets, meals, water and national-park entry fees.

SHOPPING

The following are located in Phuket Town.

Ranida   Antiques, Fashion
(Map p224; ☑076 214801; 119 Th Thalang; ☺10am-8pm Mon-Sat) An elegant antique gallery and boutique featuring antiquated Buddha statues and sculptures, organic textiles, and ambitious, exquisite high-fashion women's clothing inspired by vintage Thai garments and fabrics.

Drawing Room · Art

(Map p224; ☑086 899 4888; isara380@hotmail.com; 56 Th Phang-Nga; ☺9am-6pm) With a street-art vibe reminiscent of pre-boom Brooklyn or East London, this wide-open cooperative is by far the stand-out gallery in a town full of them. Canvases might be vibrant abstract squiggles or comical pen-and-ink cartoons. Metallic furniture and bicycles line concrete floors. House music thumps at low levels.

Weekend Market · Market

(Map p226; off Th Chao Fa West; ☺4-10pm Sat & Sun) For a classic 'market' feel, hit the massive Weekend Market, 3km southwest of Phuket Town. It flogs everything, from fake designer bags and snazzy sunglasses to *moo·ay tai* (Thai boxing; also spelled *muay Thai*) shorts and mini speakers. Things are liveliest in the evening, when it's a fantastic spot for a cheap feed. Mototaxis charge 30B from Phuket Town.

✖ EATING

For Phuket highlights, see the Phuket Dining Top Experience (p214). Other noteworthy spots:

✖ Ao Bang Thao

Pesto · Thai, International $$

(Map p226; ☑082 423 0184; Th Bandon-Cherngtalay; mains 135-530B; ☺noon-11pm; ✐) Mix a Paris-trained Thai chef with a simple street-side, semi-open-air location and you get delicious, wallet-friendly Thai and international food. Light pesto pasta and lobster lasagne whizz you to the Mediterranean. Otherwise, stay local with grilled tuna on Andaman seaweed, *đôm yam gûng* (spicy-sour prawn soup), deep-fried turmeric-spiced fish of the day and all your favourite curries.

Taste Bar & Grill · Fusion $$$

(Map p226; ☑087 886 6401; www.tastebargrill.com; 3/2 Mu 5, Th Srisoonthorn; mains 390-990B; ☺noon-11pm Tue-Sun; ☎) Minimalist modern lines, top-notch service, a sophisticated but chilled-out vibe and delicious fusion food

From left: Weekend Market; Phuket Elephant Sanctuary (p225); Shrine of the Serene Light (p224)

make this eatery an outstanding choice. The menu features Thai and Mediterranean influences, but the steaks are great too. You can't go wrong with the seafood, and there are excellent salads and a huge array of starters.

Karon

Pad Thai Shop Thai $

(Map p226; Th Patak East; mains 50-80B; ⊘8am-7pm, closed Fri) This glorified roadside food shack makes rich, savoury chicken stew and absurdly good *kôw pàt boo* (fried rice with crab), *pàt see·éw* (fried noodles) and noodle soup. It also serves up some of the best *pàt tai* we've ever tasted: spicy and sweet, packed with tofu, egg and peanuts, and plated with spring onions, bean sprouts and lime.

Don't miss the house-made chilli sauces.

Kata

Red Duck Thai $$

(Map p226; ☑084 850 2929; 88/3 Th Koktanod; mains 240-380B; ⊘noon-11pm Tue-Sun; 🛜🍴) Dishes here are more expensive than at

other Thai restaurants, but they're delicious, MSG-free and prepared with the freshest of ingredients. The seafood curries and soups are especially fine. There's also a big vegan selection of Thai classics, such as pineapple or coconut curry and a vegetable *larb*. Eat inside or on the small outdoor terrace. Service is excellent.

Patong

Ella International $$

(Map p226; ☑076 344253; 100/19-20 Soi Post Office; mains 150-400B; ⊘9am-midnight; 🛜) This moulded-concrete, industrial-feel bistro-cafe is a lovely surprise. Inventive all-day breakfasts feature spicy Rajasthani scrambled eggs, massaman (curry) chicken tacos, omelettes stuffed with chicken and veg, and baguette French toast with caramelised banana. At night, it's also a bar and a cool spot for a cocktail. There are similarly styled rooms for rent upstairs.

Georgia Restaurant Georgian $$

(Map p226; ☑076 390595; 19 Th Sawatdirak; mains 200-390B; ⊘noon-10pm, closed Sun)

BILL KINGMAN / GETTY IMAGES ©

The influx of Russian visitors to Patong has seen a corresponding rise in eateries catering to them. Georgia is the pick of the bunch, offering Russian salads and dumplings alongside delicious *khachapuri*, a cheese-filled bread; *ajapsandali*, a rich, vegetarian stew; and classic eastern European dishes such as *solyanka*, a spicy, sour meat soup served in a clay pot.

Vegetarian Festival

Deafening popping sounds fill the streets, the air is thick with smoke, and people pierce their cheeks with skewers and knives. Blood streams from their self-inflicted wounds. No, this isn't a war zone, this is the **Vegetarian Festival** (www.phuketvegetarian.com), one of Phuket's most important celebrations.

The festival takes place during the first nine days of the ninth lunar month of the Chinese calendar (late September to early October) and celebrates the beginning of 'Taoist Lent'. Those participating as mediums bring the nine deities to earth by entering a trance state and performing self-mortification. The temporarily possessed mediums (primarily men) stop at shopfront altars to pick up offerings.

Phuket Town's festival focuses on several Chinese temples, including **Jui Tui Shrine** (ศาลเจ้าจุ้ยตุ่ยเต้าโบ๊เก้ง; Map p224; Soi Puthorn; ⊙8am-8pm) **FREE**; **Bang Niew Shrine** (ศาลเจ้าบางเหนียว; Map p224; Th Ong Sim Phai; ⊙6am-6pm) **FREE**; and **Sui Boon Tong Shrine** (ศาลเจ้าซุ่ยบุ่นต๋อง; Map p224; Soi Lorong; ⊙hours vary) **FREE**.

Local Chinese claim the festival was started in 1825 in Kathu, by a theatre troupe from China who performed a nine-day penance of self-piercing, meditation and vegetarianism after becoming seriously ill for failing to propitiate the nine emperor gods of Taoism.

Phuket's Tourism Authority of Thailand office prints festival schedules.

Street procession during the Vegetarian Festival
BULE SKY STUDIO / SHUTTERSTOCK ©

No.9 2nd Restaurant — Asian $$
(Map p226; ☑076 624445; 143 Th Phra Barami; mains 165-800B; ⊙11.30am-11.30pm, closed 5th & 20th of every month) Deceptively simple, with wooden tables and photo-strewn walls, this is one of the best, busiest restaurants in Patong, thanks to the inventive and delicious mix of Thai, Japanese and Western dishes. It's a rare feat for a kitchen to be able to turn out authentic sushi, vegetarian versions of Thai curries and a lamb shank without any dip in quality.

🍷 DRINKING & NIGHTLIFE
🍸 Kata

Art Space Cafe & Gallery — Bar
(Map p226; ☑090 156 0677; Th Kade Kwan; ⊙11am-1am) Hands down the most fabulously quirky bar in Phuket, this trippy, multi-use space bursts with colour and is smothered in uniquely brushed canvases and sculptures celebrating, especially, the feminine form. It's the work of an eccentric creative and his tattoo-artist wife, who whip up both decent cocktails and veggie meals (160B to 400B). There's normally live music around 8pm.

Ska Bar — Bar
(Map p226; www.skabar-phuket.com; 186/12 Th Koktanod; ⊙1pm-2am) Tucked into the rocks on the southernmost curl of Hat Kata Yai and seemingly intertwined with the trunk of a grand old banyan tree, Ska is our choice for seaside sundowners. The Thai bartenders add to the laid-back Rasta vibe, and buoys, paper lanterns and flags dangle from the canopy. There's normally a fire show on Friday nights.

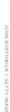

Nightlife in Patong

🍸 Patong

Nicky's Handlebar
Bar

(Map p226; 📞076 343211; www.nickyhandle
bars.com; 41 Th Rat Uthit; ⊙7am-1am; 🛜) This
fun biker bar welcomes all, wheels or no
wheels. Once a bit of a dive, Nicky's has
never looked better. There's a good selection of beers and the menu encompasses
Western and Thai, including what the bar
claims is Thailand's spiciest burger. You can
get your own wheels here by asking about
Harley **tours** (half/full-day tour incl bike hire
from 7000/9000B) and **hire** (from 4800B).

🍸 Phuket Town

Bookhemian
Cafe

(Map p224; 📞098 090 0657; www.bookhemian.
com; 61 Th Thalang; ⊙9am-7pm Mon-Fri, to
8.30pm Sat & Sun; 🛜) Every town should
have a coffee house this cool, with a
split-level design that enables it to be both
a cafe and an art exhibition space. Used
books (for sale) line the front room, bicycles hang from the wall, and the offerings
include gourmet coffee, tea and cakes, as

well as all-day breakfasts, salads, sandwiches and pasta.

ℹ️ INFORMATION

Bangkok Hospital Phuket (Map p226; 📞076
254425; www.phukethospital.com; Th Hongyok
Uthit) The Phuket outpost of this reliable Thai
chain of hospitals with international standards is
located 3km north of Phuket Town.

Police (Map p224; 📞076 212046, 191; Th Chumphon) The main police station in Phuket Town.

Tourism Authority of Thailand (TAT; Map p224;
📞076 211036; www.tourismthailand.org/Phuket;
191 Th Thalang; ⊙8.30am-4.30pm) Has maps,
brochures, transport advice and info on boat
trips to nearby islands.

ℹ️ GETTING THERE & AWAY

AIR

Phuket International Airport (📞076 632 7230;
www.phuketairportthai.com) is 30km northwest
of Phuket Town. It takes 45 minutes to an hour to
reach the southern beaches from here. A number

 Phuket for Children

There's plenty for kids to do on Phuket. **Phuket Aquarium** (สถานแสดงพันธุ์สัตว์น้ำภูเก็ต; Map p226; ☏076 391126; www.phuketaquarium.org; 51 Th Sakdidej; adult/child 180/100B; ☺8.30am-4.30pm; P) and a visit to the tiny **Phuket Gibbon Rehabilitation Project** (โครงการคืน ชะนีสู่ป่า; Map p226; ☏076 260492; www.gibbonproject.org; off Rte 4027; admission by donation; ☺9am-4.30pm, to 3pm Sat; P) ✆ are terrific animal-themed activities that are sure to please. The newest attraction for kids of all ages, but especially for tweens and above, is the **Phuket Wake Park** (Map p226; ☏076 510151; www.phuketwakepark.com; 86/3 Mu 6, Th Vichitsongkram, Kathu; adult/child 2hr visit 750/350B, day pass 1250/650B; ☺9am-6pm; ⊞), where you can learn to wake board by buzzing a lake nestled in the mountains of Kathu.

White-handed gibbon
NICKOLAY STANEV / SHUTTERSTOCK ©

of carriers serve domestic destinations including Bangkok, Chiang Mai and Ko Samui.

BUS & MINIVAN

Interprovincial buses depart from **Phuket Bus Terminal 2** (Map p226; Th Thepkrasattri), 4km north of Phuket Town. Air-con minivans go to popular tourist destinations; tickets can be bought from travel agents.

BOAT

Tha Rassada (Map p226), 3km southeast of Phuket Town, is the main pier for boats to Ko Phi-Phi and Krabi (Railay).

GETTING AROUND

Large *sŏrng·tăa·ou* (pick-up minibuses) run regularly from Phuket Town's Th Ranong near the day market to the beaches (20B to 40B, 30 minutes to 1½ hours, 7am to 5pm). Chartered túk-túk connect with the beaches.

Where to Stay

The beaches at the southern and northern ends of the west coast feel like escapes from the real world. Patong and Karon are very hyperactive.

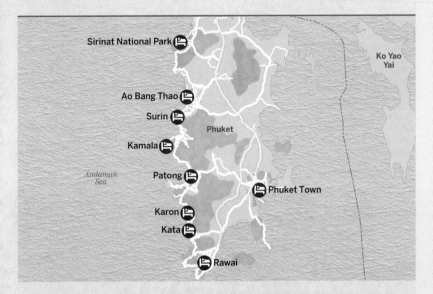

Area	Atmosphere
Phuket Town	Quirky, affordable lodging; commute to the beach
Patong	Lots of nightlife and dining; noisy, crowded and seedy
Karon	Lively beach, mix of budget lodging; slightly seedy
Kata	Lively beach, mainly high-end resorts
Rawai	Quiet beach, high-end resorts, local eats
Kamala	Relaxed beach, boutique resorts
Surin	Low-key beach, classy resorts
Ao Bang Thao	Luxury resort complex
Sirinat National Park	Natural beach, a mix of accommodation; far from dining and nightlife

AYUTHAYA

Ayuthaya at a Glance...

Ayuthaya reigned as the Siamese capital for more than 400 years. The island city was regaled at the time for its golden temples and architectural splendour. The kingdom fended off political intrigue and expansionist European powers, but after frequent wars with the Burmese, the city eventually fell in 1767. War, looting and gravity took their toll on Ayuthaya's once great temples and today the remaining ruins are designated as a Unesco World Heritage Site. A quiet provincial town sprung up around the ruins, providing a glimpse into ordinary Thai life with a historic backdrop.

Ayuthaya in Two Days

Visit the interactive exhibition at the **Ayutthaya Tourist Center** (p240) and discover why the city was once so great. Cycle around **Ayuthaya Historical Park** (p238), stopping at **Lung Lek** (p245) for the best noodles in town. The following day wander among the ruins then finish your visit with a feast at **Pae Krung Gao** (p245).

Ayuthaya in Four Days

On your third day head out of the city to visit **Bang Pa In Palace** (p243). On the way back, drop by at **Wat Phanan Choeng** (p240) to ensure good luck by releasing fish back into the river and return to the island in time to visit the nostalgic **Million Toy Museum** (p244).

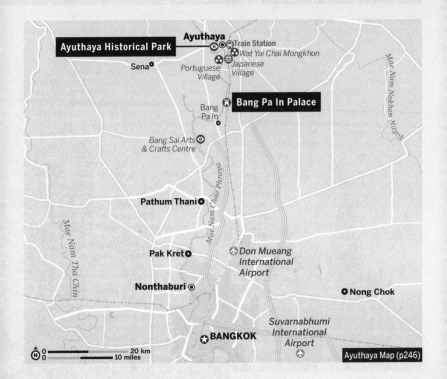

Ayuthaya

Ayuthaya Historical Park

Train Station

Wat Yai Chai Mongkhon

Sena

Portuguese Village

Japanese Village

Bang Pa In

Bang Pa In Palace

Bang Sai Arts & Crafts Centre

Mae Nam Nakhon Nayok

Pathum Thani

Mae Nam Chao Phraya

Mae Nam Tha Chin

Pak Kret

✈ *Don Mueang International Airport*

Nonthaburi

Nong Chok

Suvarnabhumi International Airport

✪ **BANGKOK**

N 0 | 20 km
0 | 10 miles

Ayuthaya Map (p246)

Arriving in Ayuthaya

Bus stop Most visitors arrive via bus or minivan from Bangkok. The bus stop is in the centre of town.

Train station Services from Bangkok's Hualamphong station make the journey here. Ayuthaya's train station is across the river from the centre of town.

Sleeping

The primary guesthouse zone is on the island around Soi 2, Th Naresuan – a convenient location with easy access to the historical park, restaurants, markets and transport – and there are also budget options close to the train station. Midrange and top-end hotels typically congregate around the river.

COWARDLION / SHUTTERSTOCK ©

Ayuthaya Historical Park

At its zenith, Ayuthaya was home to more than 400 temples. Today dozens of them have been partially restored, leaving the naked stupas, roofless chapels and headless Buddha images to evocatively tell the kingdom's tale of war with enemies and time.

Great For...

☑ Don't Miss

At night the temple ruins are dramatically lit up, providing great photo ops.

The historical park is divided into two parts: sites on the island and sites off the island. You can visit the island on a bicycle but will need a motorcycle or chartered transport to go beyond.

Wat Phra Si Sanphet

One of the holiest sites, **Wat Phra Si Sanphet** (วัดพระศรีสรรเพชญ์; 50B; ⊙8am-6pm) has three magnificent stupas and served as the model for Bangkok's Wat Phra Kaew. The temple was built in the late 15th century inside the palace grounds. It was Ayuthaya's largest temple and once contained a 16m-high standing Buddha (Phra Si Sanphet) covered with approximately 143kg of gold.

Wihan Phra Mongkhon Bophit

NATTUL / SHUTTERSTOCK ©

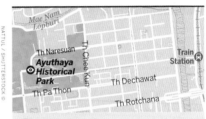

Buddha head is held above the ground by entangled bodhi tree roots.

Wihan Phra Mongkhon Bophit

Next to Wat Phra Si Sanphet, this **sanctuary hall** (วิหารพระมงคลบพิตร; ◷8am-5pm) FREE houses one of Thailand's largest bronze Buddha images. The 12.5m-high figure (17m with the base) was badly damaged by a lightning-induced fire around 1700, and again when the Burmese sacked the city. The Buddha and the building were repaired in the 20th century.

Wat Mahathat

Founded in 1374, during the reign of King Borom Rachathirat I, **Wat Mahathat** (วัดมหาธาตุ; Th Chee Kun; 50B; ◷8am-6.30pm) was the seat of the supreme patriarch and the kingdom's most important temple. Today the ruins are best known for a curious interplay between nature and art: a sandstone

Wat Ratchaburana

The prang in this **temple** (วัดราชบูรณะ; off Th Naresuan; 50B; ◷8am-6pm) is one of the best extant versions in the city, with detailed carvings of lotus and mythical creatures. You can climb inside it to visit the brightly painted crypt, if you aren't afraid of heights, small spaces or bats. The temple was founded in 1424 by King Borom Rachathirat II on the cremation site for his two brothers who died fighting each other for the throne.

Wat Chai Wattanaram

This is the most impressive off-island **site** (วัดไชยวัฒนาราม; Ban Pom; 50B; ◷8am-6pm) thanks to its 35m-high central *prang* (Khmer-style stupa) and overall good condition. It was built by King Prasat Thong beginning in 1630 (and taking around 20 years) to honour his mother.

Wat Phanan Choeng

A bevy of popular merit-making ceremonies makes this temple (วัดพนัญเชิง; Khlong Suan Plu; 20B; ⊘daylight hours) a bustling place on weekends. The temple marks the historic location of a Chinese community who settled in Ayuthaya in the 14th century and is often associated with Zheng He (known as Sam Po Khong in Thailand), the Chinese emissary who explored Southeast Asia in the 15th century.

The signature attraction is the 19m-high Phra Phanan Choeng Buddha, which was created in 1324 and sits inside a sanctuary surrounded by 84,000 small Buddha images. The Chinese shrine facing the river is especially colourful.

Wat Na Phra Men

This **temple** (วัดหน้าพระเมรุ; Lum Phli; 20B; ⊘daylight hours) was one of the few to escape the wrath of Myanmar's invading army in 1767 since it served as their main base. The *bòht* (ordination hall) is massive, larger than most modern ones, and the very holy main Buddha image wears royal attire, which was very common in the late Ayuthaya era. Despite what the English sign inside says, it's made of bronze, not gold.

Ayutthaya Tourist Center

This multi-purpose building houses the **tourist information centre** (ศูนย์ท่องเที่ยวอยุธยา; ☎035 246076; off Th Si Sanphet; ⊘8.30am-4.30pm) FREE on the ground floor.

Reclining Buddha, Wat Yai Chai Mongkhon

But the reason for a visit is the excellent upstairs museum, which puts Ayuthaya history into context with displays about the temples and daily life. Also upstairs is the tiny but interesting Ayutthaya National Art Museum.

Ayuthaya Historical Study Centre

This modern **museum** (ศูนย์ศึกษาประวัติศาสตร์ อยุธยา; ☏035 245123; Th Rotchana; adult/child 100/50B; ☉9am-4.30pm Mon-Fri, to 5pm Sat & Sun) funded by Japan features exhibitions on the lives of traditional villagers and the

✕ **Take a Break**
Drop in to Bang Ian Night Market (Th Bang Ian; snacks from 10B; mains 30-100B; ☉5-8.30pm) if you're visiting the park in the late afternoon to evening.

AMNAT30 / SHUTTERSTOCK ©

foreign communities during the Ayuthaya kingdom, plus a few dioramas of the city's former glories.

Chao Sam Phraya National Museum

The largest **museum** (พิพิธภัณฑสถานแห่งชาติ เจ้าสามพระยา; ☏035 244570; cnr Th Rotchana & Th Si Sanphet; adult/child 150B/free; ☉9am-4pm Wed-Sun) in the city displays many of the treasures unearthed during excavations of the ruins, including the golden treasures found in the crypts of Wat Mahathat and Wat Ratchaburana. Despite these treasures, the building lacks English signs and is a bit outdated.

Wat Yai Chai Mongkhon

King U Thong founded this **temple** (วัด ใหญ่ชัยมงคล; 20B; ☉6am-6pm) in 1357 to house monks returning from ordination in Sri Lanka. In 1592 King Naresuan built its fantastic bell-shaped *chedi* (stupa) after a victory over the Burmese. The landscaped gardens make this one of Ayuthaya's most photogenic ruins. There's a 7m-long reclining Buddha near the entrance and the local belief is that if you can get a coin to stick to the Buddha's feet, good luck will come your way.

Wat Phu Khao Thong

Phu Khao Thong (เจดีย์ภูเขาทอง; ☉daylight hours) FREE is a huge white stupa built by the Burmese to commemorate their occupation of Ayutthaya in 1569. The larger-than-life statue is a memorial to the all-conquering Thai King Naresuan, who ousted the Burmese. Surrounding him are reliefs of his heroic exploits, including wrestling a crocodile, and dozens of statues of fighting cockerels.

★ **Did You Know?**
Bicycles are a great way of getting around more rural, less-trafficked corners of Thailand such as Ayuthaya Historical Park.

AGFORZA / SHUTTERSTOCK ©

Bang Pa In Palace

A former summer palace for the Thai kings, Bang Pa In is an eclectic assortment of architectural styles ranging from Chinese throne rooms to Gothic churches.

Great For...

☑ Don't Miss

Feeding the fish that live in the palace lake – it is an act of merit-making for Thai Buddhists and is believed to bring luck.

Bang Pa In was built beside the Chao Phraya River in the 17th century during the reign of King Prasat Thong. The palace was abandoned by the Ayuthaya Kings and later revived by the Bangkok Kings. The European formal gardens, statuary and residences were introduced by King Rama V (Chulalongkorn), an enthusiast of Western art and architecture. At the time of use, the property was divided into two sectors by an artificial lake – the outer was for ceremonial use and inner for the royal family only.

Saphakhan Ratchaprayun

A striking European-style residence originally built for the king's brothers now houses a small history museum about the palace.

PHATHAWUT THIPAPAL / SHUTTERSTOCK ©

Phra Thinang Warophat Phiman

Built in 1876, this neoclassical building served as King Rama V's residence and throne hall. Historical paintings decorate the chambers. During the current royal family's rare visits, they stay here.

Aisawan Thiphya-At

A classical Thai-style pavilion is scenically situated in the palace lake. Inside is a statue of King Rama V.

Phra Thinang Wehut Chamrun

A grand Chinese-style palace, known as the 'Residence of Heavenly Light', was a gift to King Rama V from the Chinese Chamber of Commerce in 1889. On the ground floor is an ornate throne room.

Ho Withun Thatsana

'Sages' Lookout' is a brightly painted lookout tower. Climb the spiral staircase to reach King Rama V's favourite viewpoint.

Wat Niwet Thamaprawat

King Rama V loved mixing Thai and Western styles. This Buddhist temple located on an island across the river is a Gothic-church replica complete with stained-glass windows, a steeple and statues of knights in shining armour standing among Buddha images. Take the cable car across the river.

Memorial to Queen Sunanda

A marble obelisk remembers King Rama V's consort Queen Sunanda, who drowned on the boat journey to the palace. Thai law forbade courtiers from touching the queen, so nobody dared jump in to save her. The law was later changed.

Handmade fabric, Bang Sai Arts & Crafts Centre

CHARLIE WARADEE / SHUTTERSTOCK ©

◉ SIGHTS

Million Toy Museum Museum

(พิพิธภัณฑ์ล้านของเล่นเกริกยุ้นพันธ์; ☑081 890 5782; www.milliontoymuseum.com; Th U Thong; adult/child 50/20B; ☺9am-4pm Tue-Sun; 🅿) Thousands of toys from across the decades are amassed in this private museum. Much of the exhibition is unlabelled, so it remains a mystery why rare porcelain elephants and retro racing cars are filed alongside mass-produced Shrek and Pikachu figurines. Still, the collection is in a pleasantly cool atrium, a refreshing change from sweating it out at Ayuthaya's temple ruins.

We just pray the creepy soldiers and decaying doll babies don't awake at night.

Bang Sai Arts & Crafts Centre Cultural Centre

(ศูนย์ศิลปาชีพบางไทร; adult/child 100/50B; ☺9am-5pm Tue-Sun) Observe basket weaving, ceramic painting and myriad traditional Thai crafts at this cultural complex, 30km south of Ayuthaya. Whether you're in the market for delicate silk purses or carved wooden furniture, it's an excellent place to browse handmade souvenirs. You'll need private transport to visit the centre from Ayuthaya.

⊙ TOURS

Ayutthaya Boat & Travel Tours

(☑081 733 5687; www.ayutthaya-boat.com; cnr Th Chee Kun & Th Rotchana; ☺9am-5pm Mon-Sat) Combine cycling and paddling with cultural activities with reliable Ayutthaya Boat & Travel. Excursions include half-day cycling tours around Ayuthaya (1050B per person), day trips to Bang Pa In Palace (p243) by bike and boat (2150B per person) and two-day outings around the countryside, including an overnight stay with a local family (5050B per person).

⊗ EATING

Malakor Thai $

(www.facebook.com/malakorrestaurant; Th Chee Kun; mains 40-200B; ☺restaurant noon-10pm, coffee shop 8am-4pm; ✳️ 🛜) Touristy but satisfying, Malakor has a big menu, a great cook whipping up catfish curry and *pàd gàprow gài* (chicken with basil), and a relaxing wooden hut to enjoy it in. You will need to be patient with the service.

Sainam Pomphet   Thai $
(Th U Thong; mains 100-150B; ⏰10am-10pm; 🛜)
Spider crab – either steamed or whipped into fried rice – is the house speciality at this excellent riverside restaurant. Fish 'steamboat' dishes (in a simmering tureen) are immensely popular too. Those who aren't fans of seafood can tuck into a range of other Thai fare (try the pineapple spare ribs).

Lung Lek   Noodles $
(Th Chee Kun; mains 30-50B; ⏰8.30am-4pm)
This locally adored noodle emporium serves some of the most notable *gŏo·ay dĕe·o mŏo đun* (stewed pork noodles, aka boat noodles) in town.

Recipes have been finessed by owner Uncle Lek over more than four decades.

Pae Krung Gao   Thai $$
(Th U Thong; mains 60-1000B; ⏰10am-9.30pm; 🛜) Seemingly half the punters at this riverside restaurant are here for grilled river prawns, though fried rice dishes and the catfish and mango salad are just as tasty.

Roti Săi Măi Stalls   Desserts $
(Th U Thong; desserts from 35B; ⏰8am-8pm)
The dessert *roti săi măi* (silk thread *roti*) was invented in Ayuthaya and is sold all over town, though these stalls fronting the hospital are the most famous.

Buy a bag then make your own by rolling together thin strands of melted palm sugar and wrapping them inside the sweet flatbread.

ℹ️ INFORMATION

Phra Nakorn Si Ayuthaya Hospital (📞035 211888; www.ayhosp.go.th/ayh; Th U Thong) Has an emergency centre and English-speaking doctors.

Foreign Quarters

Ayuthaya's rulers were adroit diplomats and welcomed international merchants and immigrants. At its peak, more than 40 ethnic groups resided here. The Mon, Lao, Khmer and Chinese lived among the locals, and the Indians, Persians, Javanese and Malay were given land, mostly to the south of the island.

The Portuguese, who arrived in 1511, were the first Europeans to reach Siam. The **Portuguese Village** (หมู่บ้านโปรตุเกส; Samphao Lom; ⏰9am-4pm) 🆓 contains a Catholic church and excavation site. Later, the Dutch, English, Spanish and French arrived, bringing arms and other luxuries and returning mostly with tin, deerskins, sappan wood and rice.

The Dutch East India Company (VOC) arrived in Ayuthaya in 1604 and set up a trading post here, hoping to use Siam as a gateway to China. **Baan Hollanda** (บ้านฮอลันดา; 📞035 245683; www.baanhollanda.org; Soi Khan Rua, Mu 4; 50B; ⏰9am-5pm Wed-Sun) features an exhibition of Thai-Dutch history and the excavated foundations of centuries-old Dutch buildings.

And **Japanese Village** (หมู่บ้านญี่ปุ่น; 📞035 259867; 25/3 Mu 7, Tambon Kohrian; adult/child 50/20B; ⏰8am-5pm; 🅿️), set within manicured, hibiscus-fringed gardens, details the lives of the estimated 1500 Japanese who settled here in the early 17th century. Some came to trade, but most were Christians fleeing persecution in their homeland.

St Joseph Church
TIGERSTOCK'S / SHUTTERSTOCK ©

Ayuthaya

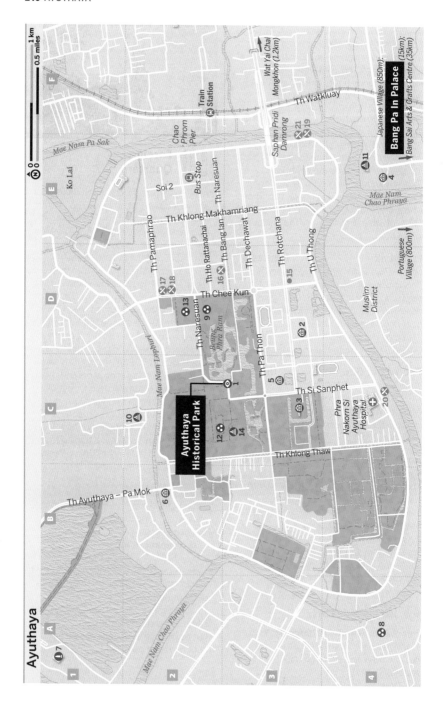

Ayuthaya Historical Park

Bang Pa In Palace

Japanese Village (850m); Bang Sai Arts & Crafts Centre (35km): (15km)

Portuguese Village (800m)

Wat Yai Chai Mongkhon (1.2km)

Train Station

Th Watkluay

Saphan Pridi Damrong

Chao Phrom Pier

Mae Nam Pa Sak

Ko Lai

Soi 2

Bus Stop

Th Naresuan

Th Khlong Makhamriang

Th Pamaphrao

Th Ho Rattanachai

Th Bang Ian

Th Dechawat

Th Rotchana

Th U Thong

Mae Nam Chao Phraya

Muslim District

Th Chee Kun

Th Naresuan

Bueng Phra Ram

Th Pa Thon

Th Si Sanphet

Phra Nakorn Si Ayuthaya Hospital

Mae Nam Lopburi

Th Khlong Thaw

Th Ayuthaya – Pa Mok

Mae Nam Chao Phraya

Ayuthaya

Tourism Authority of Thailand (TAT; ☑035 246076; tatyutya@tat.or.th; Th Si Sanphet; ⊙8.30am-4.30pm) Has an information counter with maps and good advice at the Ayutthaya Tourist Center (p240).

ℹ GETTING THERE & AWAY

BUS & MINIVAN

Ayuthaya's **minivan bus stop** (Th Naresuan) is just south of the backpacker strip, and has frequent departures for Bangkok (40B to 70B, ¾ to 1½ hours).

TRAIN

Ayuthaya's train station is near the river. For Bangkok, most trains stop at Bang Sue station (convenient for Banglamphu) before arriving at Hualamphong. Destinations from Ayuthaya include Bang Pa In (¼ hour, 16 daily), Bangkok (20B to 65B, 1½ to 2½ hours, frequent) and Chiang Mai (370B to 1850B, 11 to 14 hours, five daily) and Nong Khai (202B to 1750B, nine to 11 hours, three daily).

ℹ GETTING AROUND

Cycling is the ideal way to see the city. Many guesthouses hire bicycles (40B to 50B per day) and motorcycles (250B to 300B).

River ferries shuttle passengers across the water. The ferry nearest the train station operates from 5am to 7.30pm (5B).

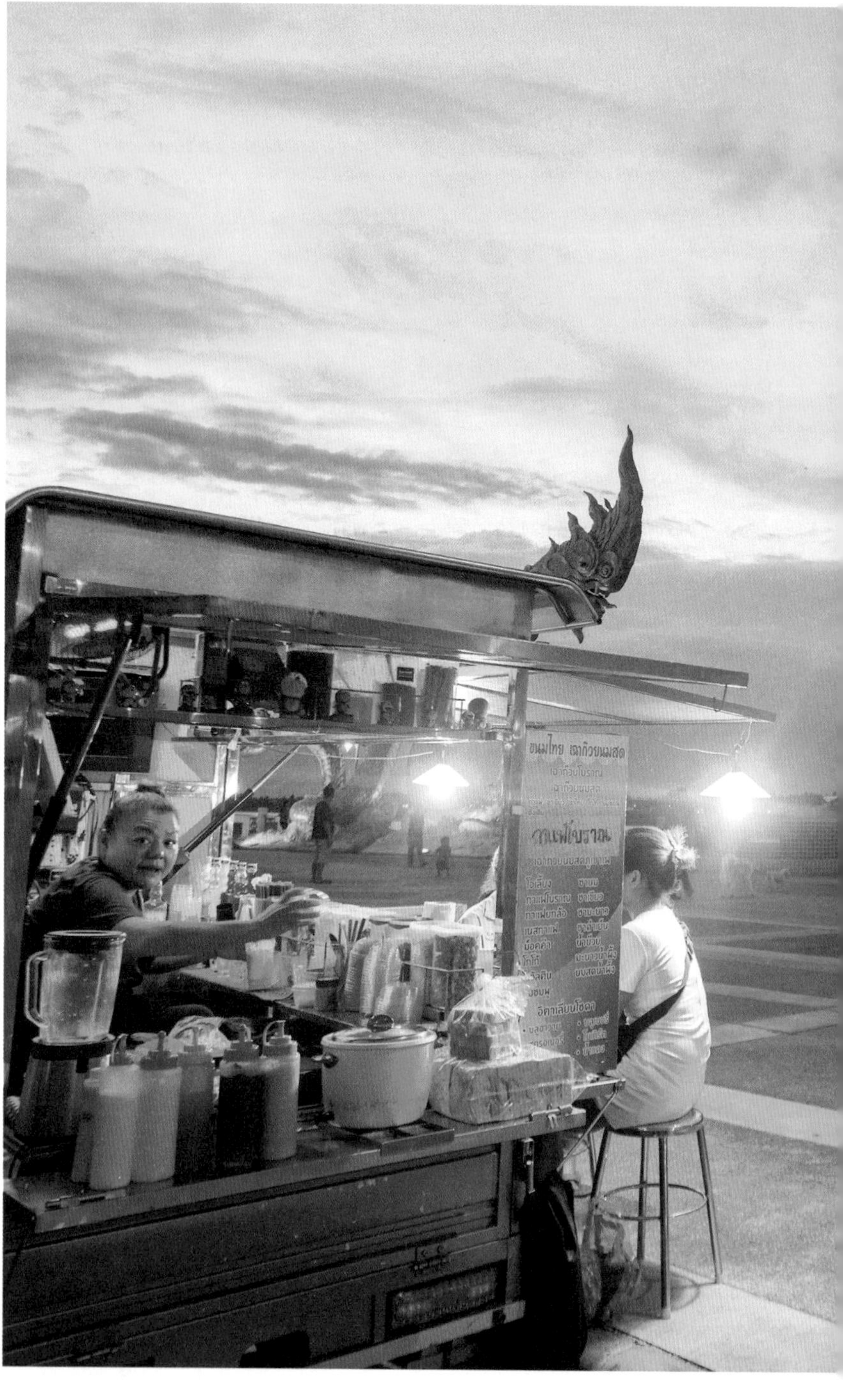

AMNAT30 / SHUTTERSTOCK ©

NONG KHAI

Nong Khai at a Glance...

Rest and relaxation are Nong Khai's draws. It is a pleasant north-eastern town perched on the banks of the muddy Mekong River, just across from Vientiane in Laos. As a border town it enjoys many Lao characteristics, including a friendly and laid-back disposition. Seduced by its dreamy pink sunsets and sluggish pace of life, many visitors who intend staying one night end up bedding down for many more.

Nong Khai in Two Days

Rent a bicycle and tour around the town enjoying the laid-back provincial lifestyle. Visit **Sala Kaew Ku** (p252) and have dinner along the riverside promenade. The next day, visit **Tha Sadet Market** (p254), filled with shoppers and diners. Experience the local food scene at **Daeng Namnuang** (p256).

Nong Khai in Four Days

Treat yourself to a whole lot of nothing. Read a book, get a massage, pick up some handicraft souvenirs. Don't worry, the time will melt away. Join the great Thai tradition of near constant eating with at least three meals plus snacks in between.

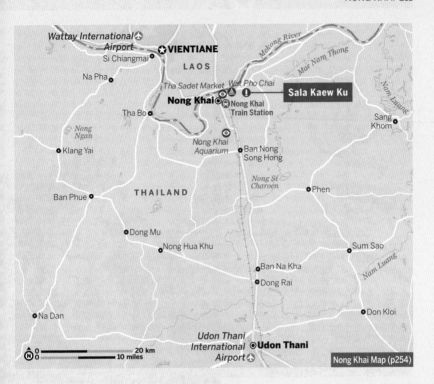

Nong Khai Map (p254)

Arriving in Nong Khai

Udon Thani Airport Located 55km south of town. Minivans run to/from the airport.

Nong Khai bus terminal Located in town.

Nong Khai train station Located 2km west of the city centre; túk-túks take you downtown.

Sleeping

Catering to the steady flow of backpackers, Nong Khai's budget lodging is the best in northeastern Thailand. Most guesthouses are centred along the river.

VIEW APART / SHUTTERSTOCK ©

Sala Kaew Ku

Tour the dream-like garden of Sala Kaew Ku, filled with larger-than-life figures from Hindu-Buddhist mythology. It is a surreal combination of art and religion that exemplifies the experimental aspects of Buddhist worship.

Great For...

☑ **Don't Miss**

The mummified body of the park's founder on the 3rd floor of the pavilion.

Built over a period of 20 years, the park features a weird and wonderful array of gigantic sculptures that merge Hindu and Buddhist imagery. The temple is locally known as Wat Kaek.

Mystic Visionary

The park's founder was a mystic shaman named Luang Pu Boun Leua Sourirat. As he tells his own story, Luang Pu tumbled into a hole as a child and met an ascetic named Kaewkoo, who introduced him to the manifold mysteries of the underworld and set him on course to become a Brahmanic-yogi-priest-shaman. Though he attracted followers, he had no formal training as a religious leader.

Shaking up his own unique blend of Hindu and Buddhist philosophy, mythology and iconography, Luang Pu developed a

ⓘ Need to Know

ศาลาแก้วกู่, Wat Khaek; 20B; ⊘7am-6pm

✕ Take a Break

Stop by Tha Sadet Market (p254) for a pre- or post-outing meal.

★ Top Tip

Mut Mee Garden Guesthouse (☎042 460717; www.mutmee.com; Soi ‖Mutmee) **distributes a map of the site with explanatory text.**

large following on both sides of the Mekong in this region. In fact, his original project was on the Lao side of the river where he had been living until the 1975 communist takeover in Laos. He died in 1996.

The main shrine building, almost as strange as the sculptures, is full of images of every description and provenance (guaranteed to throw even an art historian into a state of disorientation). There are also photos of Luang Pu at various ages and Luang Pu's corpse lying under a glass dome ringed by flashing lights.

Life-Sized Parables

The park is a smorgasbord of large and bizarre cement statues of Buddha, Shiva, Vishnu and other celestial deities born of Luang Pu's dreams and cast by workers under his direction. They crowd together like a who's who of religious celebrities. Other pieces depict stories and parables meant to teach the seekers how to gain enlightenment. Touring the grounds is a 3-D experience of Hindu-Buddhist symbols and tales.

Some of the sculptures are quite amusing. The serene elephant wading though a pack of anthropomorphic dogs teaches people to not be bothered by gossip.

The tallest sculpture, a Buddha seated on a coiled *naga* (serpent) with a spectacular seven-headed hood, is 25m high. It is a classic Thai Buddhist motif but with Luang Pu's unique twist.

Also of interest is the Wheel of Life (the process of life and rebirth), which you enter through a giant mouth. The final scene is of a young man stepping across the installation to become a Buddha figure.

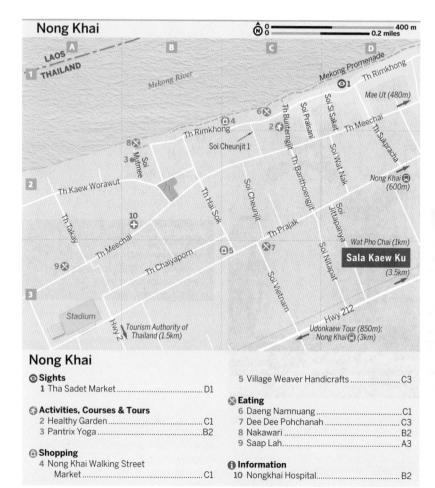

Nong Khai

◎ SIGHTS

Tha Sadet Market
Market

(ตลาดท่าเสด็จ; Th Rimkhong; ⊙8.30am-6pm) The most popular destination in town. Almost everyone loves a stroll through this covered market despite it being a giant tourist trap. It offers the usual mix of clothes, electronic equipment, food and assorted bric-a-brac, most of it imported from Laos and China, but there are also a few shops selling quirky and quality stuff.

Nong Khai Aquarium
Aquarium

(พิพิธภัณฑ์สัตว์น้ำจังหวัดหนองคาย; ☎083 459 4477; www.nongkhaiaquarium.com; off Rte 2; 100B; ⊙9am-5pm Tue-Sun) Although it's looking a little shabby these days, this large aquarium offers an interesting collection of freshwater and ocean-dwelling fish from Thailand and beyond. The highlight is the 'Big Tank', which features Mekong River species, including giant Mekong catfish, and has a walk-through tunnel. There's a scuba feeding performance daily at 2pm and also at 11am on Saturday, Sunday and public holidays. The aquarium is far out of town, on the Khon Kaen University campus off Rte 2, and not served by public transport.

Wat Pho Chai — Buddhist Temple

(วัดโพธิ์ชัย; Th Phochai; ⊘daylight hours, ubosot 6am-6.30pm) FREE Luang Po Phra Sai, a large Lan Xang–era Buddha image awash with gold, bronze and precious stones, sits at the hub of Nong Khai's holiest temple. The head of the image is pure gold, the body is bronze and the ùt·sà·nít (flame-shaped head ornament) is set with rubies. Due to the great number of miracles attributed to it, this royal temple is a mandatory stop for most visiting Thais.

Luang Po Phra Sai was one of three similar statues made for each of the daughters of Lao king Setthathirat, and they were taken as bounty after King Rama I sacked Vientiane in 1778.

The awesome murals in the hall housing the Buddha image depict their travels from the interior of Laos to the banks of the Mekong, where they were put on rafts. A storm sent one of the statues to the bottom of the river, where it remains today. It was never recovered because, according to one monk at the temple, the naga (which live in the river) wanted to keep it.

The third statue, Phra Soem, is at Wat Pathum Wanaram, next to Siam Paragon in Bangkok. Phra Sai was supposed to accompany it, but, as the murals show, the cart carrying it broke down here and so this was taken as a sign that it wished to remain in Nong Khai.

🏃 ACTIVITIES

Pantrix Yoga — Health & Wellbeing

(www.pantrix.net; Soi Mutmee) Pantrix offers week- and month-long yoga courses (they are not live-in) for serious students by experienced teachers. There's also a free daily yoga session from 2pm to 3pm.

Great Balls of Fire

Since 1983 (or for ages, depending on who you ask) the sighting of the *bâng fai pá·yah·nâhk* (loosely translated as 'naga fireworks') has been an annual event along the Mekong River. Sometime in the early evening, at the end of the Buddhist Lent (October), small reddish balls of fire shoot from the Mekong River and float into the air before vanishing.

Naga fireballs have become big business in Nong Khai Province, and curious Thais from across the country converge along the river banks for the annual show. The fireball experience is more than just watching a few small lights rise from the river; it's mostly about watching Thais (sometimes as many as 40,000 people) watching a few small lights rise from the river.

Healthy Garden — Massage

(☎042 423323; Th Banthoengjit; Thai/foot massage per hour 170/200B; ⊘8am-8pm) For the most effective treatment in Nong Khai, this place has foot massage and traditional Thai massage in air-conditioned rooms.

🛍 SHOPPING

Nong Khai Walking Street Market — Market

(⊘4pm-10pm Sat) This weekly street festival featuring music, handmade items and food takes over the promenade every Saturday night. It's smaller, but far more pleasant than the similar Walking Street markets in Chiang Mai.

Village Weaver Handicrafts — Arts & Crafts

(☎042 422651; 1020 Th Prajak; ⊘8.30am-6pm) This place sells high-quality, handwoven fabrics and clothing (ready-made or made to order) that help fund development projects around Nong Khai. The *mát·mèe* cotton is particularly good here.

From left: Nong Khai Walking Street Market (p255); Murals, Wat Po Chai (p255); Tha Sadet Market (p254)

🍴 EATING

Dee Dee Pohchanah   Thai $$

(1155/9 Th Prajak; mains 60-425B; ⏰11am-2am; 🛜) How good is Dee Dee? Just look at the dinner-time crowds. But don't be put off by them: despite having a full house every night, this open-air place is a well-oiled machine and you won't be waiting long.

Daeng Namnuang   Vietnamese $

(Th Rimkhong; mains 50-250B; ⏰8am-8pm; 🅿🛜) This massive river restaurant has grown into an Isan institution, and hordes of out-of-towners head home with car boots and carry-on bags (there's an outlet at Udon Thani's airport) stuffed with their *năam neu·ang* (DIY pork spring rolls).

Mae Ut   Vietnamese $

(Th Meechai; mains 30-50B; ⏰10am-6pm) This little place, serving just four items, including fried spring rolls and *kôw gee·ab þahk mŏr* (fresh noodles with pork), is essentially grandma's kitchen. Look for the green building with tables under a silver awning and lots of potted plants. English is limited.

Nakawari   Thai $$

(📞081 975 0516; Th Rimkhong; mains 50-480B; ⏰10am-9pm) Docked down below **Mut Mee Garden Guesthouse** (📞042 460717; www.mutmee.com; Soi Mutmee), this floating restaurant specialises in Thai and Isan fish dishes, and though the prices are a bit high, the quality is good. There's a one-hour sunset cruise most nights (80B; at least 10 guests needed before the cruise will go ahead) around 5pm or 5.30pm; order food at least 30 minutes before departure.

Saap Lah   Thai $

(Th Meechai; mains 25-150B; ⏰8.30am-7.30pm) For excellent *gài yâhng* (grilled chicken), *sôm·đam* (spicy green papaya salad) and other Isan foods, follow your nose to this no-frills shop.

ⓘ INFORMATION

Nongkhai Hospital (☏042 413456; Th Meechai; ⊙24hr) Has a 24-hour casualty department.

Tourism Authority of Thailand (TAT; ☏042 421326; tat_nongkhai@yahoo.com; Hwy 2; ⊙8.30am-4.30pm) At the time of writing it was temporarily located in front of the old provincial hall at the end of Hwy 2, but was expected to return to its inconvenient location outside of town during 2018.

ⓘ GETTING THERE & AWAY

AIR

The nearest airport is 55km south in Udon Thani; there are connections to Bangkok, Chiang Mai and Phuket. **Udon Kaew Tour** (☏042 411530; Th Pranang Cholpratan; ⊙8.30am-5.30pm) run minivans to/from the airport; book in advance.

BUS

The **bus terminal** (☏042 421246) is just off Th Prajak, about 1.5km from the riverside guest-houses. Destinations include Bangkok (330B to 660B, 10 to 11 hours, frequent afternoon and evening departures), Chiang Mai (750B to 820B, 12 hours, 7pm) and Suvarnabhumi (Airport) bus station (430B, nine to 10 hours, 8pm).

TRAIN

Nong Khai's **train station** (☏042 411637, nation-wide 1690; www.railway.co.th) is 2km west of the city centre. Four daily trains connect Bangkok (220B to 1360B, 11½ hours).

ⓘ GETTING AROUND

Nong Khai is a great place for cycling; bicycles can be hired for 50B per day.

Garuda decoration, Wat Phra Kaew (p38), Bangkok

In Focus

Thailand Today p260
Brush up on the issues that are shaping Thailand's political agenda.

History p262
From ancient kingdoms to contemporary coups, Thailand is full of interesting history.

Culture & Customs p269
Unravel the *wâi* and the what of this tolerant but complex culture.

Religion p272
Religion is a vibrant part of daily life in Thailand.

Thai Cuisine p276
Master Thai food in all of its bounty, from cheap and tasty street food to regional specialities.

Arts & Architecture p279
The Thai landscape is decorated with colourful homages to the gods and spirits.

Environment & Wildlife p285
From the northern mountains to the coral-fringed beaches of the south, Thailand's landscape is fertile and varied.

Responsible Travel p289
How to interact respectfully with Thailand's people and environment.

Grand Palace (p39), Bangkok

COWARDLION / SHUTTERSTOCK ©

Thailand Today

Many of the political loose ends that have caused insta-
bility in Thailand for nearly a decade reached a finale
in 2016. The death of the revered king brought about a
sense of national unity. The transfer of the crown from
father to son occurred peacefully. And a new constitu-
tion cemented the role of the military in the government.

A Nation in Mourning

On 13 October 2016, King Bhumibol Adulyadej (Rama IX) passed away at the age of 88 after many years of failing health. Claiming a 70-year reign, King Bhumibol was the world's longest-serving monarch and the only king that the majority of the Thai population had ever known. He was regarded as a national father figure and benevolent ruler undertaking many poverty-alleviation programs during his lifetime.

The country entered into a state-mandated and personal grieving period. The government requested a month-long hiatus from 'joyful' events (concerts, parties, festivals, football matches and the like). Civil servants were ordered to wear black clothing for one year.

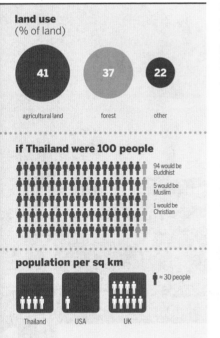

land use
(% of land)

41 agricultural land

37 forest

22 other

if Thailand were 100 people

94 would be Buddhist

5 would be Muslim

1 would be Christian

population per sq km

Thailand USA UK

≈ 30 people

Large crowds collected in public spaces and in processions to express their grief. The demand for mourning clothes outpaced supply and large bubbling vats for dyeing clothes popped up around Bangkok. The government also supplied eight million free black shirts to low-income people.

In October 2017, after Rama IX's body had been lying in state at Bangkok's Grand Palace for a year, ostensibly one of the most lavish funerals in modern history was held. A 50m-high funeral pyre was built at Sanam Luang (Royal Field), and black-clad mourners from across the country lined the streets of the capital for the various ceremonies, which allegedly ran a bill of US$90 million.

A New King

After a brief mourning period, the late king's son, the crown prince, ascended the throne as King Maha Vajiralongkorn (Rama X) on 1 December 2016. There is a close relationship between the palace and the Thai military, which currently has control over the government.

Prior to his coronation, the thrice-divorced king was not favourably viewed due to a variety of personal scandals and a jet-setting lifestyle, which included spending most of his free time in Germany with his girlfriend – an arrangement that Thais weren't used to seeing from their king. But due to strict lèse-majesté laws, the Thai public was reluctant to express candid sentiments, and they remained hopeful for stability and decorum.

A New Constitution

Thailand ratified a draft version of its 20th constitution on 7 August 2016 by popular vote. The new constitution dilutes democracy in the kingdom and gives formal governing powers to the military. The 250-member Senate (upper house) will be solely appointed with no direct elections, and includes seats reserved for the military. There is also a provision for an unelected council to have authority to remove an elected government and for the Senate to appoint a prime minister. The military-drafted constitution was described by the regime as a road map to democracy and a stable, corruption-free government.

At 55%, voter turnout was low but it passed with a 61% majority. Public information about the constitution was limited and criticisms of the provisions were repressed by the ruling military junta. Some polled voters supported the measure because the military has brought about an end to street protests in Bangkok.

Prime minister Prayut Chan-o-cha has hinted at a general election in 2018, the first since the military coup in 2014.

Wat Si Chum (p159), Sukhothai Historical Park

History

Thai history has all the dramatic elements to inspire the imagination: palace intrigue, wars waged with spears and elephants, popular protest movements and a penchant for 'smooth-as-silk' coups.

4000–2500 BC
Prehistoric inhabitants of northeastern Thailand develop agriculture and tool-making.

6th–11th centuries AD
The Mon Dvaravati thrive in central Thailand and in 10th century the Tai peoples arrive.

1240–1438
Approximate dates of Sukhothai kingdom.

Wat Chai Wattanaram (p239), Ayuthaya Historical Park

TORTOON / GETTY IMAGES ©

From the Beginning

Though there is evidence of prehistoric peoples, most scholars start the story of Thai nationhood at the arrival of the 'Tai' people during the first millennium AD. The Tai people migrated from southern China and spoke Tai-Kadai, a family of tonal languages said to be the most significant ethno-linguistic group in Southeast Asia. The language group branched off into Laos (the Lao people) and Myanmar (the Shan).

Most of these new arrivals were farmers and hunters who lived in loosely organised villages, usually near a river source, with no central government or organised military. The indigenous Mon people are often recognised as assembling an early confederation (often referred to as Mon Dvaravati) in central and northeastern Thailand from the 6th to 9th centuries. Little is known about this period, but scholars believe that the Mon Dvaravati had a centre in Nakhon Pathom, outside of Bangkok, with outposts in parts of northern Thailand.

1351	1511	1767
Legendary kingdom of Ayuthaya is founded.	Portuguese found foreign mission in Ayuthaya, followed by other European nations.	Ayuthaya falls at the hands of the Burmese.

Wat Mahathat (p157), Sukhothai Historical Park

★ **Historical Sites & Museums**

Sukhothai Historical Park (p156)

Ayuthaya Historical Park (p238)

Si Satchanalai-Chaliang Historical Park (p160)

COWARDLION / SHUTTERSTOCK ©

The ancient superpower of the region was the Khmer empire, based in Angkor (in present-day Cambodia), which expanded across the western frontier into present-day northeastern and central Thailand starting in the 11th century. Sukhothai and Phimai were regional administrative centres connected by roads with way-station temples that made travel easier and were a visible symbol of imperial power. The Khmer monuments started out as Hindu but were later converted into Buddhist temples after the regime converted. Though their power would eventually decline, the Khmer imparted to the evolving Thai nation an artistic, bureaucratic and even monarchical legacy.

Thai history is usually told from the perspective of the central region, where the current capital is. But the southern region has a separate historical narrative that didn't merge with the centre until the modern era. Between the 8th and 13th centuries, southern Thailand was controlled by the maritime empire of Srivijaya, based in southern Sumatra (Indonesia), and controlled trade between the Straits of Malacca.

The Rise of the Thai Kingdoms

While the regional empires were declining in the 12th to 16th centuries, Tai peoples in the hinterlands established new states that would eventually unite the country.

Lanna

In the northern region, the Lanna kingdom, founded by King Mengrai, built Chiang Mai (meaning 'new city') in 1292 and proceeded to unify the northern communities into one cultural identity. For a time Chiang Mai was something of a religious centre for the region. However, Lanna was plagued by dynastic intrigues, fell to the Burmese in 1556 and was later eclipsed by Sukhothai and Ayuthaya as the progenitor of the modern Thai state.

Sukhothai

Then just a frontier town on the edge of the ailing Khmer empire, Sukhothai expelled the distant power in the mid-13th century and crowned the local chief as the first king. But

1782
Chakri dynasty is founded, and the capital is moved to Bangkok.

1826
Thailand allies with Britain during the first Anglo-Burmese War.

1868–1910
King Chulalongkorn (Rama V) reigns; it's a time of modernisation and European imperialism.

it was his son Ramkhamhaeng who led the city-state to become a regional power with dependencies in modern-day Laos and southern Thailand. Sukhothai replaced Chiang Mai as a centre of Theravada Buddhism on mainland Southeast Asia. The monuments built during this era helped define a distinctive architectural style. After his death, Ramkhamhaeng's empire disintegrated. In 1378 Sukhothai became a tributary of Ayuthaya.

Ayuthaya

Close to the Gulf of Thailand, the city-state of Ayuthaya grew rich and powerful from the international sea trade. The legendary founder was King U Thong, one of 36 kings and five dynasties that steered Ayuthaya through a 416-year lifespan. Ayuthaya presided over an age of commerce in Southeast Asia. Its main exports were rice and forest products, and many commercial and diplomatic foreign missions set up headquarters outside the royal city. Ayuthaya adopted Khmer court customs, honorific language and ideas of kingship. The monarch styled himself as a Khmer *devaraja* (divine king) instead of the Sukhothai ideal of *dhammaraja* (righteous king).

Ayuthaya paid tribute to the Chinese emperor, who rewarded this ritualistic submission with generous gifts and commercial privileges. Ayuthaya's reign was constantly under threat from expansionist Burma. The city was occupied in 1569 but later liberated by King Naresuan. In 1767 Burmese troops successfully sacked the capital and dispersed the Thai leadership into the hinterlands. The destruction of Ayuthaya remains a vivid historical event for the nation, and the tales of court life are as evocative as the stories of King Arthur.

The Bangkok Era

The Revival

With Ayuthaya in ruins and the dynasty destroyed, a general named Taksin filled the power vacuum and established a new capital in 1768 in Thonburi, across the river from modern-day Bangkok. King Taksin was deposed and executed in 1782 by subordinate generals. One of the leaders of the coup, Chao Phraya Chakri, was crowned King Buddha Yot Fa (Rama I), the founder of the current Chakri dynasty. He moved the capital across the river to the Ko Ratanakosin district of present-day Bangkok. The new kingdom was viewed as a revival of Ayuthaya and its leaders attempted to replicate the former kingdom's laws, government practices and cultural achievements. They also built a powerful military that avenged Burmese aggression, kicking them out of Chiang Mai. The Bangkok rulers continued courting Chinese commercial trade.

The Reform

The Siamese elite had long admired China, but by the 1800s the West dominated international trade and geopolitics.

1932	**1939**	**1941**
A bloodless revolution ends absolute monarchy.	The country's English name is officially changed from Siam to Thailand.	Japanese forces enter Thailand during WWII.

Name Changes

The country known today as Thailand has had several monikers. The Khmers are credited for naming this area 'Siam'. In 1939 the name of the country was changed from Siam (Prathet Syam) to Thailand (Prathet Thai).

King Mongkut (Rama IV; r 1851–68), often credited with modernising the kingdom, spent 27 years prior to assuming the crown as a monk in the Thammayut sect, a reform movement he founded to restore scholarship to the faith. During his reign the country was integrated into the prevailing market system that broke up royal monopolies and granted more rights to foreign powers.

Mongkut's son, King Chulalongkorn (Rama V; r 1873–1910) took greater steps in replacing the old political order. He abolished slavery and introduced the creation of a salaried bureaucracy, a police force and a standing army. His reforms brought uniformity to the legal code, law courts and revenue offices. Schools were established along European models. Universal conscription and poll taxes made all men the king's men. Many of the king's advisors were British, and they ushered in a remodelling of the old Ayuthaya-based system. Distant sub-regions were brought under central command and railways were built to link them to population centres. Pressured by French and British colonies on all sides, the modern boundaries of Siam came into shape by ceding territory.

Democracy vs Dictatorship

The 1932 Revolution

During a period of growing independence movements in the region, a group of foreign-educated military officers and bureaucrats led a successful (and bloodless) coup against absolute monarchy in 1932. The pro-democracy party soon splintered and, by 1938, General Phibul Songkhram, one of the original democracy supporters, had seized control of the country. During WWII, Phibul, who was staunchly anti-royalist, strongly nationalistic and pro-Japanese, allowed that country to occupy Thailand as a base for assaults on British colonies in Southeast Asia. In the post-WWII era, Phibul positioned Thailand as an ally of the US in its war on communism.

The Cold War

During the Cold War and the US conflict in Vietnam, the military leaders of Thailand gained legitimacy and economic support from the US in exchange for the use of military installations in Thailand. By the 1970s a new political consciousness bubbled up from the universities. In 1973 more than half a million people – intellectuals, students, peasants and workers – demonstrated in Bangkok and major provincial towns, demanding a constitu-

1946	**1957**	**1973**
King Bhumibol Adulyadej (Rama IX) ascends the throne; Thailand joins the UN.	A successful coup by Sarit Thanarat starts a period of military rule that lasts until 1973.	Civilian demonstrators overthrow the military dictatorship; a democratic government is installed.

tion from the military government. The bloody dispersal of the Bangkok demonstration on 14 October led to the collapse of the regime and the creation of an elected constitutional government. This lasted only three years until another protest movement was brutally squashed and the military returned to restore civil order.

By the 1980s the so-called political soldier General Prem Tinsulanonda forged a period of political and economic stability that led to the 1988 election of a civilian government. Prem is still involved in politics today as the president of the palace's privy council, a powerful position that joins the interests of the monarchy with the military.

The Business Era

The new civilian government was composed of former business executives, many of whom represented provincial commercial interests, instead of Bangkok-based military officials, signalling a shift in the country's political dynamics. Though the country was doing well economically, the government was accused of corruption and vote-buying and the military moved to protect its privileged position with a 1991 coup. Elected leadership was restored shortly after the coup, and the Democrat Party, with the support of business and the urban middle class, dominated the parliament.

The 1997 Asian currency crisis derailed the surging economy and the government was criticised for its ineffective response. That same year, the parliament passed the watershed 'people's constitution', which enshrined human rights and freedom of expression and granted more power to a civil society to counter corruption. (The 1997 constitution was thrown out during the 2006 coup.)

By the turn of the millennium, the economy had recovered and business interests had succeeded the military as the dominant force in politics. The telecommunications billionaire and former police officer Thaksin Shinawatra ushered in the era of the elected CEO. He was a capitalist with a populist message and garnered support from the rural and urban poor and the working class. From 2001 to 2005, Thaksin and his Thai Rak Thai party transformed national politics into one-party rule.

The Thaksin Era

Though Thaksin enjoyed massive popular support, his regime was viewed by urban intellectuals as a kleptocracy, with the most egregious example of corruption being the tax-free sale of his family's Shin Corporation stock to the Singaporean government in 2006, a windfall of 73 billion baht (US$1.88 billion) that was engineered by special legislation. This enraged the upper and middle classes and led to street protests in Bangkok. On 19 September 2006 the military staged a bloodless coup, the first in 15 years, which brought an end to the country's longest stretch of democratic rule. The military dissolved the constitution that had sought to ensure a civilian government and introduced a new constitution that limited the resurgence of one-party rule by interests unsympathetic to the military and the aristocrats.

2004	**2006**	**2011**
A tsunami kills 5000 people and damages tourism and fishing on the Andaman Coast.	Prime Minister Thaksin Shinawatra is ousted by a military coup.	Yingluck Shinawatra becomes the first female prime minister; destructive floods hit the country.

The Coup Decade

Following Thaksin's ouster a cycle of elections-protests-coups followed. Thaksin's allies would win an election, followed by massive protests by anti-Thaksin factions, then a military coup backed by the Constitutional Court and the palace. The final scene in the political ping-pong came in 2011 when Thaksin's politically allied Puea Thai party won a parliamentary majority and Thaksin's sister Yingluck Shinawatra was elected as prime minister. Yingluck Shinawatra became both the first female prime minister of Thailand and the country's youngest-ever premier. The belief that the Yingluck government was a Thaksin administration in all but name ensured she faced bitter opposition.

The most disastrous misstep was a proposed bill granting amnesty for Thaksin, which would have allowed him to return to the country. Street demonstrations began in October 2013 with sporadic violence between Yingluck's supporters and opponents. Yingluck and nine of her ministers stepped down on 7 May of the next year. The military seized control 15 days later.

Return to Military Dictatorship

On 22 May 2014, the Thai military under General Prayut Chan-o-cha overthrew the elected government and brought to an end months of political crisis. Prayut said the coup was necessary to restore stability.

Prayut's military government is known as the National Council for Peace and Order (NCPO). The NCPO set about restoring stability by implementing martial law and silencing critics. All media were under orders to refrain from dissent. Internet providers were ordered to block any content that violated the junta's orders. Even now, some websites, including the Thailand section of the Human Rights Watch website, remain inaccessible inside Thailand. In March 2015 Prayut told journalists that he would execute those who did not toe the official line – the domestic media now self-censors its stories.

The crackdown extends into the civilian sphere as well. More than 1000 people – opposition politicians, academics, journalists, bloggers and students – have been detained or tried in military courts. In March 2015, the UN's High Commissioner for Human Rights claimed that the military is using martial law to silence opposition and to call for 'freedom of expression to ensure genuine debate'.

In preparation for the inevitable transfer of the crown, the military also increased prosecution of the country's strict lèse-majesté laws. In August 2015 one man received a 30-year prison sentence for insulting the monarchy on his Facebook page after sharing a news article. BBC Thai was investigated for defamation of the new king after a 2016 profile piece aired online.

While the NCPO was busy silencing critics, it failed to address Thailand's slumping economy. Foreign investment, exports and GDP all contracted after the coup. In 2016 a much-needed infrastructure investment plan was announced to help bolster the down-turn. Tourism continues to be the bright spot in the economy.

2014	2016	2017
Thailand's Constitutional Court finds Yingluck Shinawatra guilty of abuse of power, forcing her from office.	King Bhumibol Adulyadej (Rama IX) dies; his son succeeds the throne. Military-backed constitution wins popular referendum.	Yingluck Shinawatra flees into exile to avoid appearing in court to hear a judgement on corruption charges.

Songkran ritual (p23)

Culture & Customs

It is easy to love Thailand: the pace of life is unhurried and the people are friendly and kind-hearted. A smile is a universal key in most social situations, a cheerful disposition will be met in kind, and friendships are spontaneous requiring little more than curiosity and humour. Though Thais don't expect foreigners to know much about their country, they are delighted and grateful if they do.

The Monarchy

Thailand expresses deep reverence for its monarchy. Pictures of the king – both present and former – are enshrined in nearly every household and business, and life-size billboards of the monarchs line Th Ratchadamnoen Klang, Bangkok's royal avenue. The previous king's image, which is printed on money, is regarded as sacred, and criticising the king or the monarchy is a criminal offence. The monarchy's relationship to the people is inter-twined with religion; it is deeply spiritual and personal. Most Thais view their king with great reverence, as an exalted father figure (the previous king's birthday is recognised as national Father's Day) and as a protector of the good of the country.

Dos & Don'ts

- Always stand for the royal and national anthems.

- Don't show anger or frustration in public.

- Remove shoes before entering homes or temples; step over the threshold.

- Keep your feet off furniture.

- In temples, sit in the 'mermaid' position (with your feet tucked behind you).

- Pass and receive things with your right hand.

- Use your spoon like a fork and fork like a knife.

The National Psyche

In most social situations, establishing harmony is often a priority and Thais take personal pride in making others feel at ease.

Sà·nùk

Thais place a high value on having sà·nùk (fun). It is the underlying measure of a worthwhile activity and the reason why the country ranks so highly as a tourist destination. Thais are always up for a party, be it of their own invention or an import. Case in point: Thais celebrate three new years – the eve of the resetting of the international calendar, the Chinese lunar New Year and Songkran (the Southeast Asian Buddhist new year).

This doesn't mean that Thais are averse to work. Most offices are typically open six, and sometimes seven, days a week, and most Thais have side jobs to provide extra income. But every chore has a social aspect that lightens the mood and keeps it from being too 'serious' (a grave insult). Whether it's the backbreaking work of rice farming, the tedium of long-distance bus driving or the dangers of a construction site, Thais often mix their work tasks with socialising.

Thais in the tourism industry extend this attitude towards their guests and will often describe foreign visitors as needing a rest after a year of hard work. This cultural mindset reflects the agricultural calendar in which a farmer works from dawn to dusk during the rice-planting and harvesting season then rests until the next year's rains. That rest period involves a lot of hanging out, going to festivals and funerals (which are more party than pity) and loading up family and friends into the back of a pick-up truck for a têe·o (trip).

Status

Though Thai culture is famously non-confrontational and fun-loving, it isn't a social free-for-all. Thais are very conscious of status and the implicit rights and responsibilities. Buddhism defines the social strata, with the heads of the family, religion and monarchy sitting at the top of various tiers. Gauging where you fit into this system is a convenient ice-breaker. Thais will often ask a laundry list of questions: where are you from, how old are you, are you married, do you have children? They are sizing you up in the social strata.

In most cases, you'll get the best of both worlds: Thais will care for you as if you are a child and honour you as if you are a pôo yài (literally 'big person', or elder). When sharing a meal, don't be surprised if a Thai host puts the tastiest piece of fish on your plate.

Thais regard each other as part of an extended family and will use familial prefixes such as pêe (elder sibling) and nórng (younger sibling) when addressing friends as well as blood relations. When translated into English, this often leads foreigners to think that their Thai friends have large immediate families. Thais might also use *bâh* (aunt) or *lung* (uncle) to refer to an older person. Rarely do foreigners get embraced in this grand family reunion; *fa·ràng* is the catch-all term for foreigner. It is mostly descriptive but can sometimes express cultural frustrations.

Saving Face

Interconnected with status is the concept of 'saving face', a common consideration in Asian cultures. In a nutshell, 'face' means you strive for social harmony by avoiding firm or confrontational opinions and displays of anger. Thais regard outbursts of emotion and discourteous social interactions as shameful, whereas Westerners might shrug them off.

Social Conventions & Etiquette

Thais are generally tolerant of most social faux pas as they assume that foreign visitors know very little about their culture. Their graciousness should be returned with a concerted effort of respect.

Greetings

The traditional Thai greeting is with a prayer-like palms-together gesture known as a *wâi*. If someone shows you a *wâi*, you should return the gesture, unless the greeting comes from a child or a service person. A *wâi* can also express gratitude or an apology. Foreigners are continually baffled by when and how to use the *wâi* and such cultural confusion makes great conversation fodder. The all-purpose greeting is a cheery '*sà·wàt·dee kráp*' if you're male or '*sà·wàt·dee kâ*' if you're female. A smile usually accompanies this and goes a long way to diffuse a tense social situation. Also, Thais are great connoisseurs of beauty and a smile improves one's countenance.

Visiting Temples

When visiting a temple, it is important to dress modestly (cover yourself to the elbows and the ankles) and to take your shoes off when you enter any building that contains a Buddha image. Buddha images are sacred objects, so don't pose in front of them for pictures and definitely do not clamber on them. When visiting a religious building, act like a worshipper by finding a discreet place to sit in the 'mermaid' position (with your feet tucked behind you so that they point away from the Buddha images). Temples are maintained from the donations received and contributions from visitors are appreciated.

Touching

In the traditional parts of the country, it is not proper for members of the opposite sex to touch one another. Same-sex touching is quite common and is typically a sign of friendship, not sexual attraction. Older Thai men might grab a younger man's thigh in the same way that buddies slap each other on the back. Thai women are especially affectionate, often sitting close to female friends or linking arms. Women should not touch monks or their belongings; they should not sit next to them on public transport or accidentally brush against them on the street.

Novice monks

Religion

Religion is a fundamental component of Thai society, and colourful examples of worship can be found on every corner. Walk the streets early in the morning and you'll see the solemn progression of Buddhist monks engaged in bin·tá·bàht, *the daily house-to-house alms-food gathering. Household shrines decorate the humblest abodes, and protective amulets, ranging from discreet to overt, are common pieces of jewellery.*

Buddhism

Approximately 95% of Thai people are Theravada Buddhists. This form of Buddhism is often called the Southern School because it travelled from the Indian subcontinent to Southeast Asia.

Religious Principles

Buddhism was born in India in the 6th century. A prince named Siddhartha Gautama left his life of privilege, seeking religious fulfilment. According to the practices of the time, he became an ascetic before he realised that this was not the way to reach the end of suffering.

Adopting a more measured Middle Way, his practice became more balanced until, on the night of the full moon of the fifth month (celebrated as Visakha Bucha), he became

Spirit house (p275)

enlightened under the Bodhi tree. He became known as Buddha, 'the enlightened' or 'the awakened', and spoke of four noble truths that had the power to liberate any human being who could realise them.

The four noble truths deal with the nature and origin of suffering and the path to the cessation of suffering. Loosely explained, this includes *dukkha* (all forms of existence are subject to suffering, disease, imperfection), *samudaya* (the origin of suffering is desire), *nirodha* (cessation of suffering is the giving up desire) and *magga* (the path to cessation of suffering is the eightfold path). The eightfold path is often described as the middle path: a route between extreme asceticism and indulgence. Following the path will lead to *nibbana* ('nirvana' in Sanskrit), which literally means the 'blowing out' or extinction of all grasping and thus of all suffering. Effectively, *nibbana* is also an end to the cycle of rebirths (both moment-to-moment and life-to-life) that is existence.

Religious Practice

In reality, most Thai Buddhists aim for rebirth in a 'better' existence rather than the supramundane goal of *nibbana*. By feeding monks, giving donations to temples and worshipping regularly at their local temple, they hope to improve their lot, acquiring enough merit (*bun* in Thai) to prevent rebirths (or at least reduce their number). The concept of rebirth is almost universally accepted in Thailand, even by non-Buddhists.

Thai Buddhists look to the Triple Gems for guidance in their faith: the Buddha, the *dhamma* and the *sangha*. The Buddha is usually the centrepiece of devotional activity inside a temple and many of the most famous Thai Buddha images have supernatural tales associated with them. The *dhamma* is chanted morning and evening in every temple and

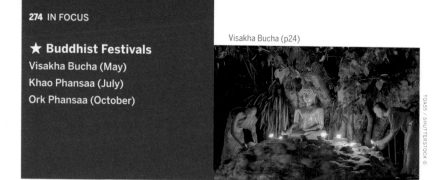
Visakha Bucha (p24)

TOA55 / SHUTTERSTOCK ©

★ **Buddhist Festivals**
Visakha Bucha (May)
Khao Phansaa (July)
Ork Phansaa (October)

taught to every Thai citizen in primary school. There are two *sangha* (monastic) sects in Thailand: the Mahanikai and Thammayut. The former is more mainstream, while the latter is aligned with the monarchy and stricter in its practices.

Hinduism & Animism

There are many enduring legacies of Hinduism and animism in Thai culture and in the practice of Thai Buddhism today. Hinduism was the religious parent of Buddhism, imparting lasting components of mythology, cosmology and symbolism.

Thais recognise the contributions of Hinduism and treat its deities with reverence. Bangkok is especially rich in Hindu shrines. Many of the royally associated ceremonies stem from Brahmanism. Spirit worship and Buddhism have commingled to the point that it is difficult to filter the two. Monks often perform obviously animistic rituals, and Thais believe that merit-making (Buddhist religious rituals) benefits deceased relatives. Trees are wrapped in sacred cloth to honour the spirits of the natural world. Altars are erected on the dashboards of taxis to ensure immunity from traffic laws and accidents. Thais often wear amulets embossed with a Buddha figure or containing sacred soil from a revered temple to protect the wearer from misfortune. In fact, many of the religious rituals of Thai Buddhists, apart from meditation, appear to be deeply rooted in the spirit world.

Monks & Monasteries

Every Thai male is expected to become a monk (*prá* or *prá pík·sù* in Thai) for a short period, optimally between the time he finishes school and the time he starts a career or marries. A family earns great merit when one of its sons 'takes robe and bowl' and many young men enter the monastery to make merit for a deceased patriarch or matriarch.

Traditionally, Buddhist Lent *(pan·săh),* which begins in July and coincides with the three-month period of the rainy season, is when most temporary monks enter the monastery. Nowadays, though, men may spend as little as a week there. Historically the temple provided a necessary social safety net for families. The monastery was a de facto orphanage and also acted as a retirement home for older rural men. Though these charitable roles are not as sought after today, the temples still give refuge and sanctuary to all living creatures. This might mean that they help feed families in need, adopt orphaned or injured animals, and give shelter to overnight travellers (usually impoverished Thai university students).

In Thai Buddhism, women who seek a monastic life are given a minor role in the temple that is not equal to full monkhood. A Buddhist nun is known as *mâa chee* (mother priest) and lives as an *atthasila* nun (following eight precepts of Buddhism's code of ethics as opposed to the five for laypeople and 227 for ordained monks), a position traditionally occupied by women who had no other place in society. Thai nuns shave their heads, wear white robes and take care of temple chores. Generally speaking, *mâa chee* aren't considered as prestigious as monks and don't have a function in the laypeople's merit-making rituals, although there are *mâa chee* who have become revered teachers in their own right, with large followings.

Temple Visits

Thai Buddhism has no particular sabbath day when the faithful are supposed to congregate weekly. Instead, Thai Buddhists visit most often on *wan prá* (holy days), which occur every seventh or eighth day, depending on phases of the moon. A temple visit is usually a social affair involving groups of friends, families or office workers. Thais will also make special pilgrimages to famous temples in other regions as sightseeing and merit-making outings. Most merit-makers visit the *wí·hăhn* (central sanctuary), which houses the primary Buddha figure. Worshippers will offer lotus buds (a symbol of enlightenment) or flower garlands, light three joss sticks and raise their hands to their forehead in a prayerlike gesture.

Houses of the Holy

Many dwellings in Thailand have a 'spirit house' for the property's *prá poom* (guardian spirits). Based on pre-Buddhist animistic beliefs, guardian spirits live in rivers, trees and other natural features and need to be honoured (and placated) like a respected but sometimes troublesome family member. Elaborate doll-house-like structures, where the spirits can 'live' comfortably separated from human affairs, are consecrated by a Brahman priest and receive daily offerings of rice, fruit, flowers and water.

Other merit-making activities include offering food to the temple sangha (community), meditating (individually or in groups), listening to monks chanting *suttas* (Buddhist discourse) and attending a *têht* or *dhamma* (teachings) talk by the abbot or some other respected teacher.

Islam & Other Religions

Although Thailand is predominantly Buddhist, its minority religions often practise alongside one another. About 5% of the population are followers of Islam. The remainder are Christian, including missionary-converted hill tribes and Vietnamese immigrants, as well as Confucians, Taoists, Mahayana Buddhists and Hindus.

The majority of Muslims in Thailand live in the southern provinces, though there are pockets elsewhere. In the southernmost provinces the Muslims are ethnic Malays, while in they north they are Yunnanese descendants. The form of Islam found in southern Thailand is mixed with elements of Malay culture and animism.

The southernmost provinces of Yala, Pattani and Narathiwat contain the country's largest Muslim majority and have long been geographically and culturally isolated to the mainstream society. These provinces were independent sultanates that were conquered by the Bangkok-based kings. During the ultra-nationalist era in the 1940s, this region responded with separatist resistance, later becoming a sanctuary for communist and insurgent activities in the 1980s. Violence flared again in the early 2000s and has persisted. Most observers classify the conflict as an ethno-nationalist struggle.

Thai Muslim women function in society as actively as their Buddhist counterparts. Headscarves are prevalent but not mandatory; sometimes a visitor only realises that someone is a Muslim when they decline an offering of pork at the dinner table. Devout Thai Muslims often encounter spiritual incompatibilities with their Buddhist neighbours. The popular view of the Thai monarch as godlike is heresy for a monotheistic religion like Islam, though many Thai Muslims respect and even love the king and do not voice open criticism. Muslims also avoid alcohol and gambling (in varying degrees) – two pursuits that define much of rural life for Buddhist Thais. In this way, religion keeps the two cultures distinct.

Floating market

Thai Cuisine

Thai food – one of the country's most famous exports – balances spicy, sweet, sour and salty flavours in complex combinations. Ingredients are fresh, flavours are assertive and the sting of the beloved chilli triggers an adrenalin rush.

Rice

In the morning Thais rise with two fundamental smells: rice being cooked and the burning joss sticks that are offered in household shrines. The start of the new day means another opportunity to eat, and eating in Thailand means eating rice (the Thai word 'to eat' is *gin kôw*, literally 'to eat rice').

Rice can be steamed, fried, boiled in a soup, formed into noodles or made into a dessert. In its steamed form it is eaten with a spoon or, in the case of *kôw nĕe·o* (sticky rice), eaten with the hands. The classic morning meal is a watery rice soup (either *jóhk* or *kôw đôm*) that is the ultimate comfort food, the equivalent of oatmeal on a cold day. The next meal of the day will probably be a stir-fry or curry, typically served over rice. In the evening in provincial towns, everyone heads to the night market to see and be seen and to eat more rice.

Noodles

When rice just won't do there is another, albeit rice-derived, alternative: *gǒo·ay dĕe·o* (rice noodles). Day or night, city or village, *gǒo·ay dĕe·o* is the original Thai fast food, served by itinerant vendors or from humble shopfronts. It demonstrates Thais' penchant for micromanaging flavours. You choose the kind of noodle and the kind of meat and you flavour it yourself with a little fish sauce, sugar, vinegar and chillies; don't shy away from the sugar.

There are three basic kinds of rice noodles – *sên yài* (wide), *sên lék* (thin) and *sên mèe* (thinner than thin) – as well as *bà·mèe,* which is a curly noodle made from wheat flour and egg. Most of these only appear in noodle soups but a few are used in various stir-fries, such as *pàt tai* (thin rice noodles stir-fried with dried or fresh shrimp, tofu and egg).

Head to the morning market for a bowl of *kà·nŏm jeen* (rice noodles doused in a thin curry). This dish is piled high with strange pickled and fresh vegetables that will make you feel as if you've grazed on the savannah and swum through the swamp. *Kà·nŏm jeen* is usually served at rickety wooden tables shared with working-class women dressed in market clothes.

Curry

The overseas celebrity of Thai cuisine, *gaang* (curry) is a humble dish on home turf. At roadside stands, especially in southern Thailand, big metal pots contain various curry concoctions of radioactive colours. When you ask vendors what they have, they'll lift the lids and name the type of meat in each: for example *gaang gài* (curry with chicken) or *gaang þlah* (shorthand for sour fish curry). In Bangkok, street-side vendors and small shops will display their curry-in-a-hurry in buffet-style trays. In either case, you point to one and it will be ladled over rice. Use a spoon to scoop it up and push the lime leaves to the side – they aren't edible.

All curries start with a basic paste that can include ingredients such as ground coriander seed, cumin seed, garlic, lemon grass, kaffir lime, galangal, shrimp paste and chillies (either dried or fresh). Most visitors know their curries by their colour, mainly red (from dried red chillies) and green (from fresh green chillies). Green curry is a classic central Thailand dish.

Regional Cuisines

Over the past 20 years there has been so much migration within Thailand that many of the once region-specific dishes have been incorporated into the national cuisine.

Northern Thai

True to its Lanna character, northern Thai cuisine is more laid-back – the flavours are mellow and the influences have migrated over the mountains from Myanmar and China. Northern cuisine is enamoured with pork, from *sâi òo·a* (local-style sausages) to *kâap mŏo* (pork rind). The Burmese influence has imparted the use of turmeric and ginger (though some could argue that northern Burmese food was influenced by Chinese) into the curry pastes used in *gaang hang·lair* (rich pork stew).

Northern flavours favour sour notes. Pickled vegetables are loaded on top of the signature noodle dishes of *kôw soy* (wheat-and-egg noodles with a thick coconut red curry) and *kà·nŏm jeen nám ngée·o* (rice noodles served with a curry broth made with pork and tomatoes); shallots and lime wedges are common seasoning garnishes. Northern Thailand shares Isan's love of *kôw nĕe·o,* which is often served in rounded bamboo baskets and accompanies such dishes as *nám prík òrng* (a chilli paste made with ground pork and tomato).

Pàt gá·prow

★ **Street-Stall Meals**

Kôw pàt – fried rice

Pàt gá·prow – stir-fried chillies, holy basil and a choice of chicken or pork

Pàt pàk ká·náh – stir-fried Chinese kale and *mŏo gròrp* (fried pork belly)

Southern Thai

Southern Thai food draws from the traditions of seafaring traders, many of whom were Muslims from India or ethnic Malays. Indian-style flat bread (known as roti) often competes with rice as a curry companion or is drizzled with sugar and sweetened condensed milk as a market dessert. Turmeric imparts its telltale yellow hue to *kôw mòk gài* (chicken biryani) and southern-style fried chicken.

The curries here are flamboyant, with dry-roasted spice bases prepared in the Indian fashion and featuring lots of locally produced coconut milk. Shaved, milked, strained and fresh, the coconut is a kitchen mainstay. Fresh seafood is plentiful. Plump squid is grilled and served on a stick with an accompanying sweet-and-spicy sauce. Whole fish are often stuffed with lemon grass and limes and barbecued over a coconut-husk fire.

Northeastern Thai

Northeasterners are known for their triumvirate dishes: *sôm·đam* (spicy green papaya salad), *kôw něe·o* (sticky rice) and *gài yâhng* (grilled chicken). In the morning, open-coal grills are loaded up with marinated chicken. Alongside the grill is a large mortar and pestle in which *sôm·đam* is prepared. In go strips of green papaya, sugar, chillies, fish sauce, green beans, tomatoes, dried shrimps and a few special requests: peanuts to make it *sôm·đam* Thai, or field crabs and *plah ráh* (fermented fish sauce) to make it *sôm·đam* Lao (referring to the ethnic Lao who live in northeastern Thailand). The vendor pounds the ingredients together with the pestle to make a musical 'pow-pow-pow' sound that is sometimes used as an onomatopoetic nickname.

What to Drink

Thai beers, such as Singha (pronounced 'sing'), are hoppy lagers which are often mixed with ice to keep them cool and palatable. Fruit shakes are refreshing on a hot day and are served with a pinch of salt to help regulate body temperature. Sweet iced coffee and tea are popular street-stall drinks. Thais get their drink on with rice whisky mixed with ice, soda water and a splash of Coke.

Thai classical dance performers

Arts & Architecture

Thais' refined sense of beauty is reflected in their artistic traditions, from Buddhist sculpture to temple architecture. Monarchs were the country's great artistic patrons; their funeral monuments were ornate stupas and handicrafts were developed specifically for royal use. Today religious artwork continues to dominate the imagination but has been adapted with multimedia installations and contemporary canvas works.

Religious Art

Temples are the country's artistic repositories, where you'll find ornate murals depicting Hindu-Buddhist mythology and Buddha sculptures. The country is most famous for its graceful and serene Buddhas that emerged during the Sukhothai era. Always instructional in intent, temple murals often depict the *Jataka* (stories of the Buddha's past lives) and the Thai version of the Hindu epic *Ramayana*. Reading the murals requires both knowledge of these religious tales and an understanding of the murals' spatial relationship. Most murals are divided into scenes, in which the main theme is depicted in the centre with resulting events taking place above and below the central action. Usually in the corner of a dramatic tableau are independent scenes of Thai village life: women carrying bamboo baskets, men fishing or a festive get-together.

Thailand's Artistic Periods

The development of Thai religious art and architecture is broken into different periods defined by the patronage of the ruling capital. A period's characteristics are seen in the depiction of the Buddha's facial features, the top flourish on the head, the dress, and the position of the feet in meditation. Another signature is the size and shape of the temples' *chedi* (stupas) – telltale characteristics are shown in the pedestal and the central bell before it begins to taper into the uppermost tower.

Period	Temple & Chedi Styles	Buddha Styles	Examples
Dvaravati period (7th–11th centuries)	Rectangular-based *chedi* with stepped tiers	Indian-influenced with a thick torso, large hair curls, arched eyebrows to represent a flying bird, protruding eyes, thick lips and a flat nose	Phra Pathom Chedi, Nakhon Pathom; Lopburi Museum, Lopburi; Wat Chama Thawi, Lamphun
Srivijaya period (7th–13th centuries)	Mahayana-Buddhist-style temples; Javanese-style *chedi* with elaborate arches	Indian influenced: heavily ornamented, humanlike features and slightly twisted at the waist	Wat Phra Boromathat, Chaiya; Wat Phra Mahathat Woramahawihaan and National Museum, Nakhon Si Thammarat
Khmer period (9th–11th centuries)	Hindu-Buddhist temples; corn-cob-shaped *prang*	Buddha meditating under a canopy of the seven-headed *naga* and atop a lotus pedestal	Phimai, Nakhon Ratchasima; Phanom Rung, Surin
Chiang Saen-Lanna period (11th–13th centuries)	Teak temples; square-based *chedi* topped by gilded umbrella; also octagonal-base *chedi*	Burmese influences with plump figure, round, smiling face and footpads facing upwards in meditation pose	Wat Phra Singh, Chiang Mai; Chiang Saen National Museum
Sukhothai period (13th–15th centuries)	Khmer-inspired temples; slim-spired *chedi* topped by a lotus bud	Graceful poses, often depicted 'walking'; no anatomical human detail	Sukhothai Historical Park
Ayuthaya period (14th–18th centuries)	Classical Thai temple with three-tiered roof and gable flourishes; bell-shaped *chedi* with tapering spire	Ayuthaya-era king, wearing a gem-studded crown and royal regalia	Ayuthaya Historical Park
Bangkok-Ratanakosin period (19th century)	Colourful and gilded temple with Western-Thai styles; mosaic-covered *chedi*	Reviving Ayuthaya style	Wat Phra Kaew, Wat Pho and Wat Arun, Bangkok

Contemporary Art

Adapting traditional themes and aesthetics to the secular canvas began around the turn of the 20th century, as Western influence surged in the region. In general, Thai painting favours abstraction over realism and continues to preserve the one-dimensional perspective of traditional mural paintings. Italian artist Corrado Feroci is often credited with being the father of modern Thai art. He was first invited to Thailand by Rama VI in 1924 and built Bangkok's Democracy Monument, among other European-style statues. Feroci founded the country's first fine arts institute in 1933, a school that eventually developed into Silpakorn University, Thailand's premier training ground for artists. In gratitude, the Thai government made Feroci a Thai citizen, with the Thai name Silpa Bhirasri.

The Modern Buddha

In the 1970s Thai artists began to tackle the modernisation of Buddhist themes through abstract expressionism. Leading works in this genre include the mystical pen-and-ink drawings of Thawan Duchanee. Montien Boonma used the ingredients of Buddhist merit-making, such as gold leaf, bells and candle wax, to create abstract temple spaces within museum galleries.

Protest & Satire

In Thailand's quickly industrialising society, many artists watched as rice fields became factories, forests became asphalt and the spoils went to the politically connected. During the student activist days of the 1970s, the Art for Life Movement was the banner under which creative discontents rallied against the military dictatorship and embraced certain aspects of communism and workers' rights. Sompote Upa-In and Chang Saetang are two important artists from that period. An anti-authority attitude continues today. Photographer Manit Sriwanichpoom is best known for his 'Pink Man on Tour' series, in which he depicted artist Sompong Thawee in a pink suit and with a pink shopping cart amid Thailand's most iconic attractions, suggesting that Thailand's cultural and natural spaces were for sale. He has since followed up this series with other socially evocative photographs poking fun at ideas of patriotism and nationalism.

During the political turmoil of the past decade, artists channelled first-person experiences into multimedia installations. Tanks, guns, violence and protest imagery are woven together to express outrage, grief, anxiety and even apathy in the collective memory during the protest-coup-election era. Vasan Sitthiket created a collection of colourful but chaotic collages in the series descriptively called 'Hypocrisy'. Chulayarnnon Siriphol's short film *A Brief History of Memory* recounts one woman's experience of violent street protests.

Public Art

In this hierarchical society, artistic innovation is often stifled by the older generation who holds prestige and power. In the 1990s there was a push to move art out of the dead zones of the museums and into the public spaces, beyond the reach of the cultural authoritarians. An artist and art organiser, Navin Rawanchaikul, started his 'in-the-streets' collaborations in his home town of Chiang Mai and then moved his big ideas to Bangkok, where he filled the city's taxi cabs with art installations, a show that literally went on the road.

His other works have had a way with words, such as the mixed-media piece *We Are the Children of Rice (Wine)* in 2002 and his rage against the commercialisation of museums in his epic painting entitled *Super (M)art Bangkok Survivors* (2004), which depicts famous artists, curators and decision-makers in a crowded Paolo Veronese setting. The piece was inspired by the struggles the Thai art community had in getting the new contemporary Bangkok art museum to open without it becoming a shopping mall in disguise.

Pop Fun

True to the Thai nature, some art is just fun. The works of Thaweesak Srithongdee are pure pop. He paints flamboyantly cartoonish human figures woven with elements of traditional Thai handicrafts or imagery. In a similar vein, Jirapat Tasanasomboon depicts traditional Thai figures in comic-book-style fights or in sensual embraces with Western icons. In

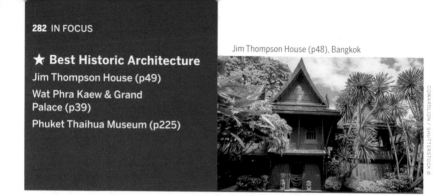

★ **Best Historic Architecture**

Jim Thompson House (p49)

Wat Phra Kaew & Grand Palace (p39)

Phuket Thaihua Museum (p225)

Hanuman Is Upset! the monkey king chews up the geometric lines of Mondrian's famous gridlike painting. Thai-Japanese artist Yuree Kensaku creates cartoon-like paintings with pop-culture references.

Sculpture

Although lacking in commercial attention, Thai sculpture is often considered to be the strongest of the contemporary arts: not surprising considering the country's relationship with Buddha figures. Moving into nonreligious arenas, Khien Yimsiri is the modern master creating elegant human and mythical forms out of bronze. Kamin Lertchaiprasert explores the subject of spirituality and daily life in his sculptural installations, which often include a small army of papier-mâché figures. His exhibit *Ngern Nang* (Sitting Money) included a series of figures made of discarded paper bills from the national bank and embellished with poetic instructions on life and love.

Theatre & Dance

Traditional Thai theatre consists of dance-dramas, in which stories are acted out by masked or costumed actors. Traditional theatre was reserved for royal or religious events but, with the modernisation of the monarchy, the once-cloistered art forms have lost their patrons and gone into decline. Classical Thai dance, on the other hand, has survived quite well in the modern era and is still widely taught in schools and universities.

Kŏhn & Lí·gair

Kŏhn is a masked dance-drama depicting scenes from the *Ramakian* (the Thai version of India's *Ramayana*). The central story revolves around Prince Rama's search for his beloved Princess Sita, who has been abducted by the evil 10-headed demon Ravana and taken to the island of Lanka.

Most often performed at Buddhist festivals by troupes of travelling performers, *lí·gair* is a gaudy, raucous theatrical art form thought to have descended from drama rituals brought to southern Thailand by Arab and Malay traders. It contains a colourful mixture of folk and classical music, outrageous costumes, melodrama, slapstick comedy, sexual innuendo and up-to-date commentary.

Classical & Folk Dance

Inherited from the Khmer, classical dance was a holy offering performed by the earthly version of *apsara* (heavenly maidens blessed with beauty and skilled in dance, who are depicted in graceful positions in temple murals and bas-reliefs). But traditional dancing enjoyed its own expressions in the villages and defined each region. In some cases the dances describe the rice-planting season, while others tell tales of flirtations. During local festivals and street parades, especially in the northeast, troupes of dancers, ranging from elementary-school age to college age, will be swathed in traditional costumes, ornate headdresses and white-powder make-up to perform synchronised steps accompanied by a marching band.

Music

Classical Thai music features a dazzling array of textures and subtleties, hair-raising tempos and pastoral melodies. The classical orchestra is called the *pèe pâht* and can include as few as five players or more than 20. Among the more common instruments is the *pèe*, a woodwind instrument that has a reed mouthpiece; it is heard prominently at Thai-boxing matches. The *rá·nâht èhk*, a bamboo-keyed percussion instrument resembling the xylophone, carries the main melodies. The slender *sor*, a bowed instrument with a coconut-shell soundbox, is sometimes played solo by street buskers.

If you take a cab in Bangkok, you're likely to hear Thailand's version of country music: *lôok tûng* (literally 'children of the fields'). Lost love, tragic early death and the plight of the hard-working farmers are popular themes sung plaintively over a melancholy accompaniment. More upbeat is *mŏr lam*, a folk tradition from the rural northeast that has been electrified with a fast-paced beat. Step into a shopping mall or a Thai disco and you'll hear the bouncy tunes of Thai pop (also dubbed 'T-pop'). The ageing hippies from the protest era of the 1970s and 1980s pioneered *pleng pêu·a chee·wít* (songs for life), which feature in the increasingly hard-to-find Thai country bars. The 1990s gave birth to an alternative pop scene – known as 'indie'.

Architecture

Traditional Homes

Traditional Thai homes were adapted to the weather, the family and artistic sensibilities. These antique specimens were humble dwellings consisting of a single-room wooden house raised on stilts. More elaborate homes, for the village chief or minor royalty for instance, might link a series of single rooms by elevated walkways. Since many Thai villages were built near rivers, the elevation provided protection from flooding during the annual monsoon. During the dry season the space beneath the house was used as a hideaway from the heat of the day, an outdoor kitchen or as a barn for farm animals. Later this all-purpose space would shelter bicycles and motorcycles.

Once plentiful in Thai forests, teak was always the material of choice for wooden structures and its use typically indicates that a house is at least 50 years old. Rooflines in central, northern and southern Thailand are steeply pitched and often decorated at the corners or along the gables with motifs related to the *naga*, a mythical water serpent long

Handicrafts

Thailand's handicrafts live on for the tourist markets, and some have been updated by chic Bangkok designers.

Ceramics The best-known ceramics are the greenish Thai-style celadon, and central Thailand's *ben·jà·rong* (five colour).

Lacquerware Northern Thailand is known for this handicraft inherited from Myanmar.

Textiles The northeast is famous for *mát·mèe* cloth – a thick cotton or silk fabric woven from tie-dyed threads. Each hill tribe has a tradition of embroidery; Chiang Mai and Chiang Rai are popular handicraft centres.

Temple Symbols

The architectural symbolism of Thai temples relies heavily on Hindu-Buddhist iconography. *Naga,* the mythical serpent that guarded Buddha during meditation, appears on hand-rails at temple entrances. A silhouette of the birdlike *chôr fáh* adorns the tip of the roof. Three-tiered roofs represent the triple gems of Buddhism: the Buddha, the *dhamma* (teachings) and the *sangha* (the Buddhist community). The lotus, a reminder of religious perfection, decorates temple gates and posts, verandah columns and spires of Sukhothai-era *chedi,* and often forms the pedestal for images of the meditating Buddha. Lotus buds are used solely for merit-making.

believed to be a spiritual protector of Tai cultures throughout Asia. In Thailand's southern provinces it's not unusual to come upon houses of Malay design, using high masonry pediments or foundations rather than wooden stilts. Residents of the south also sometimes use bamboo and palm thatch, which are more plentiful than wood. In the north, the homes of community leaders were often decorated with an ornate horn-shaped motif called *galare,* a decorative element that has become shorthand for old Lanna architecture. Roofs of tile or thatch tend to be less steeply pitched, and rounded gables – a feature inherited from Myanmar – can also be found further north.

Temples

The most striking examples of Thailand's architectural heritage are the Buddhist temples (wát), which dazzle in the tropical sun with wild colours and soaring rooflines. Thai temples are compounds of different buildings serving specific religious functions. The most important structures include the *uposatha* (*bòht* in central Thai, *sĭm* in northern and northeastern Thai), which is a consecrated chapel where monastic ordinations are held, and the *wí·hăhn,* where important Buddha images are housed.

A classic component of temple architecture is the presence of one or more *chedi* (stupas), a solid mountain-shaped monument that pays tribute to the enduring stability of Buddhism. *Chedi* come in myriad styles, from simple inverted bowl-shaped designs imported from Sri Lanka to the more elaborate octagonal shapes found in northern Thailand. Many are believed to contain relics (often pieces of bone) belonging to the historical Buddha. Some *chedi* also house the ashes of important kings and royalty. A variation of the stupa inherited from the Angkor kingdom is the corn-cob-shaped *prang,* a feature in the ancient Thai temples of Sukhothai and Ayuthaya.

Contemporary Architecture

Thais began mixing traditional architecture with European forms in the late 19th and early 20th centuries, as exemplified by certain buildings of the Grand Palace. The port cities of Thailand, including Bangkok and Phuket, acquired fine examples of Sino-Portuguese architecture – buildings of stuccoed brick decorated with an ornate facade – a style that followed the sea traders during the colonial era. In Bangkok this style is often referred to as 'old Bangkok' or Ratanakosin. In the 1960s and 1970s the European Bauhaus movement shifted contemporary architecture towards a stark functionalism. During the building boom of the mid-1980s, Thai architects used high-tech designs such as ML Sumet Jumsai's famous Robot Building on Th Sathon Tai in Bangkok. In the new millennium, shopping centres and hotels have reinterpreted the traditional Thai house through an industrial modernist perspective, creating geometric cubes defined by steel beams and glass curtains.

Elephants, Chiang Mai

Environment & Wildlife

Thailand clings to a southern spur of the Himalaya in the north, cradles fertile river plains at its core and tapers between two shallow seas fringed by coral reefs. Its shape is likened to an elephant's head, with the Malay Peninsula representing the trunk. Spanning 1650km and 16 latitudinal degrees from north to south, Thailand is one of the most environmentally diverse countries in Southeast Asia.

Northern Thailand

Northern Thailand is fused to Myanmar, Laos and southern China through the south-east-trending extension of the Himalayan mountain range known as the Dawna-Tenasserim. The tallest peak is Doi Inthanon (measured heights vary from 2565m to 2576m), which is topped by a mixed forest of evergreen and swamp species, including a thick carpet of moss. Monsoon forests comprise the lower elevations and are made up of deciduous trees, which are green and lush during the rainy season but dusty and leafless during the dry season. Teak is one of the most highly valued monsoon forest trees but it now exists only in limited quantities and is illegal to harvest. The cool mountains of northern Thailand are considered to be some of the most accessible and rewarding birding

Environmental Trivia

o Thailand is equivalent in area to the size of France.

o Bangkok sits at about N14° latitude, level with Madras, Manila, Guatemala and Khartoum.

o The Mekong rivals the Amazon River in terms of biodiversity.

o Thailand is home to venomous snakes, including the pit viper and the king cobra.

o Thailand's limestone formations are a soft sedimentary rock created by shells and coral from an ancient sea bed 250 to 300 million years ago.

destinations in Asia and are populated by montane species and migrants with clear Himalayan affinities, such as flycatchers and thrushes.

Central Thailand

In the central region the topography mellows into a flat rice basket, fed by rivers that are as revered as the national monarchy. Thailand's most exalted river is the Chao Phraya, which is formed by the northern tributaries of the Ping, Wang, Yom and Nan – a lineage as notable as any aristocrat's. The river delta spends most of the year in cultivation, changing with the seasons from fields of emerald-green rice shoots to golden harvests. This region has been heavily sculpted by civilisation: roads, fields, cities and towns have transformed the landscape into a working core. In the western frontier, bumping into the mountainous border with Myanmar is a complex of forest preserves that cover 17,800 sq km – the largest protected area in Southeast Asia and a largely undisturbed habitat for endangered elephants and tigers. These parks have little in the way of tourist infrastructure or commercial development.

Northeastern Thailand

The landscape of Thailand's northeastern region is occupied by the arid Khorat Plateau rising some 300m above the central plain. This is a hardscrabble land where the rains are meagre, the soil is anaemic and the red dust stains as stubbornly as the betel nut chewed by the local grandmothers. The dominant forest is dry dipterocarp, which consists of deciduous trees that shed their leaves in the dry season to conserve water. The region's largest forest preserve is Khao Yai National Park, which, together with nearby parks, has been recognised as a Unesco World Heritage Site. The park is mainly arid forest, a favourite of hornbills and more than 300 other bird species. There is a small population of wild elephants in the park but development around the perimeter has impacted important wildlife corridors.

Southern Thailand

The kingdom's eastern rivers dump their waters and sediment into the Gulf of Thailand, a shallow basin off the neighbouring South China Sea. In the joint of the fishhook-shaped gulf is Bangkok, surrounded by a thick industrial zone that has erased or polluted much of the natural environment. The extremities of the gulf, both to the east and to the south, are more characteristic of coastal environments: mangrove swamps form the transition between land and sea and act as the ocean's nursery, spawning and nurturing fish, bird and amphibian species. Thailand is home to nearly 75 species of these salt-tolerant trees that were once regarded as wastelands and were vulnerable to coastal development.

The long slender 'trunk' of land that runs between the Gulf of Thailand and the Andaman Sea is often referred to as the Malay Peninsula. This region is Thailand's most tropical: rainfall is plentiful, cultivating thick rainforests that stay green year-round. Malayan flora and fauna predominate and a scenic range of limestone mountains meanders from land to sea. On the west coast, the Andaman Sea is an outcropping of the larger Indian Ocean and home to astonishing coral reefs that feed and shelter thousands of varieties of fish and act as breakwaters against tidal surges. Many of the coral-fringed islands are designated marine national parks, limiting – to some degree – coastal development and boat traffic. The 2010 global coral bleaching phenomenon (in which El Niño weather conditions contributed to warmer sea temperatures) killed or damaged significant portions of Thailand's reefs.

National Parks & Protected Areas

With 15% of the kingdom's land and sea designated as park or sanctuary, Thailand has one of the highest percentages of protected areas of any Asian nation. There are more than 100 national parks, plus more than 1000 'nonhunting areas', wildlife sanctuaries, forest reserves, botanic gardens and arboretums. Thailand began its conservation efforts in 1960 with the creation of a national system of wildlife sanctuaries under the Wild Animals Reservation and Protection Act, followed by the National Parks Act of 1961. Khao Yai National Park was the first wild area to receive this new status. Despite promises, official designation as a national park or sanctuary does not guarantee protection from development or poaching. Local farmers, hunters and moneyed interests often circumvent conservation efforts. Enforcement of environmental regulations lacks political will and proper funding. Foreign visitors are often confused by resort development in national parks despite their protected status. In some cases private ownership of land pre-dated the islands' protected status, while in other cases rules are bent for powerful interests.

Mekong River

Defining the contours of Thailand's border with Laos is the Mekong River, Southeast Asia's artery. The Mekong is a workhorse, having been dammed for hydroelectric power, and a mythmaker, featuring in local people's folktales and festivals. The river winds in and out of the steep mountain ranges to the northeastern plateau where it swells and contracts according to seasonal rainfall. In the dry season, riverside farmers plant vegetables in the muddy floodplain, harvesting the crop before the river reclaims its territory. Scientists have identified the Mekong River as having impressive biodiversity. As many as 1000 previously unidentified species of flora and fauna have been discovered in the last decade in the Mekong region (which includes Vietnam, Laos and Cambodia).

Environmental Issues

Thailand has put enormous pressure on its ecosystems as it has industrialised. Natural forest cover now makes up about 28% of land area, compared to 70% some 50 years ago. Thailand's coastal region has experienced higher population and economic growth than the national average and these areas suffer from soil erosion, water pollution and degradation of coral reef systems. Seasonal flooding is a common natural occurrence in some parts of Thailand due to the nature of the monsoon rains. But high-level floods have increased in frequency and severity. The record-busting 2011 flooding was one of the world's costliest natural disasters. Of the country's 77 provinces, 65 were declared flood disaster zones; there were 815 deaths and an estimated US$45.7 billion worth of damage.

Ang Thong Marine National Park (p116)

★ National Parks

Ang Thong Marine National Park (p116)

GANG PENG / 500PX ©

Fisheries continue to experience declining catches as fish stocks plummet, and an industry once dominated by small family fisherfolk has shifted to big commercial enterprises that can go into deeper waters.

In 2013 a pipeline unloading an oil tanker off the coast of Rayong spilled 50,000L of crude into the sea, coating the western side of Ko Samet. While the outward condition of beaches quickly recovered with the use of dispersants, experts say there may be considerable long-term effects of the spill on both human health and the marine ecosystem.

Akha women, Chiang Rai (p126)

Responsible Travel

*Thais are a warm and friendly people who generally
welcome foreign visitors and appreciate efforts to
understand their culture and society. There are
numerous volunteer organisations for travellers who
are keen on contributing, and they can be a rewarding
way to learn more about Thailand, its people and
environment.*

Cultural Etiquette

The monarchy and religion (which are interconnected) are treated with extreme deference
in Thailand. Thais avoid criticising or disparaging the royal family for fear of offending
someone or, worse, being charged with a violation of the country's very strict lèse-majesté
laws, which carry a jail sentence.

Buddha images are sacred objects. Thais consider it bad form to pull a silly pose in front
of one for a photo, or to clamber upon them (in the case of temple ruins). Instead they
would show respect by performing a *wâi* (a prayer-like gesture) to the figure no matter how
humble it is. As part of their ascetic vows, monks are not supposed to touch or be touched
by women. If a woman wants to hand something to a monk, the object is placed within
reach of the monk or on the monk's 'receiving cloth'.

Essential Etiquette – Dos

Stand respectfully for the royal and national anthem They are played on TV and radio stations as well as in public and government places.

Smile a lot It makes everything easier.

Bring a gift if you're invited to a Thai home Fruit, drinks or snacks are acceptable.

Take off your shoes When you enter a home or temple building.

Dress modestly for temple visits Cover to the elbows and ankles and always remove your shoes when entering any building containing a Buddha image.

Sit in the 'mermaid' position inside temples Tuck your feet beside and behind you.

Give and receive politely Extend the right hand out while the left hand gently grips the right elbow when handing an object to another person or receiving something.

From a spiritual viewpoint, Thais regard the head as the highest and most sacred part of the body and the feet as the dirtiest and lowest. Many of the taboos associated with the feet have a practical derivation as well. Traditionally Thais ate, slept and entertained on the floor of their homes with little in the way of furniture. To keep their homes and eating surfaces clean, the feet (and shoes) contracted a variety of rules.

Shoes aren't worn inside private homes and temple buildings, both as a sign of respect and for sanitary reasons. Thais can kick off their shoes in one fluid step and many lace-up shoes are modified by the wearer to become slip-ons. Thais also step over – not on – the threshold, which is where the spirit of the house is believed to reside. On some buses and 3rd-class trains you'll see Thais prop their feet up on the adjacent bench, and while this isn't the height of propriety, do notice that they always remove their shoes before doing so. Thais also take off their shoes if they need to climb onto a chair or seat.

Thais don't touch each others' heads or ruffle hair as a sign of affection. Occasionally you'll see young people touching each others' heads, which is a teasing gesture, maybe even a slight insult, between friends.

Thais hold modesty in personal dress in high regard, though this is changing among the younger generation. The importance of modesty extends to the beach as well. Except for urbanites, most provincial Thais swim fully clothed. For this reason, sunbathing nude or topless is not acceptable and in some cases it is even illegal. Remember that swimsuits are not proper attire off the beach; wear a cover-up in between the sand and your hotel.

Tourism

Most forms of tourism, despite the prevailing prejudices, have a positive economic effect on the local economy in Thailand, providing jobs for young workers and business opportunities for entrepreneurs. But in an effort to be more than just a consumer, many travellers look for opportunities to spend where their money might be needed, either on charitable causes or activities that preserve traditional ways of life. Thailand has done a surprisingly good job at adapting to this emerging trend by promoting village craft programs and homestays. Unfortunately, much of this is aimed at the domestic market rather than international visitors. But more and more, foreign tourists can engage in these small-scale tourism models that offer an insight into traditional ways. Travellers should also consider the environmental impact of their activities.

Diving

The popularity of Thailand's diving industry places immense pressure on fragile coral sites. To help preserve the ecology, adhere to these simple rules:

o Avoid touching living marine organisms, standing on coral or dragging equipment (such as fins) across reefs. Coral polyps can be damaged by even the gentlest contact.

o When treading water in shallow reef areas, be careful not to kick up clouds of sand, which can easily smother the delicate reef organisms.

o Take great care in underwater caves where your air bubbles can be caught within the roof and leave previously submerged organisms high and dry.

o Join a coral clean-up campaign that's sponsored by dive shops.

o Don't feed the fish or allow your dive operator to dispose of excess food in the water. The fish become dependent on this food source and don't tend to the algae on the coral, causing harm to the reef.

Elephant Encounters

Throughout Thai history, elephants have been revered for their strength, endurance and intelligence, working alongside their mahouts harvesting teak, transporting goods through mountainous terrain or fighting ancient wars.

Many of the elephants' traditional roles have either been outsourced to machines or outlawed, leaving the 'domesticated' animals and their mahouts without work. Some mahouts turned to begging on the streets in Bangkok and other tourist centres, but most elephants find work in Thailand's tourism industry. Their jobs vary from circus-like shows and elephant camps giving rides to tourists to 'mahout-training' schools, while sanctuaries and rescue centres provide modest retirement homes to animals that are no longer financially profitable to their owners.

It costs about 30,000B (US$1000) a month to provide a comfortable living for an elephant, an amount equivalent to the salary of Thailand's upper-middle class. Welfare standards within the tourism industry are not standardised or subject to government regulations, so it's up to the conscientious consumer to encourage the industry to ensure safe conditions for elephants.

With more evidence available than ever to support claims by animal welfare experts that elephant rides and shows are harmful to these gentle giants, who are often abused to force them to perform for humans, a small but growing number of sanctuaries offer more sustainable interactions, such as walking with and bathing retired and rescued elephants.

Lonely Planet does not recommend riding on elephants or viewing elephant performances. We also urge visitors to be wary of organisations that advertise as being a conservation centre but actually offer rides and performances.

Hill-Tribe Hiking

Though marginalised within mainstream society, Thailand's hill-tribe minorities remain a strong tourism draw, with large and small businesses organising 'trekking' tours (these can range from proper hikes to leisurely walks) to villages for cultural displays and interactions. Economically it is unclear whether hill-tribe trekking helps alleviate the poverty of the hill-tribe groups, which in turn helps to maintain their separate ethnic identity. Most agree that a small percentage of the profits from trekking filters down to individual families within hill-tribe villages, giving them a small source of income that might prevent urban migration.

In general, the trekking business has become more socially conscious than in past decades. Most companies now tend to limit the number of visits to a particular area to lessen the impact of outsiders on the daily lives of ordinary villagers. But the industry still has a long way to go. It should be noted that trekking companies are Thai owned and employ Thai guides, another bureaucratic impediment regarding citizenship for ethnic minorities. Without an identification card, guides from hill tribes do not qualify for a Tourist Authority of Thailand (TAT) tour guide licence and so are less than desirable job candidates.

Trekkers should also realise that the minority tribes maintain their own distinct cultural identity and many continue their animistic traditions, which define social taboos and conventions. If you're planning on visiting hill-tribe villages on an organised trek, talk to your guide about acceptable behaviour.

Here is a general prescription to get you started:

o Always ask for permission before taking any photos of tribes people, especially at private moments inside their dwellings. Many traditional belief systems regard photography with suspicion.

o Show respect for religious symbols and rituals. Don't touch totems at village entrances or sacred items hanging from trees. Don't participate in ceremonies unless invited.

o Avoid cultivating the practice of begging, especially among children. Talk to your guide about donating to a local school instead.

o Avoid public nudity and be careful not to undress near an open window where village children might be able to peep in.

o Don't flirt with members of the opposite sex unless you plan on marrying them.

o Don't drink or do drugs with the villagers; altered states sometimes lead to culture clashes.

o Smile at villagers even if they stare at you. Ask your guide how to say 'hello' in the tribal language.

o Avoid public displays of affection, which in some traditional systems are viewed as offensive to the spirit world.

o Don't interact with the villagers' livestock, even the free-roaming pigs; these creatures are valuable possessions, not entertainment. Also avoid interacting with jungle animals, which in some belief systems are viewed as visiting spirits.

o Don't litter.

o Adhere to the same feet taboos that apply to Thai culture. Don't step on the threshold of a house, prop your feet up against the fire or wear your shoes inside.

Homestays

A visit to a homestay is one of the best ways to experience Thailand's rural culture, not to mention a way to ensure that your baht are going directly to locals. More popular with domestic tourists, homestays differ from guesthouses in that visitors are welcomed into a family's home, typically in a small village that isn't on the tourist trail. Accommodation is basic: usually a mat or foldable mattress on the floor, or occasionally a family will have a private room. Rates include lodging, meals with the family and cultural activities that highlight the region's traditional way of life, from rice farming to silk weaving. English fluency varies, so homestays are also an excellent way to exercise your spoken Thai.

Essential Etiquette – Don'ts

Get a tattoo of the Buddha Nor display one you already have. It is considered sacrilegious.

Criticise the monarchy The monarchy is revered and protected by defamation laws – more so now than ever.

Prop your feet on tables or chairs Feet are considered dirty and people have to sit on chairs.

Step on a dropped bill to prevent it from blowing away Thai money bears a picture of the king. Feet + monarchy = grave offence.

Step over someone or their personal belongings Aaah, attack of the feet.

Tie your shoes to the outside of your backpack They might accidentally brush against someone: gross.

Touch a Thai person on the head It is considered rude, not chummy.

Touch monks or their belongings Women are expected to step out of the way when passing a monk on the footpath and should not sit next to them on public transport.

Volunteering

There are myriad volunteer organisations in Thailand to address both the needs of the locals and visitors' desires to help. A regularly updated resource for grassroots-level volunteer opportunities is Volunteer Work Thailand (www.volunteerworkthailand.org). Be aware, though, that so-called 'voluntourism' has become a big business and that not every organisation fulfils its promise of meaningful experiences. It is essential that you do your own thorough research before agreeing to volunteer with any organisation.

A number of NGOs undertake local conservation efforts and run rescue and sanctuary centres for wild animals that have been adopted as pets or veterinarian clinics that tend to the domesticated population of dogs and cats. At centres and sanctuaries that rely on volunteer labour, your hard work is often rewarded with meaningful interactions with the animals.

Northern Thailand, especially Chiang Mai and Chiang Rai, has a number of volunteer opportunities working with disadvantaged hill-tribe groups. There are also many volunteer teaching positions in northeastern Thailand, the country's agricultural heartland.

When looking for a volunteer placement, it is essential to investigate what your chosen organisation does and, more importantly, how it goes about it. If the focus is not primarily on your skills and how these can be applied to help local people, that should ring alarm bells. Any organisation that promises to let you do any kind of work, wherever you like, for as long as you like, is unlikely to be putting the needs of local people first.

For any organisation working with children, child protection is a serious concern, and organisations that do not conduct background checks on volunteers should be regarded with extreme caution. Experts recommend a three-month commitment for volunteering with children. Visit www.thinkchildsafe.org for more information.

Bangkok (p34)

ELENA ERMAKOVA / SHUTTERSTOCK ©

Survival Guide

Directory A–Z

Accommodation

Thailand offers a wide variety of accommodation, from cheap and basic to pricey and luxurious. In places where spoken English might be limited, it is handy to know the following: *hôrng pát lom* (room with fan) and *hôrng aa* (room with air-con).

Customs Regulations

You do not have to fill in a customs form on arrival unless you have imported goods to declare. In that case you can get the proper form from Thai customs officials at your point of entry. The **Customs Department** (02 667 6000; www.customs.go.th) maintains a helpful website with specific information about regulations for travellers.

Thailand allows the following items to enter duty-free:

- reasonable amount of personal effects (clothing and toiletries)
- professional instruments
- 200 cigarettes
- 1L of wine or spirits

Thailand prohibits the import of the following items:

- firearms and ammunition (unless registered in advance with the police department)
- illegal drugs
- pornographic media

When leaving Thailand, you must obtain an export licence for any antique reproductions or newly cast Buddha images. Submit two front-view photos of the object(s), a photocopy of your passport, the purchase receipt and the object(s) in question to the **Office of the National Museum** (02 224 1370; National Museum, 4 Th Na Phra That, Bangkok; 9am-4pm Tue-Fri; Chang Pier, Maharaj Pier, Phra Chan Tai Pier). Allow four days for the application and inspection process to be completed.

Climate

Bangkok
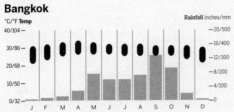

Chiang Mai
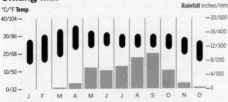

Phuket
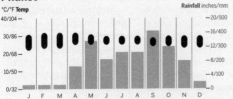

Electricity

Thailand uses 220V AC electricity. Power outlets most commonly feature two-prong round or flat sockets.

Type A
220V/50Hz

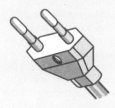

Type C
220V/50Hz

Food

The following price ranges indicate how much you should expect to pay for a main dish in Thailand.

$ less than 150B
$$ 150–350B
$$$ more than 350B

Health

Health risks and the quality of medical facilities vary depending on where and how you travel in Thailand. The majority of cities and popular tourist areas have adequate, and even excellent, medical care. However, travel to remote rural areas can expose you to some health risks and less adequate medical care.

Travellers tend to worry about contracting exotic infectious diseases when visiting the tropics, but these are far less common than problems with pre-existing medical conditions, such as heart disease, and accidental injury (especially as a result of traffic accidents).

Other common illnesses are respiratory infections, diarrhoea and dengue fever. Fortunately most common illnesses can be prevented or are easily treated.

Our advice is a general guide and does not replace the advice of a doctor trained in travel medicine.

Before You Go

Pack medications in clearly labelled original containers and obtain a signed and dated letter from your physician describing your medical conditions, medications and syringes or needles. If you have a heart condition, bring a copy of your electrocardiogram (ECG) taken just prior to travelling.

If you take any regular medication bring double your needs in case of loss or theft. In Thailand you can buy many medications over the counter without a doctor's prescription, but it can be difficult to find the exact medication you are taking.

Contact your home country's Department of Foreign Affairs or the equivalent and register your trip; this is a helpful precaution in the event of a natural disaster

Insurance

Don't travel without health insurance – accidents do happen. You may require extra cover for adventure activities such as rock climbing or diving, as well as scooter or motorcycle riding. If your home health insurance doesn't cover you for medical expenses abroad, ensure you get specific travel insurance.

Most hospitals require an upfront guarantee of payment (from yourself or your insurer) prior to admission. Enquire before your trip about payment of medical charges and retain all documentation (medical reports, invoices etc) for claim purposes.

Medical Checklist

Recommended items for a personal medical kit include the following, most of which are available in Thailand.

- antifungal cream, eg Clotrimazole
- antibacterial cream, eg Muciprocin
- antibiotic for skin infections, eg Amoxicillin/ Clavulanate or Cephalexin
- antibiotics for diarrhoea include Norfloxacin, Ciprofloxacin or Azithromycin for bacterial diarrhoea; for giardiasis or amoebic dysentery, take Tinidazole
- antihistamine – there are many options, eg Cetrizine for daytime and Promethazine for night-time
- antiseptic, eg Betadine
- antispasmodic for stomach cramps, eg Buscopan
- contraceptives
- decongestant
- DEET-based insect repellent
- oral rehydration solution for diarrhoea (eg Gastrolyte), diarrhoea 'stopper' (eg Loperamide) and antinausea medication
- first-aid items such as scissors, Elastoplasts, bandages, gauze, thermometer (but not one with mercury), sterile needles and syringes (with a doctor's letter), safety pins and tweezers
- alcohol-based hand gel or wipes
- ibuprofen or another anti-inflammatory
- indigestion medication, eg Quick-Eze or Mylanta
- laxative, eg Coloxyl
- migraine medicine – for migraine sufferers
- paracetamol
- permethrin to impregnate clothing and mosquito nets if at high risk
- steroid cream for allergic/ itchy rashes, eg 1% to 2% hydrocortisone
- sunscreen, sunglasses and hat
- throat lozenges
- thrush (vaginal yeast infection) treatment, eg Clotrimazole pessaries or Diflucan tablet
- Ural or equivalent if prone to urinary-tract infections

Recommended Vaccines

Arrange your vaccines six to eight weeks prior to departure through a specialised travel-medicine clinic.

The Centers for Disease Control and Prevention (www.cdc.gov) has a traveller's health section that contains recommendations for vaccinations. The only vaccine required by international regulations is yellow fever. Proof of vaccination will only be required if you have visited a country in the yellow-fever zone within the six days prior to entering Thailand. If you are travelling to Thailand from Africa or South America you should check to see if you require proof of vaccination.

In Transit

Deep-vein thrombosis (DVT) occurs when blood clots form in the legs during long trips chiefly because of prolonged immobility. Though most blood clots are reabsorbed uneventfully, some may break off and travel through the blood vessels to the lungs, where they can cause life-threatening complications.

The chief symptom of DVT is swelling or pain of the foot, ankle or calf, usually but not always on one side. When a blood clot travels to the lungs, it may cause chest pain and difficulty in breathing. Travellers with any of these symptoms should immediately seek medical attention.

To prevent the development of DVT on long flights, you should walk about the cabin periodically, and drink plenty of fluids (nonalcoholic).

Jet lag is common when crossing more than five time zones. It results in insomnia, fatigue, malaise or nausea. To avoid jet lag, drink plenty of fluids (nonalcoholic) and eat light meals. Upon arrival, seek exposure to natural sunlight and readjust your sleep schedule. Some people find melatonin helpful to relieve symptoms.

In Thailand

Infectious Diseases

Cuaneous Larva Migrans

This disease, caused by dog or cat hookworm, is particularly common on the beaches of Thailand. The rash starts as a small lump, and then slowly spreads like a winding line. It is intensely itchy, especially at night. It is easily treated with medications and should not be cut out or frozen.

Dengue Fever

This mosquito-borne disease is increasingly problematic in Thailand, especially in the cities. As there is no vaccine, it can only be prevented by avoiding mosquito bites. The mosquito that carries dengue is a daytime biter, so use insect-avoidance measures at all times. Symptoms include high fever, severe headache (especially behind the eyes), nausea and body aches (dengue was previously known as 'breakbone fever'). Some people develop a rash (which can be very itchy) and experience diarrhoea.

There is no specific treatment, just rest and paracetamol – do not take aspirin or ibuprofen as they increase the risk of haemorrhaging. See a doctor to be diagnosed and monitored.

Dengue can progress to the more severe and life-threatening dengue haemorrhagic fever, but this is very uncommon in tourists. The risk of this increases substantially if you have previously been infected with dengue and are then infected with a different serotype.

Hepatitis A

The risk of hepatitis A in Bangkok is decreasing, but there is still significant risk in most of the country. This food- and waterborne virus infects the liver, causing jaundice (yellow skin and eyes), nausea and lethargy. There is no specific treatment for hepatitis A. All travellers to Thailand should be vaccinated against hepatitis A.

Hepatitis B

The only sexually transmitted disease (STD) that can be prevented by vaccination, hepatitis B is spread by body fluids, including sexual contact. In some parts of Thailand up to 20% of the population are carriers of hepatitis B, and usually are unaware of this. The long-term consequences can include liver cancer, cirrhosis and death.

HIV

HIV is now one of the most common causes of death in people under the age of 50 in Thailand. Always practice safe sex, and avoid getting tattoos or using unclean syringes.

Influenza

Present year-round in the tropics, influenza (flu) symptoms include high fever, muscle aches, runny nose, cough and sore throat. Flu is the most common vaccine-preventable disease contracted by travellers and everyone should consider vaccination. There is no specific treatment, just rest and paracetamol. Complications such as bronchitis or middle-ear infection may require antibiotic treatment.

Leptospirosis

Leptospirosis is contracted from exposure to infected surface water – most commonly after river rafting or canyoning. Early symptoms are very similar to flu and include headache and fever. It can vary from a very mild ailment to a fatal disease. Diagnosis is made through blood tests and it is easily treated with Doxycycline.

Malaria

There is an enormous amount of misinformation concerning malaria. Malaria is caused by a parasite transmitted by the bite of an infected mosquito. The most important symptom of malaria is fever, but general symptoms such as headache, diarrhoea, cough or chills may also occur – the same symptoms as many other infections. A diagnosis can only be made by taking a blood sample.

Most parts of Thailand visited by tourists, particularly city and resort areas, have minimal to no risk of malaria, and the risk of side effects from taking antimalarial tablets is likely to outweigh the risk of getting the disease itself. If you are travelling to high-risk rural areas (unlikely for most visitors), seek medical advice on the right medication and dosage for you.

Measles

This highly contagious viral infection is spread through coughing and sneezing and remains prevalent in Thailand. Measles starts with a high fever and rash and can be complicated by pneumonia and brain disease. There is no specific treatment. Ensure you are fully vaccinated.

Rabies

This disease, fatal if left untreated, is spread by the bite or lick of an infected animal – most commonly a dog or monkey. You should seek medical advice immediately after any animal bite and commence postexposure treatment. Having a pretravel vaccination means the postbite treatment is greatly simplified.

STDs

Sexually transmitted diseases most common in

Rare But Be Aware

○ **Avian Influenza** Most of those infected have had close contact with sick or dead birds.

○ **Filariasis** A mosquito-borne disease that is common in the local population; practice mosquito-avoidance measures.

○ **Hepatitis E** Transmitted through contaminated food and water and has similar symptoms to hepatitis A. Can be a severe problem in pregnant women. Follow safe eating and drinking guidelines.

○ **Japanese B Encephalitis** Viral disease transmitted by mosquitoes, typically occurring in rural areas. Vaccination is recommended for travellers spending more than one month outside cities, or for long-term expats.

○ **Meliodosis** Contracted by skin contact with soil. Affects up to 30% of the local population in northeastern Thailand. The symptoms are very similar to those experienced by tuberculosis (TB) sufferers. There is no vaccine, but it can be treated with medications.

○ **Strongyloides** A parasite transmitted by skin contact with soil; common in the local population. It is characterised by an unusual skin rash – a linear rash on the trunk that comes and goes. An overwhelming infection can follow. It can be treated with medications.

○ **Tuberculosis** Medical and aid workers and long-term travellers who have significant contact with the local population should take precautions. Vaccination is recommended for children spending more than three months in Thailand. The main symptoms are fever, cough, weight loss, night sweats and tiredness. Treatment is available with long-term multidrug regimens.

○ **Typhus** Murine typhus is spread by the bite of a flea; scrub typhus is spread via a mite. Symptoms include fever, muscle pains and a rash. Follow general insect-avoidance measures; Doxycycline will also prevent it.

Thailand include herpes, warts, syphilis, gonorrhoea and chlamydia. People carrying these diseases often have no signs of infection. Condoms will prevent gonorrhoea and chlamydia, but not warts or herpes. If after a sexual encounter you develop any rash, lumps, discharge or pain when passing urine, seek immediate medical attention. If you have been sexually active during your travels, have an STD check on your return home.

Typhoid

This serious bacterial infection is spread through food and water. It gives a high and slowly progressive fever, severe headache and may be accompanied by a dry cough and stomach pain. It is diagnosed by blood tests and treated with antibiotics. Vaccination is recommended for all travellers spending more than a week in Thailand, or travelling outside of the major cities. Be aware that vaccination is not 100% effective, so you must still be careful with what you eat and drink.

Traveller's Diarrhoea

Traveller's diarrhoea is by far the most common problem affecting travellers. In over 80% of cases, traveller's diarrhoea is caused by a bacteria (there are numerous potential culprits) and responds promptly to treatment with antibiotics.

Here we define traveller's diarrhoea as the passage

of more than three watery bowel movements within 24 hours, plus at least one other symptom such as vomiting, fever, cramps, nausea or feeling generally unwell.

Treatment consists of staying well hydrated; rehydration solutions such as Gastrolyte are the best for this. Antibiotics such as Norfloxacin, Ciprofloxacin or Azithromycin will kill the bacteria quickly. Seek medical attention if you do not respond to an appropriate antibiotic.

Loperamide is just a 'stopper' that only treats the symptoms. It can be helpful, for example, if you have to go on a long bus ride. Don't take Loperamide if you have a fever, or blood in your stools.

Giardia lamblia is a parasite that is relatively common. Symptoms include nausea, bloating, excess gas, fatigue and intermittent diarrhoea. 'Eggy' burps are often attributed solely to giardiasis. The treatment of choice is Tinidazole, with Metronidazole being a second-line option.

Amoebic dysentery is very rare in travellers, but may be misdiagnosed by poor-quality labs. Symptoms are similar to bacterial diarrhoea. You should always seek reliable medical care if you have blood in your diarrhoea. Treatment involves two drugs: Tinidazole or Metronidazole to kill the parasite in your gut and then a second drug to kill the cysts. If left untreated

complications, such as liver abscesses, can occur.

Environmental Hazards

Jellyfish Stings

Box jellyfish stings are extremely painful and can even be fatal. There are two main types of box jellyfish – multi-tentacled and single-tentacled.

Multi-tentacled box jellyfish are present in Thai waters – these are the most dangerous and a severe envenomation can kill an adult within two minutes. They are generally found along sandy beaches near river mouths and mangroves during the warmer months.

There are many types of single-tentacled box jellyfish, some of which can cause severe symptoms known as the Irukandji syndrome. The initial sting can seem minor; however severe symptoms such as back pain, nausea, vomiting, sweating, difficulty breathing and a feeling of impending doom can develop between five and 40 minutes later.

There are many other jellyfish in Thailand that cause irritating stings but no serious effects. The only way to prevent these stings is to wear protective clothing.

Heat

For most people it takes at least two weeks to adapt to the hot climate. Prevent swelling of the feet and ankles as well as muscle cramps caused by excessive sweating by avoiding dehydration and excessive activity in the heat of the day.

Heatstroke requires immediate medical treatment. Symptoms come on suddenly and include weakness, nausea, a hot dry body with a body temperature of more than 41°C, dizziness, confusion, loss of coordination, fits and eventually collapse and loss of consciousness.

Insect Bites & Stings

◉ Bedbugs live in the cracks of furniture and walls and then migrate to the bed at night to feed on humans. You can treat the itch with an antihistamine.

◉ Ticks are contracted when walking in rural areas. They are commonly found behind the ears, on the belly and in armpits. If you've been bitten by a tick and a rash develops at the site of the bite or elsewhere, along with fever or muscle aches, see a doctor. Doxycycline prevents tick-borne diseases.

◉ Leeches are found in humid rainforests. They do not transmit disease, but their bites are often itchy for weeks afterwards and can easily become infected. Apply an iodine-based antiseptic to the bite to help prevent infection.

◉ Bee and wasp stings mainly cause problems for people who are allergic to them. Anyone with a serious allergy should carry an injection of adrenalin (eg an EpiPen) for emergencies.

For others, pain is the main problem – apply ice to the sting and take painkillers.

Parasites

Numerous parasites are common in local populations in Thailand, but most of these are rare in travellers. To avoid parasitic infections, wear shoes and avoid eating raw food, especially fish, pork and vegetables.

Skin Problems

Prickly heat is a common skin rash in the tropics, caused by sweat being trapped under the skin. Treat by taking cool showers and using powders.

Two fungal rashes commonly affect travellers. The first occurs in the groin, armpits and between the toes. It starts as a red patch that slowly spreads and is usually itchy. Treatment involves keeping the skin dry, avoiding chafing and using an antifungal cream such as Clotrimazole or Lamisil. The fungus *Tinea versicolor* causes small and light-coloured patches, most commonly on the back, chest and shoulders. Consult a doctor.

Cuts and scratches become easily infected in humid climates. Immediately wash all wounds in clean water and apply antiseptic. If you develop signs of infection, see a doctor. Coral cuts can easily become infected.

Snakes

Though snake bites are rare for travellers, there are more than 85 species of venomous snakes in Thailand. Wear boots and long pants if walking in an area that may have snakes.

The Thai Red Cross produces antivenom for many of the poisonous snakes in Thailand.

Sunburn

Even on a cloudy day, sunburn can occur rapidly.

Avoiding Mosquito Bites

Travellers are advised to prevent mosquito bites by taking these steps:

◉ Use a DEET-containing insect repellent on exposed skin.

◉ Sleep under a mosquito net, ideally impregnated with permethrin.

◉ Choose accommodation with screens and fans.

◉ Impregnate clothing with permethrin in high-risk areas.

◉ Wear long sleeves and trousers in light colours.

◉ Use mosquito coils.

◉ Spray room with insect repellent before going out.

Tap Water

Although it's deemed potable by the authorities, the Thais don't drink the tap water, and neither should you. Stick to bottled or filtered water during your stay.

Use a strong sunscreen (at least factor 30+), making sure to reapply after a swim, and always wear a wide-brimmed hat and sunglasses outdoors. If you become sunburnt stay out of the sun until you have recovered, apply cool compresses and take painkillers for the discomfort. One-percent hydrocortisone cream applied twice daily is also helpful.

Children's Health

Consult a doctor who specialises in travel medicine prior to travel to ensure your child is appropriately prepared. A medical kit designed specifically for children includes liquid medicines for children who cannot swallow tables. Azithromycin is an ideal paediatric formula used to treat bacterial diarrhoea, as well as ear, chest and throat infections.

Good resources include Lonely Planet's *Travel with Children* and, for those spending longer away, Jane Wilson-Howarth's *Your Child's Health Abroad*.

Women's Health

● In 2016, the Zika virus was confirmed in Thailand, and two cases of birth defects related to the virus were reported. Check the International Association for Medical Assistance for Travellers (www.iamat.org) website for updates on the situation.

● Sanitary products are readily available in Thailand's urban areas.

● Bring adequate supplies of your personal birth-control option, which may not be available.

● Heat, humidity and antibiotics can all contribute to thrush, which can be treated with antifungal creams and Clotrimazole. A practical alternative is one tablet of fluconazole (Diflucan).

● Urinary-tract infections can be precipitated by dehydration or long bus journeys without toilet stops; bring suitable antibiotics for treatment.

Insurance

A travel-insurance policy to cover theft, loss and medical problems is a good idea. Be sure that your policy covers ambulances or an emergency flight home. Some policies specifically exclude 'dangerous activities', which can include scuba diving, motorcycling and even trekking. A locally acquired motorcycle licence is not valid under some policies. You may prefer a policy that pays doctors or hospitals directly rather than you having to pay on the spot and claim later. If you have to claim later, make sure you keep all documentation.

Worldwide travel insurance is available at www.lonelyplanet.com/travel-insurance. You can buy, extend and claim online any time – even if you're already on the road.

Internet Access

Wi-fi is almost standard in hotels, guesthouses and cafes. Signal strength deteriorates in the upper floors of a multistorey building; request a room near a router if wi-fi is essential. Cellular data networks continue to expand and increase in capability.

Legal Matters

In general Thai police don't hassle foreigners, especially tourists. They usually go out of their way to avoid having to speak English with a foreigner, especially regarding minor traffic issues. Thai police do, however, rigidly enforce laws against drug possession. Do be aware that some police divisions, especially on the Thai islands, might view foreigners and their legal infractions as a money-making opportunity.

If you are arrested for any offence, the police will allow

you the opportunity to make a phone call, either to your embassy or consulate in Thailand if you have one, or to a friend or relative if not. There's a whole set of legal codes governing the length of time and the manner in which you can be detained before being charged or put on trial, but a lot of discretion is left to the police. In the case of foreigners the police are more likely to bend these codes in your favour. However, as with police worldwide, if you don't show respect you will make matters worse.

Thai law does not presume an indicted detainee to be either guilty or innocent but rather a 'suspect', whose guilt or innocence will be decided in court. Trials are usually speedy.

The **tourist police** (☎24hr 1155) can be very helpful in cases of arrest. Although they typically have no jurisdiction over the kinds of cases handled by regular cops, they may be able to help with translations or with contacting your embassy. You can call the hotline to lodge complaints or to request assistance with regards to personal safety.

LGBTIQ Travellers

Thai culture is relatively tolerant of both male and female homosexuality. There is a fairly prominent LGBTIQ scene in Bangkok, Pattaya and Phuket. With regard to dress or mannerism, the LGBTIQ community are generally accepted without comment. However, public displays of affection – whether heterosexual or homosexual – are frowned upon.

It's worth noting that, perhaps because Thailand is still a relatively conservative place, lesbians generally adhere to rather strict gender roles. Overtly 'butch' lesbians, called tom (from 'tomboy'), typically have short hair, and wear men's clothing. Femme lesbians refer to themselves as dêe (from 'lady'). Visiting lesbians who don't fit into one of these categories may find themselves met with confusion.

Utopia (www.utopia-asia.com) posts lots of Thailand information for LGBTIQ travellers and publishes a gay guidebook to the kingdom.

Money

Most places in Thailand deal only with cash. Some foreign credit cards are accepted in high-end establishments.

ATMs

Debit and ATM cards issued by a bank in your own country can be used at ATMs around Thailand to withdraw cash (in Thai baht only) directly from your account back home. ATMs are extremely ubiquitous throughout the country and can be relied on for the bulk of your spending cash. Most ATMs allow a max of 20,000B in withdrawals per day.

The downside is that Thai ATMs charge a 200B foreign-transaction fee on top of whatever currency conversion and out-of-network fees your home bank charges. Before leaving home, shop around for a bank account that has free international ATM usage and reimburses fees incurred at other institutions' ATMs.

Changing Money

Banks or private money changers offer the best foreign-exchange rates. When buying baht, US dollars is the most accepted currency, followed by British pounds and euros. Most banks charge a commission and duty for each travellers cheque cashed. Current exchange rates are posted at exchange counters.

Credit & Debit Cards

Credit and debit cards can be used for purchases at some shops, hotels and restaurants. The most commonly accepted cards are Visa and MasterCard. American Express is typically only accepted at high-end hotels and restaurants.

Contact your bank and your credit-card provider before you leave home and notify them of your upcoming trip so that your accounts aren't suspended due to suspicious overseas activity.

Tipping

Tipping is not generally expected in Thailand, though it is appreciated. The exception is loose change from a large restaurant bill – if a meal costs 488B and you pay with a 500B note, some Thais will leave the change. It's a way of saying 'I'm not so money grubbing as to grab every last baht'. At many hotel restaurants and upmarket eateries, a 10% service charge will be added to your bill.

Opening Hours

Banks and government offices close for national holidays. Some bars and clubs close during elections and certain religious holidays when alcohol sales are banned. Shopping centres have banks that open late.

Banks 8.30am to 4.30pm; 24hr ATMs

Bars 6pm to midnight or 1am

Clubs 8pm to 2am

Government Offices 8.30am to 4.30pm Monday to Friday; some close for lunch

Restaurants 8am to 10pm

Shops 10am to 7pm

Photography

Be considerate when taking photographs of locals. Learn how to ask politely in Thai and wait for an embarrassed nod. In some of the regularly visited hill-tribe areas, be prepared for the photographed subject to ask for money in exchange for a picture. Other hill tribes will not allow you to point a camera at them.

Public Holidays

Government offices and banks close their doors on the following public holidays. For the precise dates of lunar holidays, see Events & Festivals on the Tourism Authority of Thailand (www.tourismthailand. org/Events-and-Festivals) website.

1 January New Year's Day

February (date varies) Makha Bucha; Buddhist holy day

6 April Chakri Day; commemorating the founder of the Chakri dynasty, Rama I

13–15 April Songkran Festival

1 May Labour Day

5 May Coronation Day

May/June (date varies) Visakha Bucha; Buddhist holy day

28 July King Maha Vajiralongkorn's Birthday

July/August (date varies) Asanha Bucha; Buddhist holy day

12 August Queen Sirikit's Birthday/Mother's Day

23 October Chulalongkorn Day

5 December Commemoration of Late King Bhumiphol/Father's Day

10 December Constitution Day

31 December New Year's Eve

Safe Travel

The following government websites offer travel advisories and information on current hot spots.

Australian Department of Foreign Affairs (www.smarttraveller.gov.au)

British Foreign Office (www.gov.uk/foreign-travel-advice)

Canadian Department of Foreign Affairs (http://www.fait-maeci.gc.ca)

New Zealand Foreign Affairs & Trade (www.safetravel.govt.nz)

US State Department (www.travel.state.gov/traveladvisories)

Telephone

The telephone country code for Thailand is ☏66 and is used when calling the country from abroad. All Thai telephone numbers are preceded by a '0' if you're dialling domestically (the '0' is omitted when calling from overseas). After the initial '0', the next three numbers represent the provincial area code, which is now integral to the telephone number. If the initial '0' is followed by a '6', an '8' or a '9' then you're dialling a mobile phone.

International Calls

If you want to call an international number from a telephone in Thailand, you must first dial an international access code plus the country code followed by the subscriber number.

In Thailand there are various international access codes charging different rates per minute. The standard direct-dial prefix is ☎001; it is operated by CAT and is considered to have the best sound quality. It connects to the largest number of countries, but it is also the most expensive. The next best is ☎007, a prefix operated by TOT with reliable quality and slightly cheaper rates. Economy rates are available through different carriers – do an internet search to determine promotion codes.

Mobile Phones

The easiest option is to acquire a mobile (cell) phone equipped with a local SIM card. Buying a prepaid SIM is as simple as finding a 7-Eleven. SIM cards include talk and data packages and you can add more funds with a prepaid reload card.

Important Phone Numbers

Thailand country code	☎66
Bangkok city code	☎02
Mobile numbers	☎06, ☎08, ☎09
Operator-assisted international calls	☎100
Free local directory assistance	☎1133

Time

Thailand is seven hours ahead of GMT/UTC (London). Times are often expressed according to the 24-hour clock.

Toilets

The Asian-style squat toilet is increasingly less the norm in Thailand. There are still specimens in rural areas, provincial bus stations, older homes and modest restaurants, but Western-style toilets are becoming more prevalent and appear wherever foreign tourists are found.

If you encounter a squat, here's what you should know. You should straddle the two foot pads and face the door. To flush use the plastic bowl to scoop water out of the adjacent basin and pour into the toilet bowl. Some places supply a small pack of toilet paper at the entrance (5B), otherwise bring your own stash or wipe the old-fashioned way with water.

Even in places where sit-down toilets are installed, the septic system may not be designed to take toilet paper. In such cases there will be a waste basket where you're supposed to place used toilet paper and feminine hygiene products. Some toilets also come with

a small spray hose – Thailand's version of the bidet.

Tourist Information

The government-operated tourist information and promotion service, **Tourism Authority of Thailand** (TAT; ☎1672; www.tourismthailand. org), was founded in 1960 and produces excellent pamphlets on sightseeing. The TAT head office is in Bangkok and there are 35 regional offices throughout the country; check the website for contact information.

Travellers with Disabilities

Thailand presents one large, ongoing obstacle course for the mobility impaired. With high kerbs, uneven footpaths and nonstop traffic, Thai cities can be particularly difficult. In Bangkok many streets must be crossed on pedestrian bridges flanked by steep stairways, while buses and boats don't stop long enough even for the fully mobile. Rarely are there any ramps or other access points for wheelchairs.

A number of more expensive top-end hotels make consistent design efforts to provide disabled access to their properties. Other deluxe hotels with high employee-to-guest ratios are usually good about accommodating the mobility impaired by providing staff help where building design fails. For the rest, you're pretty much left to your own resources.

Download Lonely Planet's free Accessible Travel guide from http://lptravel.to/AccessibleTravel. Alternatively, some organisations and publications that offer tips on international travel include the following:

Accessible Journeys (www.disabilitytravel.com)

Asia Pacific Development Centre on Disability (www.apcdfoundation.org)

Mobility International USA (www.miusa.org)

Society for Accessible Travel & Hospitality (www.sath.org)

Wheelchair Holidays @ Thailand (www.wheelchairtours.com)

Visas

Thailand has visa-exemption and visa-on-arrival agreements with most nations (including European countries, Australia, New Zealand and the USA). Nationals from these countries can enter Thailand at no charge without pre-arranged documentation. Depending on nationality, these citizens are issued a 14- to 90-day visa exemption. Note that for some nationalities, less time (15 days rather than 30 days) is given if arriving by land rather than air. Check

the **Ministry of Foreign Affairs** (☏02 203 5000; www.mfa.go.th) website for more details.

Without proof of an onward ticket and sufficient funds for your projected stay, you can be denied entry, but in practice this is a formality that is rarely checked.

Women Travellers

Women travellers face relatively few problems in Thailand. It is respectful to cover up if you're going deep into rural communities, entering temples or going to and from the beach. But on the whole, local women dress in a variety of different styles (particularly in cities), so you can usually wear spaghetti strap tops and short skirts without offending Thais' modesty streak.

As in most countries, attacks and rapes do occur, especially when an attacker observes a vulnerable target. If you return home from a bar alone, be sure to have your wits about you. Avoid accepting rides from strangers late at night. Some women may prefer to avoid travelling around isolated areas alone.

Keep Thai etiquette in mind during social interactions. A Thai man could feel a loss of face if conversation, flirting or other attention is directed towards him and then diverted to another person. In extreme

cases (or where alcohol is involved), this could create an unpleasant situation or even lead to violence. Women who aren't interested in romantic encounters should not presume that Thai men have merely platonic motives.

Transport

Getting There & Away

Flights and tours can be booked online at www.lonelyplanet.com/bookings.

Air

Airports with international connections include the following:

Suvarnabhumi International Airport (☏02 132 1888; www.suvarnabhumiairport.com) The country's main air terminal is located in Samut Prakan, 30km east of Bangkok and 110km from Pattaya. The airport's name is pronounced *sù·wan·ná·poom*.

Don Mueang International Airport (☏02 535 2111; www.donmueangairportthai.com) Located 25km north of central Bangkok, Don Mueang was retired from service in 2006 only to reopen later as the city's de facto budget and domestic hub.

Phuket International Airport (☏076 632 7230; www.phuket

airportthai.com) With several domestic and international destinations.

Chiang Mai International Airport (☏05 327 0222; www.chiangmaiairportthai.com) International destinations include many Asian and Southeast Asian cities.

Chiang Rai International Airport (Mae Fah Luang International Airport; ☏053 798 000; www.chiangraiairportthai.com) International destinations include Kunming, China.

Samui International Airport (www.samuiairportonline.com) International destinations include Singapore.

Krabi International Airport International destinations include Doha, Kuala Lumpur, Singapore and a few cities in China.

Land

Thailand shares land borders with Cambodia, Laos, Malaysia and Myanmar. Land travel between all of these countries can be done at sanctioned border crossings. With improved highways and new bridges, it is also easier to travel from Thailand to China via Laos.

Getting Around

Air

Hopping around the country by air continues to be affordable. Most routes originate from Bangkok (both Don Mueang and Suvarnabhumi International Airports), but Chiang Mai, Hat Yai, Ko Samui, Phuket and Udon Thani all have a few routes to other Thai towns.

Bicycle

Lack of infrastructure and dangerous roads mean that cycling isn't generally recommended as a means of transport for the casual tourist. Exceptions are the guided bicycle tours of Bangkok and some other large cities that stick to rural routes.

Boat

The true Thai water transport is the *reu·a hǎhng yow* (long-tail boat), so-called because the propeller is mounted at the end of a long driveshaft extending from the engine. The long-tail boats are a staple of transport on rivers and canals in Bangkok and neighbouring provinces, and between islands.

Between the mainland and small, less-touristed islands, the standard craft is a wooden boat, 8m to 10m long, with an inboard engine, a wheelhouse and a simple roof to shelter passengers and cargo. To more popular destinations, faster hovercraft (jetfoils) and speedboats are the norm.

Bus

The bus network in Thailand is prolific and reliable. The Thai government subsidises the Transport Company (*bò·rí·sàt kǒn sòng*), usually abbreviated to Baw Khaw Saw (BKS). Every city and town in Thailand linked by bus has a BKS station, even if it's just a patch of dirt by the side of the road.

By far the most reliable bus companies in Thailand are the ones that operate out of the BKS stations. In some cases the companies are entirely state owned; in others they are private concessions.

We do not recommend using bus companies that

Climate Change & Travel

Every form of transport that relies on carbon-based fuel generates CO_2, the main cause of human-induced climate change. Modern travel is dependent on aeroplanes, which might use less fuel per kilometre per person than most cars but travel much greater distances. The altitude at which aircraft emit gases (including CO_2) and particles also contributes to their climate change impact. Many websites offer 'carbon calculators' that allow people to estimate the carbon emissions generated by their journey and, for those who wish to do so, to offset the impact of the greenhouse gases emitted with contributions to portfolios of climate-friendly initiatives throughout the world. Lonely Planet offsets the carbon footprint of all staff and author travel.

operate directly out of tourist centres, such as Bangkok's Th Khao San, because of repeated instances of theft and commission-seeking stops. Be sure to be aware of bus scams and other common problems.

For an increasing number of destinations, minivans are superseding buses. Minivans are run by private companies and because their vehicles are smaller, they can depart from the market (instead of the out-of-town bus stations) and in some cases will deliver passengers directly to their hotel. Just don't sit in the front – that way you can avoid watching the driver's daredevil techniques!

Car & Motorcycle

Hire

Cars, 4WDs and vans can be hired in most major cities and airports from local companies as well as all the usual international chains. Local companies tend to have cheaper rates, but the quality of their fleets vary. Check the tyre tread and general upkeep of the vehicle before committing.

Motorcycles can be hired in major towns and tourist centres from guesthouses and small mom-and-pop businesses. Hiring a motorcycle in Thailand is relatively easy and a great way to independently tour the countryside. For daily hires most businesses will ask that you leave your passport as a deposit. Before hiring a motorcycle, check the vehicle's condition and ask for a helmet (which is required by law).

Road Rules & Hazards

Thais drive on the left-hand side of the road – most of the time! Other than that, just about anything goes, in spite of road signs and speed limits.

The main rule to be aware of is that right of way goes to the bigger vehicle – this is not what it says in the Thai traffic laws, but it's the reality. Maximum speed limits are 50km/h on urban roads and 80km/h to 100km/h on most highways – but on any given stretch of highway you'll see various vehicles travelling as slowly as 30km/h and as fast as 150km/h.

Indicators are often used to warn passing drivers about oncoming traffic. A flashing left indicator means it's OK to pass, while a right indicator means that someone's approaching from the other direction. Horns are used to tell other vehicles that the driver plans to pass. When drivers flash their lights, they're telling you not to pass.

In Bangkok traffic is chaotic, roads are poorly signposted and motorcycles and random contraflows mean you can suddenly find yourself facing a wall of cars coming the other way.

Outside of the capital, the principal hazard when driving in Thailand, besides the general disregard for traffic laws, is having to contend with so many different types of vehicles on the same road – trucks, bicycles, túk-túk and motorcycles. This danger is often compounded by the lack of working lights. In village areas the vehicular traffic is lighter but you have to contend with stray chickens, dogs and water buffaloes.

Insurance

Thailand requires a minimum of liability insurance for all registered vehicles on the road. The better hire companies include comprehensive coverage for their vehicles. Always verify that a vehicle is insured for liability before signing a rental contract; you should also ask to see the dated insurance documents. If you have an accident while driving an uninsured vehicle, you're in for some major hassles.

Local Transport

City Bus & Sŏrng·tăa·ou

Bangkok has the largest city-bus system in the country, while Udon Thani and a few other provincial capitals have some city-bus services. The etiquette for riding public buses is to wait at a bus stop and hail the vehicle by waving your hand palm-side downward. You typically pay the fare once you've taken a seat or, in some cases, when you disembark.

Elsewhere, public transport is provided by sŏrng·tăa·ou ('two rows'; a small pick-up truck outfitted with two facing benches for passengers). They sometimes operate on fixed routes, just like buses, but they may also run a shared taxi service where they pick up passengers going in the same general direction. In tourist centres, *sŏrng·tăa·ou* can be chartered just like a regular taxi, but you'll need to negotiate the fare beforehand. You can usually hail a *sŏrng·tăa·ou* anywhere along its route and pay the fare when you disembark.

Depending on the region, *sŏrng·tăa·ou* might also run a fixed route from the centre of town to outlying areas, or even points within the provinces.

Mass Transit

Bangkok is the only city in Thailand to have an above-ground (BTS) and underground light-rail (MRT) public transport system.

Taxi

Bangkok has the most formal system of metered taxis, although other cities have growing 'taxi meter' networks. In some cases, fares are set in advance or require negotiation.

In bigger cities, traditional taxi alternatives and app-based taxi hailing initiatives are also available – at least, sort of.

Introduced to Thailand in 2014, Uber (www.uber.com) quickly gained popularity among those looking to avoid the usual Bangkok taxi headaches: communication issues, perpetual lack of change and inability to get a taxi during peak periods. Later that year, however, the service was banned because drivers and the payment system didn't meet government standards. It continues to operate, although less visibly.

Other app-based services include GrabTaxi (www.

grabtaxi.com/th), All Thai Taxi (www.allthaitaxi.com) and Easy Taxi (www.easytaxi.com).

Motorcycle Taxi

Many cities in Thailand have *mor·deu·sai ráp jâhng*, motorcycle taxis that can be hired for short distances. If you're empty-handed or travelling with a small bag, they can't be beaten for transport in a pinch.

In most cities, you'll find motorcycle taxis clustered near street intersections. Usually they wear numbered jerseys. You'll need to establish the price beforehand.

Săhm·lór & Túk-túk

Săhm·lór (also spelt săam-láw) are three-wheeled pedicabs that are typically found in small towns where traffic is light and old-fashioned ways persist.

The modern era's version of the human-powered săhm·lór is the motorised

Dangerous Roads

Thailand's roads are dangerous: in 2015 the World Health Organization declared Thailand the second-deadliest country for road fatalities in the world. Several high-profile bus accidents involving foreign tourists have prompted some Western nations to issue travel advisories for highway safety due to disregard for speed limits, reckless driving and long-distance bus drivers' use of stimulants.

Fatal bus crashes make headlines, but nearly 75% of vehicle accidents in Thailand involve motorcycles. Less than half of the motorcyclists in the country wear helmets and many tourists are injured riding motorcycles because they don't know how to handle the vehicles and are unfamiliar with local driving conventions. British consular offices cited Thailand as a primary destination for UK citizens experiencing road-traffic accidents, often involving motorcyclists.

If you are a novice motorcyclist, familiarise yourself with the vehicle in an uncongested area of town and stick to the smaller 100cc automatic bikes. Drive slowly, especially when roads are slick or when there is loose gravel. Remember to distribute weight as evenly as possible across the frame of the bike to improve handling. And don't expect that other vehicles will look out for you: motorcycles are low on the traffic totem pole.

túk-túk (pronounced *đúk đúk*). They're small utility vehicles, powered by screaming engines (usually LPG-powered) with a lot of flash and sparkle.

With either form of transport the fare must be established by bargaining before departure. In tourist centres, túk-túk drivers often grossly overcharge foreigners, so have a sense of how much the fare should be before soliciting a ride. Hotel staff are helpful in providing reasonable fare suggestions.

Readers interested in pedicab lore and design may want to have a look at Lonely Planet's *Chasing Rickshaws* by Lonely Planet founder Tony Wheeler.

Train

Thailand's train system connects the four corners of the country and is a scenic, if slow, alternative to buses for the long journey north to Chiang Mai or south to Surat Thani. The train is also ideal for short trips to Ayuthaya and Lopburi from Bangkok, where traffic is a consideration.

The 4500km rail network is operated by the **State Railway of Thailand** (SRT; ☐1690; www.railway. co.th) and covers four main lines: northern, southern, northeastern and eastern. All long-distance trains originate from Bangkok's Hualamphong Train Station.

Most train stations have printed timetables in English, though this isn't always the case for smaller stations.

Classes

The SRT operates passenger trains in three classes – 1st, 2nd and 3rd – but each class varies considerably depending on whether you're on an ordinary, rapid or express train. In 2016, SRT announced the purchase of 115 modern train carriages with seat-mounted TV screens and more comfortable bathrooms, currently in use on the northern and northeastern routes.

1st class Private, two-bunk cabins define the 1st-class carriages, which are available only on rapid, express and special-express trains.

2nd class The seating arrangements in a 2nd-class, non-sleeper carriage are similar to those on a bus, with pairs of padded seats, usually recliners, all facing towards the front of the train. On 2nd-class sleeper cars, pairs of seats face one another and convert into two fold-down berths. The lower berth has more headroom than the upper berth and this is reflected in a higher fare. Children are always assigned a lower berth. Second-class carriages are found only on rapid and express trains. There are air-con and fan 2nd-class carriages.

3rd class A typical 3rd-class carriage consists of two rows of bench seats divided into facing pairs. Each bench seat is designed to seat two or three passengers, but on a crowded rural line nobody seems to care. Express trains do not carry 3rd-class carriages at all. Commuter trains in the Bangkok area are all 3rd class.

Costs

Fares are determined on a base price with surcharges added for distance, class and train type (special express, express, rapid, ordinary). Extra charges are added if the carriage has air-con and for sleeping berths (either upper or lower).

Reservations

Advance bookings can be made from one to 60 days before your intended date of departure. You can make bookings in person from any train station. Train tickets can also be purchased at travel agencies, which usually add a service charge to the ticket price. If you're making an advance reservation from outside the country, contact a licensed travel agent; the SRT previously had an online ticket service but that has been discontinued.

It is advisable to make advanced bookings for long-distance sleeper trains between Bangkok and Chiang Mai, or from Bangkok to Surat Thani, as seats fill up quickly.

For short-distance trips you should purchase your ticket at least a day in advance for seats (rather than sleepers).

Partial refunds on tickets are available depending on the number of days prior to your departure that you arrange a cancellation. These arrangements can be handled at the train station booking office.

Language

There are different ways of writing Thai in the Roman alphabet – we have chosen one method below. The hyphens indicate syllable breaks within words, and some syllables are further divided with a dot to help you pronounce them. Thai is a tonal language – the accent marks on vowels represent these low, mid, falling, high and rising tones.

Note that after every sentence, men add the polite particle *káp*, and women *ká*.

To enhance your trip with a phrasebook, visit **lonelyplanet.com**. Lonely Planet iPhone phrasebooks are available through the Apple App store.

Basics

Hello.
สวัสดี · sà-wàt-dee

How are you?
สบายดีไหม · sà-bai dee măi

I'm fine.
สบายดีครับ/ค่ะ · sà·bai dee kráp/kâ (m/f)

Excuse me.
ขออภัย · kŏr à-pai

Yes./No.
ใช่/ไม่ · châi/mâi

Thank you.
ขอบคุณ · kòrp kun

You're welcome.
ยินดี · yin dee

Do you speak English?
คุณพูดภาษา
อังกฤษได้ไหม · kun pôot pah-săh
ang-grìt dâi măi

I don't understand.
ผม/ดิฉันไม่เข้าใจ · pŏm/dì-chăn mâi kôw jai (m/f)

How much is this?
เท่าไร · tôw-rai

Can you lower the price?
ลดราคาได้ไหม · lót rah-kah dâi măi

Accommodation

Where's a hotel?
โรงแรมอยู่ที่ไหน · rohng raam yòo têe năi

Do you have a single/double room?
มีห้องเดี่ยว/
เตียงคู่ไหม · mee hôrng dèe·o/
đee·ang kôo măi

Eating & Drinking

I'd like (the menu), please.
ขอ (รายการ
อาหาร) หน่อย · kŏr (rai gahn
ah-hăhn) nòy

What would you recommend?
คุณแนะนำอะไรบ้าง · kun náa-nam à-rai bâhng

That was delicious.
อร่อยมาก · à-ròy mâhk

Cheers!
ไชโย · chai-yoh

Please bring the bill/check.
ขอบิลหน่อย · kŏr bin nòy

I don't eat ...
ผม/ดิฉัน ไม่กิน ... · pŏm/dì-chăn mâi gin ...
(m/f)

eggs	ไข่	kài
fish	ปลา	þlah
nuts	ถั่ว	tòo·a
red meat	เนื้อแดง	néu·a daang

Emergencies

I'm ill.
ผม/ดิฉันป่วย · pŏm/dì-chăn þòo·ay (m/f)

Help!
ช่วยด้วย · chôo·ay dôo·ay

Call a doctor!
เรียกหมอหน่อย · rêe·ak mŏr nòy

Call the police!
เรียกตำรวจหน่อย · rêe·ak đam-ròo·at nòy

Where are the toilets?
ห้องน้ำอยู่ที่ไหน · hôrng nám yòo têe năi

Directions

Where's (a market/restaurant)?
(ตลาด/ร้านอาหาร) · (đà-làht/ráhn ah-hăhn)
อยู่ที่ไหน · yòo têe năi

What's the address?
ที่อยู่คืออะไร · têe yòo keu à-rai

Could you please write it down?
เขียนลงให้ได้ไหม · kĕe·an long hâi dâi măi

Can you show me (on the map)?
ให้ดู (ในแผนที่) · hâi doo (nai păan têe)
ได้ไหม · dâi măi

Behind the Scenes

Writers' Thanks

Austin Bush

A big thanks to Destination Editors Dora Ball and Clifton Wilkinson, as well as to all the people on the ground in Bangkok and northern Thailand.

Tim Bewer

A hearty *kòrp jai lăi lăi dêu* to the perpetually friendly people of Isan who rarely failed to live up to their reputation for friendliness and hospitality when faced with my incessant questions, in particular Prapaporn Sompakdee (especially for her crispy pork expertise) and Julian Wright. Special thanks to my wife Suttawan for everything.

Celeste Brash

Thanks to Chiang Mai University and my beloved professors; to Samui Steve, Iain Leonard, Frans Betgem, Lee at Akha Ama and Catherine Bodry. A huge hug to Janine Brown of the Smithsonian Conservation Biology Institute for passion and insight on a tricky subject; and my family – Josh, Jasmine and Tevai – who I wish could come with me on every trip.

David Eimer

Thanks to my fellow island writers and all the Lonely Planet crew in London. Thanks also to Alex and co for the nights out on Phuket. As ever, much gratitude to everyone I met on the road who passed on tips, whether knowingly or unwittingly.

Damian Harper

Huge thanks to the late Neil Bambridge, much gratitude for everything, may you rest in peace. Also thanks to Neil's wife Ratchi, to Maurice Senseit, the jolly staff at Nira's in Thong Sala, Piotr, Gemma, James Horton, George W, Celeste Brash and everyone else who helped along the way, in whatever fashion.

Anita Isalska

Big thanks to everyone who helped me on my travels in Thailand. Gratitude to Sai and Anna for the warm welcome and insights into the wild west, to the Tourism Authority Thailand team in Kanchanaburi, and to Tim Bewer for helpful suggestions. I'd also like to thank the kids in Lopburi who helped this perplexed travel writer wriggle free from a prematurely locked temple ground. Thanks always to Normal Matt for crackly Skype calls and support.

Acknowledgements

Climate map data adapted from Peel MC, Finlayson BL & McMahon TA (2007) 'Updated World Map of the Köppen-Geiger Climate Classification', Hydrology and Earth System Sciences, 11, 163344.

Illustrations pp40-1, pp44-5 by Michael Weldon.

This Book

This 2nd edition of Lonely Planet's *Best of Thailand* guidebook was curated by Austin Bush and researched and written by Austin, Tim Bewer, Celeste Brash, David Eimer, Damian Harper and Anita Isalska. The previous edition was curated by China Williams and researched and written by Mark Beales, Tim Bewer, Joe Bindloss, Austin Bush, David Eimer, Bruce Evans, Damian Harper and Isabella Noble. This guidebook was produced by the following:

Destination Editors Dora Ball, Tanya Parker, Clifton Wilkinson

Product Editor Amanda Williamson

Senior Product Editor Kate Chapman

Senior Cartographer Alison Lyall

Regional Senior Cartographer Diana Von Holdt

Book Designer Wibowo Rusli

Assisting Editors Judith Bamber, Katie Connolly, Melanie Dankel, Andrea Dobbin, Jennifer Hattam, Gabrielle Innes, Rosie Nicholson, Susan Paterson, Tamara Sheward, Gabrielle Stefanos

Cover Researcher Naomi Parker

Thanks to Bruce Evans, James Hardy, Pedro Melo, Virginia Moreno, Rachel Rawling

Send Us Your Feedback

We love to hear from travellers – your comments keep us on our toes and help make our books better. Our well-travelled team reads every word on what you loved or loathed about this book. Although we cannot reply individually to postal submissions, we always guarantee that your feedback goes straight to the appropriate authors, in time for the next edition. Each person who sends us information is thanked in the next edition, the most useful submissions are rewarded with a selection of digital PDF chapters.

Visit lonelyplanet.com/contact to submit your updates and suggestions or to ask for help. Our award-winning website also features inspirational travel stories, news and discussions.

Note: We may edit, reproduce and incorporate your comments in Lonely Planet products such as guidebooks, websites and digital products, so let us know if you don't want your comments reproduced or your name acknowledged. For a copy of our privacy policy visit lonelyplanet.com/privacy.

A – Z
Index

Symbols & Map Key

Look for these symbols to quickly identify listings:

- ⊙ Sights
- ⊕ Activities
- ⊜ Courses
- ⊙ Tours
- ⊛ Festivals & Events
- ⊗ Eating
- ⊖ Drinking
- ⊛ Entertainment
- ⊞ Shopping
- ⊙ Information & Transport

These symbols and abbreviations give vital information for each listing:

🌿 Sustainable or green recommendation

FREE No payment required

- ☑ Telephone number
- ⊙ Opening hours
- Ⓟ Parking
- ⊝ Nonsmoking
- ✳ Air-conditioning
- @ Internet access
- 🛜 Wi-fi access
- ⊠ Swimming pool
- 🚍 Bus
- 🚢 Ferry
- 🚋 Tram
- 🚆 Train
- 🍱 English-language menu
- 🥗 Vegetarian selection
- 👪 Family-friendly

Find your best experiences with these Great For... icons.

 Art & Culture

 Beaches

 Budget

 Cafe/Coffee

 Cycling

 Detour

 Drinking

 Entertainment

Events

Family Travel

🍴 Food & Drink

 History

 Local Life

 Nature & Wildlife

 Photo Op

 Scenery

 Shopping

 Short Trip

 Sport

 Walking

Winter Travel

Sights

- 🏖 Beach
- 🐦 Bird Sanctuary
- 🕌 Buddhist
- 🏰 Castle/Palace
- ✝ Christian
- ☯ Confucian
- 🕉 Hindu
- ☪ Islamic
- 卍 Jain
- ✡ Jewish
- 🗼 Monument
- 🏛 Museum/Gallery/ Historic Building
- ⊕ Ruin
- ⛩ Shinto
- ☬ Sikh
- ☯ Taoist
- 🍷 Winery/Vineyard
- 🦁 Zoo/Wildlife Sanctuary
- ⊙ Other Sight

Points of Interest

- Ⓒ Bodysurfing
- 🏕 Camping
- ☕ Cafe
- 🛶 Canoeing/Kayaking
- Course/Tour
- 🤿 Diving
- 🍸 Drinking & Nightlife
- ⊗ Eating
- 🎭 Entertainment
- ♨ Sento Hot Baths/ Onsen
- 🛍 Shopping
- ⛷ Skiing
- 🛏 Sleeping
- 🤿 Snorkelling
- 🏄 Surfing
- 🏊 Swimming/Pool
- 🚶 Walking
- 🏄 Windsurfing
- 🚩 Other Activity

Information

- 🏦 Bank
- 🏛 Embassy/Consulate
- ➕ Hospital/Medical
- @ Internet
- 👮 Police
- 📮 Post Office
- 📞 Telephone
- 🚻 Toilet
- ⓘ Tourist Information
- • Other Information

Geographic

- 🏖 Beach
- ⊢ Gate
- ⌂ Hut/Shelter
- 🗼 Lighthouse
- 🔭 Lookout
- ▲ Mountain/Volcano
- 🌴 Oasis
- 🌳 Park
-)(Pass
- 🌳 Picnic Area
- 💧 Waterfall

Transport

- ✈ Airport
- Ⓑ BART station
- ⊗ Border crossing
- 🅣 Boston T station
- 🚍 Bus
- 🚠 Cable car/Funicular
- 🚲 Cycling
- ⛴ Ferry
- Ⓜ Metro/MRT station
- 🚝 Monorail
- Ⓟ Parking
- 🛢 Petrol station
- Ⓢ Subway/S-Bahn/ Skytrain station
- 🚕 Taxi
- 🚉 Train station/Railway
- 🚊 Tram
- 🚇 Tube Station
- Ⓤ Underground/ U-Bahn station
- • Other Transport

David Eimer

David has been a journalist and writer ever since abandoning the idea of a law career in 1990. After spells working in his native London and in Los Angeles, he moved to Beijing in 2005, where he contributed to a variety of newspapers and magazines in the UK. Since then he has travelled and lived across China and in numerous cities in Southeast Asia, including Bangkok, Phnom Penh and Yangon. He has been covering China, Myanmar and Thailand for Lonely Planet since 2006.

Damian Harper

With two degrees (one in modern and classical Chinese from SOAS University of London), Damian has been writing for Lonely Planet for more than two decades, contributing to titles on places as diverse as China, Vietnam, Thailand, Ireland, London, Mallorca, Malaysia, Singapore, Brunei, Hong Kong and the UK. A seasoned guidebook writer, Damian has penned articles for numerous newspapers and magazines, including the *Guardian* and the *Daily Telegraph*, and currently makes Surrey, England, his home. Follow Damian on Instagram @damian.harper.

Anita Isalska

Anita is a travel journalist, editor and copywriter whose work for Lonely Planet has taken her from Greek beach towns to Malaysian jungles, and plenty of places in between. After several merry years as an in-house editor and writer – with a few of them in Lonely Planet's London office – Anita now works freelance between the UK, Australia and any Balkan guesthouse with a good wi-fi connection. Anita writes about travel, food and culture for a host of websites and magazines. Read her writing on www.anitaisalska.com.

Our Story

A beat-up old car, a few dollars in the pocket and a sense of adventure. In 1972 that's all Tony and Maureen Wheeler needed for the trip of a lifetime – across Europe and Asia overland to Australia. It took several months, and at the end – broke but inspired – they sat at their kitchen table writing and stapling together their first travel guide, *Across Asia on the Cheap*. Within a week they'd sold 1500 copies. Lonely Planet was born.

Today, Lonely Planet has offices in Franklin, London, Melbourne, Oakland, Dublin, Beijing, and Delhi, with more than 600 staff and writers. We share Tony's belief that 'a great guidebook should do three things: inform, educate and amuse'.

Our Writers

Austin Bush

Austin originally came to Thailand in 1999 as part of a language study program hosted by Chiang Mai University. The lure of city life, employment and spicy food eventually led him to Bangkok. City life, employment and spicy food have managed to keep him there ever since. These days, Austin works as a writer and photographer, and in addition to having contributed to numerous books, magazines and websites, has contributed text and photos to more than 20 Lonely Planet titles including *Bangkok*; *The Food Book*; *Food Lover's Guide to the World*; *Laos*; *Malaysia, Singapore & Brunei*; *Myanmar (Burma)*; *Pocket Bangkok*; *Thailand*; *Thailand's Islands & Beaches*; *Vietnam, Cambodia, Laos & Northern Thailand*; and *The World's Best Street Food*.

Tim Bewer

After briefly holding fort behind a desk as a legislative assistant, Tim decided he didn't have the ego to succeed in the political world (or the stomach to work around those who did). He quit his job at the capitol to backpack around West Africa, during which time he pondered what to do next. His answer was to write a travel guide to parks, forests, and wildlife areas of the gorgeous state of Wisconsin. He's been a freelance travel writer and photographer ever since.

Celeste Brash

Like many California natives, Celeste now lives in Portland, Oregon. She arrived, however, after 15 years in French Polynesia, 18 months in Southeast Asia and a stint teaching English as a second language (in an American accent) in Brighton, England – among other things. She's been writing guidebooks for Lonely Planet since 2005 and her travel articles have appeared in publications from *BBC Travel* to *National Geographic*.

 More Writers

STAY IN TOUCH LONELYPLANET.COM/CONTACT

AUSTRALIA The Malt Store, Level 3, 551 Swanston St, Carlton, Victoria 3053
☎ 03 8379 8000,
fax 03 8379 8111

IRELAND Digital Depot, Roe Lane (off Thomas St), Digital Hub, Dublin 8, D08 TCV4, Ireland

USA 124 Linden Street, Oakland, CA 94607
☎ 510 250 6400,
toll free 800 275 8555,
fax 510 893 8572

UK 240 Blackfriars Road, London SE1 8NW
☎ 020 3771 5100,
fax 020 3771 5101

 twitter.com/
lonelyplanet
 facebook.com/
lonelyplanet
 instagram.com/
lonelyplanet
 youtube.com/
lonelyplanet
 lonelyplanet.com/
newsletter